TABLE OF CONTENTS

Using On This Spot

This is not a standard guidebook, the kind that tells you where to go, how to get there, what to see, and where to eat and sleep. Instead, it is a historical guide, or "sitebook," a book that carries you back in time. This historical guide takes the reader to those spots in and around the city of Washington where history was made.

A historical guide is by its nature more realistic, yet also more dramatic and romantic than a book that steers you to museums and monuments. A historical guide speaks of spies, murderers, bartenders, and writers, the unflinching reality of history. In this guide, for example, the reader is taken to the tennis courts at Fort McNair, which now cover the site of the mass hanging of the Lincoln assassination conspirators. And to the Capitol Hill digs of a notorious band of grave robbers.

Although it might appear so because of the grandeur of the monuments and the Mall area, Washington is not a theme park in which the past is neatly preserved or replicated. It is more than a repository of Senate debates and Supreme Court decisions, more than an august national capital. It is also a living, growing city, and for many decades it was a rough, dirty, and noisy place. Our book reflects this occasionally raucous growth and change.

We expect that this book will be read in bits and pieces rather than from beginning to end, as readers browse or pick and choose areas of interest or explore the city using it as a guide.

For this reason, we have repeated key information in several places. For example, the destruction of the city's public buildings by the British on August 24, 1814, is mentioned in the sections on Capitol Hill, Downtown, the White House, and Georgetown. We've also added a brief chronology of important events and dates in the physical shaping of the city.

Most sites are located in the parts of the city with the longest history—Downtown, Capitol Hill, Georgetown. The sites are grouped according to their locations, often bunched under "locators" in cases where a single large building or development now covers several former sites (such as the Library of Congress or John Marshall Park). Sites in more recently developed areas are fewer and more scattered, such as those in the northern sections of the city beyond Florida Avenue NW. (This area was Washington County before all sections of the District of Columbia were merged into a single municipality in 1895 as population expanded from the downtown.)

The book is not a series of walking tours, but is intended for people who wish to fashion their own based on their free time and fascinations. We have, therefore, attempted to cluster sites in small finite areas rather than lay them out in a given direction from the Capitol or another central location.

For those not familiar with the city, this book should still be easy to use because of Washington's layout. It is, in fact, one of the few cities whose basic street dynamics can be described in less than 250 words:

The Mall and three streets–North Capitol, South Capitol, and East Capitol—converge at the Capitol building and divide the city into four quadrants: Northeast, Northwest, Southeast, and Southwest. There is no West Capitol Street, but if there were it would run down the center of the Mall. The Mall is a broad plaza lined with

ON THIS SPOT

Pinpointing the Past in
Washington, D.C.

By Douglas Evelyn and Paul Dickson

NATIONAL
GEOGRAPHIC
WASHINGTON, D.C.

Published by the National Geographic Society
1145 17th Street NW
Washington, D.C. 20036

ON THIS SPOT ™ is a trademark for a series of historical guidebooks owned by
Douglas E. Evelyn and Paul Dickson.

Based on an original design by Barkin & Davis, Inc. Revised design and typography
by Elizabeth Evelyn and Nick Pimentel.

Library of Congress Cataloging-in-Publication Data

Evelyn, Douglas E., 1941-
      On this spot : pinpointing the past in Washington, D.C. / by
Douglas Evelyn and Paul Dickson.
          p.   cm.
      This new issue of "On this spot" is greatly revised, per
Publisher's information.
      Includes bibliographical references and index.
      ISBN 0-7922-7499-7
      1. Washington (D.C.) Guidebooks. 2. Historic sites--Washington
(D.C.) Guidebooks. 3. Washington (D.C.)--History. I. Dickson,
Paul. II. Title.
F192.3.E84 1999
917.5304'41--dc21   99-36102
                                                      CIP

View of Pennsylvania Avenue with the Willard Hotel in the upper left and the Treasury Department to the far left. The image is from September, 1911 and nicely displays the shade trees on either side of the Avenue as well as a parade and various modes of transportation.

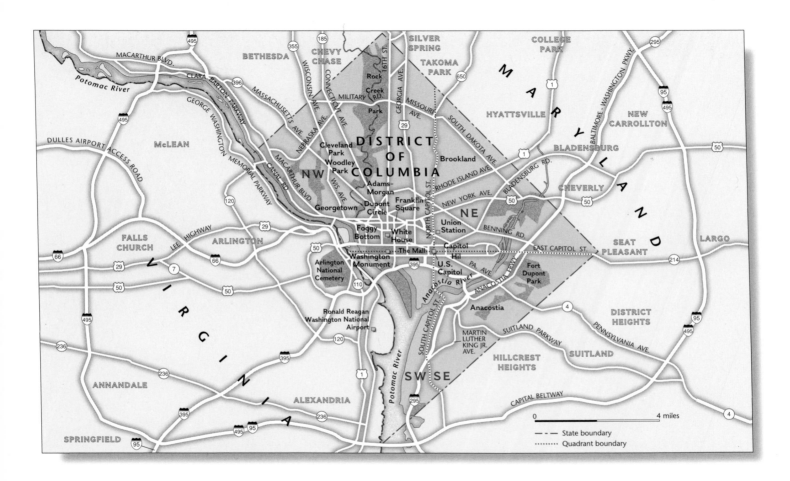

museums and monuments. There is no Main Street, although Pennsylvania Avenue comes close to playing that role.

Lettered streets run east and west, while those with numbers run north and south. As one moves away from the Capitol in any direction the street addresses become higher, as do the numbered and lettered streets. Street addresses also correspond to blocks, so the Martin Luther King Memorial Library at 901 G Street NW is at 9th and G Streets. Correspondingly, Ford's Theatre at 511 10th Street NW is between E (the 5th letter) and F (the 6th letter) on 10th Street. Odd-numbered addresses fall on the north and east and even-numbered on the south and west sides of the streets. After there are no more single letters left (no X, Y, or Z Streets), the streets have one-syllable names that are almost all in alphabetical order, then come two-syllable names, and lastly three-syllable street names to the far north and south. Wide avenues named for the states cut diagonally across the grid. Rock Creek and its surrounding park bisect Washington from north to south. Thanks to the Potomac and the Anacostia, the city can boast much riverfront.

A word about change. Because Washington has been a constantly changing city, many of the spots we have pinpointed no longer resemble what they were when they made history. We have tried in every instance to make it clear to the reader whether he or she is looking at the original building or the site of the original. When not, we use phrases such as "on this site" or "formerly on this spot" or explicitly state that the original structure has been demolished.

When the first edition of *On This Spot* was published in 1992, we knew that we were working with a canvas that was ever-changing. In creating a fresh, new edition we have incorporated as many of those changes as possible.

Speaking of change, this new edition of the book contains a vastly improved set of maps for each of the 17 sectors of the city visited. There is also a new system for locating sites on those maps.

The 1992 edition prompted letters from scores of readers who had personal memories of sites described or pictured in the book. We are delighted to incorporate a number of comments from these mostly older readers and only wish we had room for more. We are most indebted to those who contributed and look forward to continuing this relationship with our readers.

At the time of this revision, summer 1999, the rate of change seems to be accelerating. So, by the time you use this book, there will undoubtedly be other changes. This point was brought home to us during our final check of sites in 1999. Structures that were in place for the earlier work had either vanished or been altered by the time we paid our next visit. Even though the preservation movement is thriving, we cannot expect that all of our "spots" will remain unchanged.

Therefore, if that charming old building you were anticipating has been replaced by a high-rise office building or a parking lot, bring your imagination into play. This is the key to enjoying and getting the most from a historical tour.

Stand in front of the National Gallery of Art and imagine the scene here in 1932, when federal troops, cavalry, and tanks led by the likes of Douglas MacArthur and Dwight D. Eisenhower routed thousands of impoverished World War I veterans who had marched on Washington as the "Bonus Army." Or look from the White House grounds toward the Commerce Department and picture a notorious red-light district, part of a squalid slum known as Murder Bay. Stroll to the National Archives, on the former site of Center Market, where Daniel Webster did his grocery shopping. Walk out the F Street entrance of the Willard Hotel, look across the street, and see not the structure that was once Washington's grandest department store, but the house in which Mark Twain wrote *Innocents Abroad*.

Imagine. And have fun. D.E.E. and P.A.D.

A HISTORICAL TIME LINE OF WASHINGTON, D.C.

JULY 16, 1790 • Following the use of eight cities as temporary capitals, Congress designates land on the Maryland side of the Potomac River to be the permanent capital of the United States, with the exact site to be chosen by the President.

JANUARY 24, 1791 • George Washington selects as the site of the future capital the junction of the Eastern Branch (now known as the Anacostia) and Potomac Rivers, an area that includes the existing town of Georgetown.

FEBRUARY 24, 1791 • Congress adds to the federal territory land on the Virginia side of the Potomac, including the town of Alexandria. All public buildings are to be built on the Maryland side. Eager for the economic benefits they anticipate from having the capital as a neighbor, Maryland and Virginia cede the necessary land to the federal government at no cost and contribute $72,000 and $120,000 respectively to its development.

MARCH 9, 1791 • Maj. Pierre Charles L'Enfant arrives in Georgetown under assignment from President Washington to plan the new city. L'Enfant, a young French artist, came to the attention of national leaders while serving in the Continental Army during the Revolutionary War.

APRIL 15, 1791 • Well-known surveyor Andrew Ellicott and prominent mathematician and astronomer Benjamin Banneker, a free black, begin surveying the territory—a square, each side 10 miles long.

JUNE 22, 1791 • L'Enfant lays before the President the first version of a plan for the city. By the standards of its day it is considered grand. Based on the baroque tradition of European cities, it is to include elegant buildings, panoramic vistas, and public squares connected by stately boulevards.

1800 • Territory's population totals 14,093, half living in the established towns of Alexandria and Georgetown. Of the total, 783 are free blacks and 3,244 are slaves.

NOVEMBER 1, 1800 • President John Adams moves into the President's House, later to be known as the White House. Later that month Congress arrives from Philadelphia, followed by the rest of the federal establishment.

FEBRUARY 24, 1801 • Congress formally designates the federal territory the District of Columbia. It includes the town of Alexandria and the County of Alexandria on the Virginia side of the Potomac. On the Maryland side are the City of Washington, Georgetown, and Washington County.

MAY 3, 1802 • Congress charters the city government, allowing for a mayor to be appointed by the President and a city council to be elected by white male taxpayers.

AUGUST 24, 1814 • British troops sack and burn most of Washington's public buildings, including the Capitol and the President's House.

NOVEMBER 21, 1815 • City Canal is completed, connecting the Potomac and Eastern Branch Rivers and running along what is now Constitution Avenue.

1820 • District's population reaches 33,039, of which 15,705 live in Alexandria and Georgetown. Total includes 4,048 free blacks and 6,277 slaves.

MAY 20, 1836 • Congress absorbs the District's 1.8-million-dollar debt for canal construction and agrees to begin regular contributions for street and other improvements.

1840 • District's population totals 43,712, including 30,657 whites, 8,361 free blacks, and 4,694 slaves. Of the total population, 8,459 live in Alexandria, 7,312 in Georgetown.

AUGUST 10, 1846 • Smithsonian Institution established by Congress in response to British scientist James Smithson's $500,000 bequest.

SEPTEMBER 7, 1846 • Virginia portions of the District retroceded to Virginia.

DECEMBER 29, 1849 • First gas works established by newly formed Washington Gas Light Company and used to light the President's House. Plant located at what is now Constitution Avenue and 10th street.

1850 • District's population (without retroceded Virginia portions) reaches 51,687. The City of Washington population is 17,000, or nearly 75 percent greater than it was in previous decade.

SEPTEMBER 20, 1850 • Congress abolishes the slave trade in the District; owning slaves remains legal.

1860 • Foreign immigration swells the District's population to 75,080, including 60,764 whites, 11,131 free blacks, and 3,185 slaves.

APRIL 12, 1861 • Civil War begins with attack on Fort Sumter, South Carolina.

APRIL 16, 1862 • Slavery abolished in the District

JULY 11, 1864 • Confederate Gen. Jubal A. Early's forces attack Washington but are repelled at Fort Stevens.

1870 • Post-Civil War population of the District reaches 131,720, a 75 percent increase during the decade. It includes 88,298 whites and 43,422 free blacks. Growth reflects the thousands of newly emancipated blacks who came to Washington during and after the war as well as the thousands of government employees who were drawn to the capital by the war and remained.

MARCH 16, 1871 • Congress appoints powerful Board of Public Works, independent of the District government. With Alexander R. "Boss" Shepherd as chief operating officer, the board implements a 20-million-dollar improvement program that transforms the face of the city, fills in the Mall's canal, and substantially exceeds debt authority.

JUNE 1, 1871 • A new, congressionally mandated, territorial form of government, led by a presidentially appointed governor, begins managing the District. Georgetown and Washington County abolished as separate legal entities and merged into the District.

JUNE 26, 1874 • Overspending by the territorial government prompts Congress to replace it with a three-member commission appointed by the President.

1880 • Population of the District reaches 177,624.

FEBRUARY 1881 • Severe flooding spurs reclamation and flood control measures along the Potomac.

1882-1890 • Maj. Gen. Peter Conover Hains supervises reclamation of over 600 acres of Potomac river flatlands, creating Hains Point and East and West Potomac Parks.

JULY 30, 1883 • Chesapeake and Potomac Telephone Company founded; takes over fledgling telephone system. (First telephones appeared in Washington in 1878. By 1879 there were about 400 phones—and a single operator.) One of C&P's earliest steps is to take down ugly telephone poles and run wires underground.

OCTOBER 1888 • Electric streetcars begin operating in Washington, between Eighth and K streets NW and Fourth and T Streets NE. Cars use tracks laid in 1862 for horse-drawn omnibuses. By 1900, streetcar systems will total 190 miles and encourage growth of suburbs.

MARCH 2, 1889 • National Zoo established.

1890 • District's population totals 230,392. Federal employees increase from 13,000 to 20,000 during 1880s.

SEPTEMBER 27, 1890 • Rock Creek Park established.

1899 • Congress limits downtown building heights in Washington and thereby precludes a future of skyscrapers for the city.

1900 • District's population reaches 278,718.

JANUARY 15, 1902 • McMillan Plan, recommending improvements to the Mall and monumental areas downtown and along the Potomac, is presented to President Theodore Roosevelt. The plan will determine the 20th-century development of Washington's grand vistas, classical buildings, and monuments along lines envisaged by L'Enfant.

JULY 4, 1906 • District Building, Washington's new city hall, opens at 14th and E Streets NW.

1910 • District's population totals 331,069.

JULY 19-23, 1919 • Race riots in Washington claim nine lives, many wounded.

1920 • District's population increases by more than 100,000 over the decade including World War I, reaching 437,571 by 1920. Dozens of temporary buildings erected to house new residents and offices.

JANUARY 28, 1922 • Knickerbocker Theater roof collapses from 26-inch snowfall, killing 97 and injuring 140. New standards for theater construction result.

MAY 30, 1922 • Lincoln Memorial dedicated. Black officials at opening ceremony segregated from whites.

SEPTEMBER 21, 1924 • Baseball's Washington Senators beat New York Giants in 12-inning final game to win their first and only World Series.

MAY 25, 1926 • Congress launches Federal Triangle project, an immense complex of government office buildings between Pennsylvania Avenue and the Mall.

1930 • Population of the District climbs to 486,869; number of automobiles registered reaches 155,000, up from 56,000 in 1920.

SEPTEMBER 16, 1937 • Washington Redskins beat New York Giants 13-3 at Griffith Stadium, the professional football team's first game after moving from Boston.

1940 • District's population soars to 663,091, climbing by more than 200,000 and reflecting the New Deal-inspired growth of the 1930s. Black population increases at double the rate of the 1920s.

JUNE 1941 • First plane lands at National Airport.

DECEMBER 7, 1941 • Japanese attack Pearl Harbor; United States enters World War II.

1949 • Whitehurst Freeway completed along Georgetown waterfront.

1950 • District's population, swelled by wartime workers, reaches 802,178.

APRIL 26, 1954 • Urban renewal begins in Southwest Washington, resulting in the replacement of most of the section's structures by 1960 and the displacement of thousands of poor residents.

MAY 17, 1954 • Supreme Court declares segregated schools unconstitutional, paving the way for desegregation of District public schools in September. On the same day, the District integrates recreational facilities.

1960 • For the first time in its history, the District records a decline in population, dropping during the decade to 763,956. The metropolitan area, however, passes two million.

JANUARY 27, 1962 • Streetcar service comes to an end in Washington.

AUGUST 28, 1963 • More than 200,000 take part in the March on Washington to bring about passage of the Civil Rights Act. The day culminates with Martin Luther King, Jr.'s "I Have a Dream" speech at the Lincoln Memorial.

1964 • Capital Beltway completed.

NOVEMBER 3, 1964 • Citizens of the District of Columbia cast their first votes for President after ratification of the 23rd Amendment to the Constitution.

AUGUST 11, 1967 • President Johnson replaces commissioner form of government, in place since 1874, with a presidentially appointed mayor and council.

APRIL 4, 1968 • Rioting erupts following assassination of Martin Luther King, Jr., resulting in 12 deaths and 24 million dollars in damages. Troops and police restore order after two nights of turmoil, but city will bear physical and social scars for years.

1970 • District's population declines slightly, to 756,668, while metropolitan area grows to 2.8 million.

DECEMBER 24, 1973 • President Nixon signs legislation allowing District citizens to vote on home rule charter. In May of following year voters approve the charter.

JANUARY 2, 1975 • Limited home rule comes to the District of Columbia. Mayor Walter Washington and City Council, elected previous November, take office and begin governing. Although self-government has been granted, Congress and President retain authority to intervene in local affairs.

MARCH 28, 1976 • Metrorail opens first route of projected 100-mile metropolitan area subway system. Downtown building boom follows.

1980 • District population declines to 638,333, lowest figure since the eve of World War II.

1990 • Population drops further, to 606,900.

1991 • District of Columbia marks its bicentennial. The official slogan: "Celebrate the City Beyond the Monuments."

January 2, 1999 • Anthony A. Williams is sworn into office as the city's fourth mayor. He calls for a "back to basics" era of efficient good government. "Our citizens deserve the best city in America," he declares.

This time line draws from a "Chronology of Events in the History of the District of Columbia," prepared by Philip W. Ogilvie, former District of Columbia Public Records Administrator; Constance McLaughlin Green's *Washington, A History of the Capital, 1800-1950;* Frederick Gutheim's *Worthy of a Nation;* and the D.C. History Curriculum Project's *City of Magnificent Intentions.*

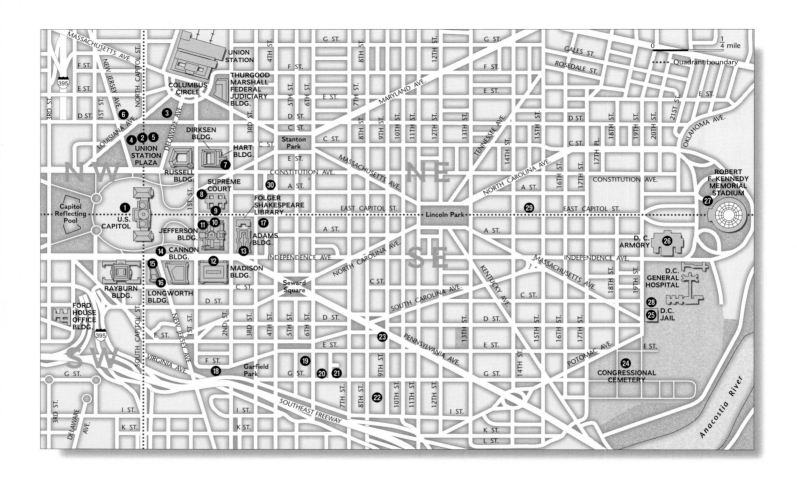

The Capitol and Capitol Hill

1 **The Capitol and its grounds, the point where the four quadrants of the city converge, once called Jenkins Hill and now Capitol Hill**

"A PEDESTAL WAITING FOR A MONUMENT"—In his report to George Washington of June 28, 1791, Pierre Charles L'Enfant, the Frenchman engaged to plan the new Federal City, described the placement of the Capitol: "After much menutial search for an eligible situation, prompted, I may say, from a fear of being prejudiced in favor of a first opinion, I could discover no one so advantageously to greet the congressional building as is that on the West End of Jenkins Heights, which stands as a pedestal waiting for a monument."

Almost all of the nation's political leaders have a direct association with this site. George Washington laid the cornerstone of the Capitol on September 18, 1793. Repeated attempts over the years to locate that cornerstone have failed, and its whereabouts remains a mystery.

William Thornton, a gentleman architect, won the architectural competition. The building was begun according to his plans, supervised by Steven Hallet and then James Hoban. Professionally trained architect Benjamin Henry Latrobe took over in 1803 when President Thomas Jefferson appointed him surveyor of public buildings. Over the next 14 years, Latrobe replaced earlier interior work and clashed frequently and publicly with Thornton.

By the War of 1812, the Senate and House wings were finished but the center and dome had not yet been filled in. After the British burned the Capitol on August 24, 1814, Latrobe began to rebuild,

Early Vision. The Capitol from the east as it appears in a John Plumbe, Jr., daguerreotype of about 1846. The building is capped with its early Charles Bulfinch dome. This is the earliest known photographic image of the Capitol, which was then known as Congress House.

CAPITOL HILL. The neighborhood known as the Hill for the last 200 or so years is roughly bounded on the north by F Street NE, on the south by the Southwest Freeway, and on the east by 14th Street SE and NE. The western boundary is usually vaguely said to be a few blocks down the Mall from the Capitol.

This is how Secretary of the Treasury Albert Gallatin found the neighborhood in January 1801: "Our local situation is far from being pleasant or even convenient. Around the Capitol are seven or eight boarding houses, one tailor, one shoemaker, one printer, a washing woman, a grocery shop, a pamphlets and stationery shop and an oyster house. This makes the whole of the Federal City as connected with the Capitol."

By 1862 the Civil War made the Hill and the city an armed camp and refugee center. Mary Clemmer Ames described it in her *Ten Years in Washington:* "Capitol Hill, dreary, desolate and dirty stretched away into an uninhabited desert, high above the mud of the West End. Arid hill and sodden plain showed alike the horrid trail of war. Forts bristled above every hill-top. Soldiers were entrenched at every gate-way. Shed hospitals covered acres on acres in every suburb."

retaining Thornton's exterior. Latrobe was replaced in 1817 by Boston architect Charles Bulfinch, who completed the original building and dome by 1829. Thomas U. Walter, assisted by Edward Clark, extended the building between 1851 and 1865, including the enlarged cast iron dome (1863) capped by the statue of Freedom designed by Thomas Crawford and cast in bronze by Clark Mills.

John Adams was the first president to address a joint session of Congress here (November 22, 1800), using the Senate Chamber, located in the only portion of the building then completed. A generation later his son, John Quincy Adams, was inaugurated President in the Old House Chamber (now Statuary Hall) on March 4, 1825. Later, as a member of the House of Representatives, he was fatally stricken in the same room on February 23, 1848. Many famous figures have lain in state in the Rotunda here including Pierre Charles L'Enfant (who died in 1825 but was honored at the Capitol in 1909 when his remains were transferred from suburban Maryland to Arlington National Cemetery), Abraham Lincoln (1865), John F. Kennedy (1963), and the bodies of the Unknown Dead from the nation's wars.

Statuary Hall honors leaders selected by each state. In 1996 Congress decided that a portrait monument of three activists for women's rights—Susan B. Anthony, Elizabeth Cady Stanton, and Lucretia Mott—should be moved from the basement of the Capitol into the Rotunda. The statue was designed and carved by Adelaide Johnson and commissioned by Alice Paul, founder of the National Women's Party. The sculpture was moved in 1997.

The next four sites were within the area now occupied by Union Station Plaza, a parklike area between the Capitol and Union Station bounded by Delaware, Constitution, New Jersey, and *Louisiana Avenues NW and created after the completion of Union Station. Most of the grading and construction was done in the 1930s, and resulted in the elimination of the three blocks of North Capitol Street nearest the Capitol and the demolition of several other historic blocks. (For Union Station itself, see Chapter 2, p. 29.)*

② Union Station Plaza, near Delaware and Constitution Avenues NW

THE HOUSES GEORGE BUILT—George Washington demonstrated his confidence in the city's real estate market by investing in two lots on North Capitol Street near the Capitol in October 1798. According to his will, dated July 1799, he purchased the original lots for $963.

A plaque along the west side of the walk at the Capitol end of Union Station Plaza, about two-thirds of a block north of Constitution Avenue, informs us that the lots on this site were improved with houses designed by William Thornton. (Architect Benjamin Henry Latrobe—a bitter rival of Thornton's—referred to them as "two indifferent houses.") Washington died before work was completed, and the buildings became congressional boarding houses. Eventually the dwellings were remodeled into a single residence for Adm. Charles Wilkes, best known for leading an American exploring expedition to the South Pacific in 1838-42. The expedition was the first to determine that Antarctica is a separate continent.

③ The area in front of Union Station, bounded by Delaware Avenue, Columbus Circle, and North Capitol and C Streets NE

LADIES' ROOMS—Over 30 temporary buildings were erected on this site to house government workers during World War I. One group of these buildings, the Union Plaza Dormitories, was built between 1918 and 1920 specifically for 2,000 female government

Old Capitol Prison. This former boarding house, temporary Capitol, and infamous prison was located at First Street and Maryland Avenue NE, where the Supreme Court Building is today. This photograph shows it as it appeared just after the Civil War.

NEW JERSEY AVENUE. When President John Adams brought the government to the city in 1800, a congressman from Connecticut wrote of the great avenues that were to be a feature of the new capital: "not one was visible, unless we except a road, with two buildings on each side of it, called the New Jersey Avenue."

workers. According to historian James M. Goode's *Capital Losses,* amenities included a dining room, infirmary, and maid services. Monthly rates reached $50.50 in the 1920s.

The "Government Hotels" were razed starting in July 1931 to clear the area for Union Station Plaza.

4 East side of New Jersey Avenue opposite C Street NW

ALL ABOARD—From 1852 to 1907 this was the site of the Baltimore and Ohio Railroad station. The B&O served points to the north and west. Abraham Lincoln's funeral train departed from here on its ceremonial journey back to Illinois in April 1865. Sidings, switchyards, and work and supply sheds spread throughout the area. This station and the Baltimore and Potomac Terminal at Constitution Avenue and Sixth Street NW (where the West Building of the National Gallery of Art is now located) were consolidated into Union Station in 1907.

5 Union Station Plaza, between New Jersey and Delaware Avenues at C Street NE

GAS MAN—In 1846 James Crutchett moved from Dayton, Ohio, to this site, then the intersection of North Capitol and C Streets NE, and lighted his house with "solar gas" that he produced on his property. He convinced Congress to let him demonstrate his lighting inventions on the dome of the Capitol in 1847, and within months the Washington Gas Light Company was formed.

6 419-423 New Jersey Avenue NW

HOUSE OF THE BODY SNATCHERS—In the mid-19th century this was the site of "Ryder's Castle," which housed a large group of "resurrectionists," or body snatchers, who stole their treasures from freshly filled graves. The grotesque but long-lived operation was headed by a woman named Maude Brown who claimed to be the daughter of a noted Russian physician and anatomist. It was a few doors from the old No. 6 Police Station.

Before 1894, when the police recorded the last snatch, the theft and sale of bodies, usually to out-of-town medical schools, was a major problem in the city. Breaking rings of such thieves was a prime concern of police. A major crackdown in the early 1890s brought an end to the practice. One of the biggest breakthroughs in the investigation occurred at the B&O Terminal on New Jersey Avenue when a collection of barrels labeled "pork" was found to contain pickled human remains. Many years later Capt. J. Walter Mitchell wrote about the body snatchers in the *Times-Herald* with a certain amount of sympathy, adding that they "furnished the old-time reporters of the city with many thrilling stories."

❼ 144 Constitution Avenue NE

ARMED RESISTANCE AND WOMEN'S RIGHTS—Here was the home of Robert Sewall, the only place in the District of Columbia where armed resistance was encountered by the British during the 1814 invasion. A shot fired from the garden killed the horse of Gen. Robert Ross, who was leading the British column into the city. Incensed, Ross had the house burned and that evening, August 24, 1814, torched the Capitol, the White House, and other public buildings as well.

Rebuilt in 1820, this house continued as a residence until acquired by Alva Belmont in 1929. Her divorce in 1895 from William Kissam Vanderbilt, on grounds of adultery, left her with a settlement of $100,000 per year. She then married Oliver H.P. Belmont, son of wealthy banker August Belmont. Oliver died in 1908, and Alva devoted her money and leadership to the cause of women's rights. She helped found the National Woman's Party in 1913 and organized an enormous rally in Washington that year to

Great Hall. This stunning public area of the Library of Congress provides lavish testimony to the tastes of the 1890s, when it was declared a masterpiece of contemporary architecture.

End of an Era. Three fire horses—Gene, Tom, and Barney—make their last run with the District's horse-drawn fire apparatus from Engine Company 19, the last to be motorized. The ceremonial run took place along East Capitol Street on June 15, 1925.

gain women the right to vote. During the suffragettes' march on Woodrow Wilson's inauguration, March 5, 1913, unruly behavior among opponents of women's rights required the intervention of the police to keep order. But the march built momentum for the women's suffrage movement, which succeeded in 1920 with ratification of the 19th Amendment to the Constitution.

Belmont bought the Sewall house when the National Woman's Party was forced to vacate its nearby quarters to make way for construction of the Supreme Court building. The house, now known as the Sewall-Belmont House, was converted into offices and continues to serve as headquarters for the organization. It is considered the oldest house on Capitol Hill because it incorporates a farmhouse constructed in 1680.

❽ Southeast corner of 1st Street and Maryland Avenue NE, now the grounds of the Supreme Court

THE "OLD BRICK CAPITOL"—A large brick building was erected hurriedly on this site after the burning of the Capitol by the British in 1814. Congress met here in 1815-19. The inauguration of President James Monroe took place here in 1817, making Monroe the only President with the exception of John Adams and George Washington whose inaugural ceremony was not held at the Capitol. Historian James M. Goode points out that Monroe decided to take the oath in the open air—starting a tradition—when the House and Senate could not decide which chamber to use inside the building. Other reasons for the outdoor ceremony advanced by 1920s Washington journalist George Rothwell Brown were that the event would thereby be more democratic and, finally, that Congress feared the building wouldn't support the crowd.

John C. Calhoun died here in 1850 when the building was known as Hill's boarding house. In 1860, it was used as a schoolhouse before being taken over by the government in 1861 for use as a prison. Renamed the Old Capitol Prison during the Civil War, the building primarily held spies and political suspects. Belle Boyd, the celebrated Confederate spy, was confined here. General McClellan was supposed to have said that Boyd "knows my plans better than Lincoln." Capt. Henry Wirz, the commandant of the notorious Andersonville Prison, was hanged in the prison yard on November 19, 1865.

The building was partially demolished in 1867, and the remaining portion was converted into three large houses. They were known as Trumbull Row because they were financed by Senator Lyman Trumbull of Illinois. Trumbull Row later served as headquarters for the National Woman's Party during and after its successful effort to secure voting rights for women with the adoption of the 19th amendment to the Constitution in 1920. Trumbull Row was removed in the l930s to make room for the Supreme Court, now located on the east portion of the site upon which the Old Brick Capitol stood.

❾ North side of East Capitol Street, between 1st and 2nd Streets NE

EARLY POST OFFICE—Now part of the grounds of the Supreme Court, this site was once the location of the home of Lund Washington, Jr., son of George Washington's cousin and estate manager at Mount Vernon. Lund became city postmaster in 1796 and established a post office in his house.

❿ East Capitol Street between 1st and 2nd Streets

CAPITOL HILL MARKET—On February 1, 1813, the Capitol Hill Market was opened here in the middle of the street.

The Marquis de Lafayette, the French aristocrat whose service with the American Army in the Revolutionary War made him a national hero, made a triumphal visit to the city in 1824 and was escorted to the Capitol by way of this market. Every stand was decorated in his honor. The market was removed in 1838 after Capitol Hill residents petitioned Congress, stating that the market-house standing on East Capitol Street was "a common nuisance, and great annoyance to all persons residing in the neighborhood of it; that it affords no commensurate benefit to any, and is not required by the population of the place, and tends materially to injure and lessen the value of all the property on the street, which is thought one of the handsomest in the city, particularly when viewed from the east portico of the Capitol, if not obstructed by this unsightly, useless old building."

Three buildings housing the Library of Congress now occupy the sites of the next three entries. The most imposing and historic of these is the Thomas Jefferson Building located on First Street SE, between Independence Avenue and East Capitol Street. Designed by John L. Smithmeyer and Paul J. Pelz, the building was constructed by Army engineers Thomas Lincoln Casey and Bernard R. Green between 1886 and 1897. Its total cost was just under the 6.5 million dollars authorized by Congress. Library of Congress staffer John Y. Cole has credited the engineers with keeping the cost within budget, while still enabling the most extensive decoration—murals, polychrome stonework, sculpture, and extraordinary detailing—of any American public building. Cole notes that they engaged over 40 American artists and made the building a showcase of American artistic talent as well as a home for the national library.

Map on page 12

TOURIST TIP

BEWARE OF COUNTERFEIT CONGRESSMEN. Almost every guidebook to the city ever published has offered advice to strangers. Often the advice is instructive and telling, such as this warning from the 1869 version of John B. Ellis's *The Sights and Secrets of the National Capital:*

"Persons visiting Washington on business, are very frequently the dupes of impostors, with which the city abounds. These scoundrels represent themselves as members of Congress, or as belonging to one of the important branches of government, and offer their services to facilitate your business in any way that lies within their power, for which they ask a sum which varies with the nature of the business, or of the service they propose to render. Such men are simply impostors, who are constantly on the watch for strangers, out of whose simplicity and ignorance of public affairs they expect to reap a rich harvest. It is best to decline all offers of assistance in Washington, whether gratuitous or for a stated compensation, unless the party making the offer is known to you as a man of integrity and capable of carrying out his promises."

Then, as an afterthought, the guide adds, "Men are not the only persons thus engaged."

 Southeast corner of East Capitol and 1st Streets SE

CARROLL ROW—A five-house block of buildings called Carroll Row once occupied a site from First Street to the center of the west front of the Library of Congress, where A Street SE formerly was cut through. Carroll Row was occupied and used as headquarters by Gen. Robert Ross and Adm. Sir George Cockburn, leaders of the invading British forces who burned the city on the night of August 24, 1814.

Abraham Lincoln, while a member of the 30th Congress (1847-49), lived in Mrs. Anna G. Sprigg's boarding house, also part of Carroll Row. During this period, the Hill was an active marketplace of the local slave trade (slave trading was not abolished in the District until 1850), and Lincoln could see slaves being bought and sold from the windows of this house or of the Capitol itself. In *Mr. Lincoln's City*, Richard M. Lee writes of an incident at the boarding house: "A black servant, who had paid all but $60 of the $300 price for his freedom, was seized by two men, carried off to a slave pen, then sent to the auction block in New Orleans. An effort by Mr. Lincoln and his friends to redress this injustice in the House of Representatives failed."

Another building in Carroll Row was Long's Hotel, where the 1809 inaugural ball was held in honor of President Madison. An eyewitness described the guests as a "moving mass" that crowded into the ballroom and broke an upper window sash for ventilation when the air became oppressive. When the music stopped at midnight, she said, "we all came home tired and sick."

Conveniently near the Capitol, the hotel was used later that year to house sessions of the Supreme Court, according to Architect of the Capitol Benjamin Henry Latrobe's 1809 annual report, because the Capitol's library became "so inconvenient and cold."

During the Civil War this site and others on Carroll Row were combined into Carroll Prison. The buildings were razed in 1886 for the construction of what is today the Thomas Jefferson Building of the Library of Congress.

12 122 Independence Avenue SE

STONECUTTER'S COTTAGE—Site of what was once the home of Giuseppe Antonio Franzoni, a sculptor of the Capitol and the first of a long string of Italian artists, stonecutters, and craftsmen brought to Washington to work on public buildings. The James Madison Building of the Library of Congress now occupies the site.

13 206 Pennsylvania Avenue SE

SAVING THE COURT—A residence on this site figured in the history of the United States Supreme Court, originally located in the Capitol. Owner Elias Boudinot Caldwell was serving as clerk of the Court when the British attacked in 1814. He hastily relocated the court's library to his nearby home in time to prevent its loss when the British burned the Capitol. The report that this house served as a temporary Court has been proved false, but Caldwell did indeed save the books. The house survived until 1933 when it was demolished to make way for the Library of Congress annex, completed in 1938 and named the John Adams Building in 1980.

14 Northeast corner of New Jersey and Independence Avenues SE

EARLY BOOKSHOP—In 1801 Daniel Rapine opened one of the first bookstores in Washington on this site, which has since been incorporated into the Capitol grounds. Rapine operated his shop for 13 years before relocating to Pennsylvania Avenue between 4 1/2 and 6th Streets NW.

Backdrop. The U.S. Capitol is used as a photographic backdrop for all sorts of events and causes. Here it is fronted by the truck of an itinerant crusader with a strong message, in a 1939 Farm Security Administration photograph by John Vachon.

Map on page 12

Naked George. Horatio Greenough's seven-ton statue of George Washington proved too heavy for the Capitol Rotunda in 1842 and was placed at various sites in front of the Capitol before being moved to the Smithsonian in 1908. The story of this immodest, bare-chested, toga-clad "Father of Our Country" continues in Chapter 5 with the discussion of the National Museum of American History, where it now resides.

The following two sites are where the Longworth House Office Building is now located.

⑮ 3 Independence Avenue SE

TEMPORARY COURT—A house on this site was used for offices by the United States Supreme Court for a year or so after the Capitol was burned by the British on August 24, 1814. Later, architect Robert Mills lived there while supervising construction of the Washington Monument and the Patent, Treasury, and General Post Office buildings at various times between 1836 and his death in 1855. In about 1873, the house was demolished and replaced by an enormous four-story stone house erected by Gen. Benjamin F. Butler, who fought for the Union in the Civil War and was later a candidate for President on the Greenback and Anti-Monopoly Party tickets in 1884. *The Oxford Companion to American History* describes him as "an erratic soldier and administrator, and a controversial politician." The new building contained a residence for Butler and two town houses for rent. Chester Arthur was living here when he succeeded to the Presidency upon the death by assassination of James Garfield in 1881. Later the building was occupied by the offices of the United States Surgeon General, before being cleared in 1929 for the Longworth House Office Building.

⑯ Northwest corner of New Jersey Avenue and C Street SE

FIREPROOFING—Here was the Coast and Geodetic Survey building, an early iron-beamed "fireproof" structure erected in 1847-48. This agency surveyed the coastal waters of the United States and was especially active as the nation's territory and maritime and naval enterprises expanded during the mid-19th century. Next door at the corner of C Street, real estate developer

Thomas Law—who speculated heavily on properties along New Jersey Avenue and in the southern areas of the city—built three five-story row houses for boarders in the 1790s. George Washington visited them and Thomas Jefferson lived in one of them before becoming President in 1801. This complex later became the Varnum Hotel and finally the Congress Hall Hotel. The block was razed to make way for the Longworth House Office Building in 1929.

🕦 20 3rd Street SE

RED BAITER—The last home of Senator Joseph R. McCarthy. When the Wisconsin Republican began making his headline-grabbing "disclosures" of Communists in government, he lived at 335 C Street SE.

🕦 The portion of Garfield Park bounded by New Jersey and Virginia Avenues and F and 2nd Streets SE

FORMER MARKETS—One of the earliest markets in the city operated here along New Jersey Avenue in 1803, according to historian W.B. Bryan. City authorities took over the New Jersey Avenue Market and by 1806 opened Eastern Branch Market on the nearby square initially set aside on the city plan for a market site (bounded by Fifth, Seventh, K, and L Streets SE). The city's first Eastern Market remained near the Navy Yard and was often referred to as the Navy Yard Market until the city markets were reorganized after the Civil War. (The present Eastern Market was established at Seventh Street and North Carolina Avenue NE in 1873.)

🕦 517 6th Street SE

LOVE NEST—Former residence of senator and presidential aspirant Gary Hart. In April 1987 he was spotted here by *Miami*

Herald reporters with "model and actress" Donna Rice, who was not his wife. In 1989 the *Los Angeles Times* described this as "the juiciest morsel" of a popular "Scandal Tour" of Washington.

🕦 620 G Street SE

CHRIST CHURCH—This church was erected in 1807. Presidents Jefferson, Madison, and John Quincy Adams attended services here.

🕦 636 G Street SE

THE MARCH KING—The birthplace on November 6, 1854, of John Philip Sousa. It was built in 1844.

Sousa was bandmaster of the U.S. Marine Band from 1880 to 1892. He had joined the band at 13, after his father talked him out of running off with a circus band. For many years, Sousa was a great national celebrity and perhaps the leading local figure not directly associated with politics. Notable among the many works of the man they called the "March King" were "Semper Fidelis" (1888), "Stars and Stripes Forever" (1897), and "The Washington Post March" (1889). The nearby area east of 11th Street to the Anacostia River was called Pipetown, and Sousa commemorated this neighborhood in his "Pipetown Sandy." Sousa died on March 6, 1932, just after conducting his own "Stars and Stripes Forever." He was given a military funeral at the Marine Barracks and buried in Congressional Cemetery.

🕦 8th and I Streets SE

MARINE BARRACKS—Nicknamed "8th and I" by the Marines who served here, this site contains the official home of the commandant of the Marine Corps and occupies the spot picked for this purpose by Thomas Jefferson in 1801. Six years later former Vice President Aaron Burr was confined here while awaiting his trial for treason. The Marine Band is based here.

23 **Southwest corner of 9th Street and Pennsylvania Avenue SE**

NEIGHBORHOOD TAVERN—Site of Tunnicliff's Tavern, an early watering hole and political meeting place. President John Adams stopped here at least twice in 1800 while overseeing the relocation of the federal government from Philadelphia. It was named for William Tunnicliff, its manager from 1796 through 1799. In December 1796 the Washington Dancing Academy used the site for the first ball in the city of which there is any record.

In *Capital Losses,* James M. Goode says the tavern was one of the earliest hotels in the city and the only 18th-century example to survive to be photographed. The building was demolished in 1932 to make room for a gas station, and one stands on the site today.

24 **1801 E Street SE**

CONGRESSIONAL CEMETERY—Established in 1807 with the burial of Maj. Gen. Uriah Tracy of Connecticut, it was originally planned to contain the graves of congressmen and officials who died in Washington. For years it was termed the "American Westminster Abbey." It is the oldest national cemetery. Here rest the remains of Elbridge Gerry, signer of the Declaration of Independence, inspiration for the term "gerrymander," and Vice President; Tobias Lear, private secretary to George Washington; Philip P. Barbour, Justice of the Supreme Court; Gen. Jacob Brown, United States Army; William Wirt, President Monroe's attorney general; Joseph Gales and William W. Seaton, editors of the *National Intelligencer;* George Watterston, first librarian of Congress; J. Edgar Hoover, long-time FBI director; John Philip Sousa, Marine Band leader; Robert Mills, designer of the Washington Monument; Civil War photographer Mathew Brady; and others who have been eminent in the history of this country.

Tragedy has left its mark on this cemetery. It holds the graves for what remained of 21 young women who died in the explosion of the Federal Arsenal—now the site of the Army War College at Fort McNair—during the Civil War. Just inside the main gate is the final resting place of all five members of the Reed family, killed in the fire on the Potomac steamer *Wawaset* on August 8, 1873. The story of the Reed family was for many years symbolic of a particularly nasty tragedy, marked by many safety violations and irregularities, the most notable being that life jackets had been packed away so well that when the fire broke out nobody could get to them. There was villainy too; locals waited by the shore to rob the dead as they drifted into shallow water.

Then there is the grave of Colonel Beau Hickman, the city's great gentleman loafer—the man they called the King of Bummers—who came to the city in 1833 at age 20 with some money from his Virginia family. He ran out of money in two years and spent the next 38 years charming people with his wit and his patrician demeanor while living on other people's money. When he died on September 1, 1873, it could be said that he had never worked a day in his life. He was quickly buried in a pauper's grave, but friends immediately contributed money to have him moved to this cemetery. Many showed up for the move and the second funeral and were shocked when the original grave was opened and it was found that body snatchers had stolen his brains and heart.

A number of what appear to be tombs for members of Congress are in fact empty, making them cenotaphs (a memorial to a person buried elsewhere). Only about 80 of these sandstone monuments are occupied, making them true graves. From 1839 to 1870 one was created for every member, but Congress voted to end the program. During debate on the subject, Senator Hoar of Massachusetts pointed out that being buried under one of these stubby monuments added a new terror to death.

In *Washington: Magnificent Capital,* A. Robert Smith and Eric Sevareid note that the demise of this place as a congressional burial ground had much to do with transportation:

"Until the advent of the railroad made preferred home-state burials feasible, the death of a VIP in Washington meant burial in Congressional. President Zachary Taylor, dead of an intestinal disorder after a year in the White House, Dolly [sic] Madison and John C. Calhoun were temporarily interred here but reburied elsewhere."

After House Majority Leader T. Hale Boggs and Representative Nicholas Begich were lost in a 1972 Alaskan plane flight, a new cenotaph for them was placed in the cemetery.

25 Opposite 19th and C Streets SE

HISTORIC LOCKUP—Site of the present D.C. Jail, which first opened in 1875 as the "Washington Bastille." The most famous 19th-century occupant was Charles Guiteau, who shot President James Garfield. He was committed to the jail on July 2, 1881, sentenced on February 4, 1882, and hanged on June 30, 1882. J. Walter Mitchell, a reporter for the *Times-Herald,* witnessed this execution and wrote in 1918 that "Guiteau was drunk when he ascended the stairs to the scaffold...." He had been made to drink "a heaping" glass of brandy. Guiteau declared it the first strong drink he had ever tasted. As Mitchell recalled later, the effect was magical, and Guiteau's gloomy demeanor changed to one of foolish cheerfulness. He became gay and chattered like a trained magpie. When the procession was formed Guiteau visibly staggered from intoxication, and two guards steadied him by holding onto

Special Chamber. When the Supreme Court vacated its old chamber in the basement of the East Front of the Capitol in 1860, it became the Law Library of the Library of Congress and continued as such until 1950. This is what it looked like before it closed. Because of its bad light and ventilation, the room was considered an architectural disaster. In 1834 architect Robert Mills said of the room, "The floor is sunk below the general level, and makes it very uncomfortable to the members of the bar. Indeed the early death of some of our most distinguished lawyers at this bar has been attributed to the cold damps and want of ventilation in this room."

his arms. As he neared the scaffold he began to sing discordantly: "I'm so glad I'm going to the Lordy...O-O-O I'm so glad I'm going to the Lordy."

26 2001 East Capitol Street SE

DISTRICT OF COLUMBIA ARMORY—Work began on this building in 1940 after a 75-year effort to get an adequate armory for the District National Guard. (An earlier armory was located on the Mall.) Armory Hall, a column-free space of 66,000 square feet, has been a major venue for expositions, sports activities, boat shows, and political events.

27 19th and East Capitol Streets NE

ROBERT F. KENNEDY STADIUM—Completed in 1961 as D.C. Stadium, it was renamed by Interior Secretary Stewart L. Udall on the last day of Lyndon B. Johnson's Presidency in memory of the former attorney general and New York senator who was assassinated in 1968 while seeking the Democratic presidential nomination.

This was the first of the combined baseball-football stadiums known as a "cookie-cutter." In his 1992 book on stadiums, *Green Cathedrals*, Philip J. Lowry describes it as looking like "a wet straw hat, or waffle whose center stuck to the griddle because of its curved dipping roof." Washingtonian Francis W. Brown remembers it was dedicated with a football game between George Washington University and Virginia Military Institute.

In terms of baseball, it stands as the only federally owned ballpark ever used in the majors. The first home run here was hit by Roger Maris. The stadium's last regular-season game, played on September 30, 1971, ended in a forfeit as angry fans of the Texas-bound Senators destroyed seats and stormed the field with the home team leading the Yankees 7-5 in the ninth. The area had now lost two major league teams, one moving to Minneapolis to become the Minnesota Twins, the other to the Dallas area and renamed the Texas Rangers.

That this site was originally a swamp was graphically displayed during the initial 1962 baseball season when sections of left and center field sank as much as six feet.

RFK was long the home of the Washington Redskins, who played their first game here on October 1, 1961, drawing 37,767 who saw the Giants beat the locals 24-21. The team's first win at the stadium did not come until December 17, 1961, when they beat Dallas 34-24 to end a 23-game winless streak dating back to the 1960 season. The team went on to win three Super Bowl championships and compiled a record of 173 wins, 102 losses, and 3 ties before relocating to the new Jack Kent Cooke Stadium in 1997. RFK is home to the D.C. United professional soccer team and is the site of concerts, festivals, and sports events.

28 The open area immediately east of the triangle created by C Street, 19th Street, and the last block of Massachusetts Avenue SE, just south of the Stadium-Armory Metro stop

POOR HOUSE—Officially called the Washington Asylum but better known as the District Poorhouse, the building once on this site held a certain grotesque fascination in the late 19th century when tourists and locals alike could obtain permits to visit from the mayor, a physician, or the Poor Commissioner. In his 1873 book *Washington, Outside and Inside*, George Alfred Townsend described what he saw in one section of the building: "Strolling into the syphilitic wards, where, in the awful contemplation of their daily, piecemeal decay, the silent victims were stretched all day upon their cots; amongst the idiotic and the crazed; into the apartments of the aged poor, seeing let us hope, blessed visions of life beyond these shambles; and drinking in, as we walked, the solumn [sic] but needful lessons of our possibilities, and the mutations of our nature, we stood at last amongst the graves of the Almshouse dead—those who have escaped the dissecting knife."

㉙ East Capitol Street between 14th and 15th Streets NE

CAR BARN—Site of a 19th-century trolley barn that sat idle for many years before being transformed into a striking housing complex in the early 1980s.

㉚ 316 A Street NE

DOUGLASS RESIDENCE—This house was Frederick Douglass' first Washington home after he relocated in 1870 to edit the *New Era* newspaper. A former slave who had escaped to the North in 1838 to become a famous anti-slavery lecturer, he spent his last 25 years in Washington as an editor, lecturer, and District and federal government official.

For many years this was the Museum of African Art, a bureau of the Smithsonian. The museum relocated to larger quarters on the Mall in 1987.

Wartime Washington. A street photographer plies his trade in front of the Capitol in an Esther Bubley photograph of March 1943. Literary critic Malcolm Cowley wrote of Washington at war in *The New Republic* for June 1942: "Washington in wartime is a combination of Moscow (for overcrowding), Paris (for its trees), Wichita (for its way of thinking), Nome (in the gold-rush days, and Hell (for its livability)."

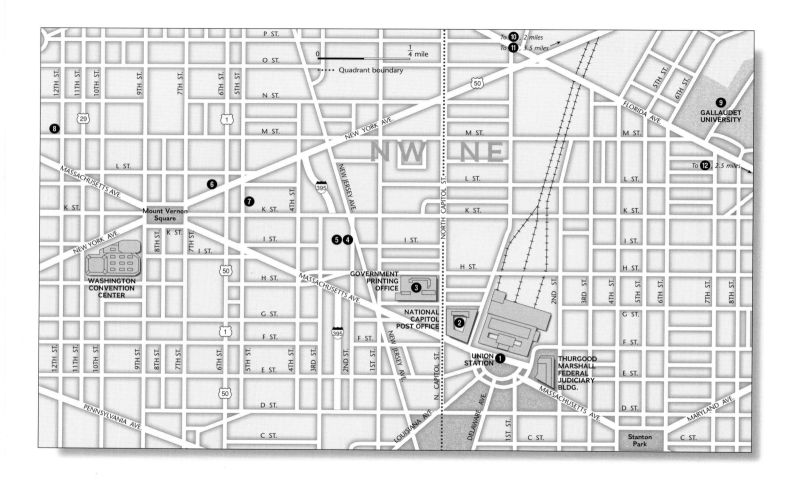

The Union Station Area

① 50 Massachusetts Avenue NE (1st Street and Louisiana and Massachusetts Avenues NE)

UNION STATION—A wooded swampy area until the 20th century, it was picked as the site of a united terminal for the railroad lines whose smaller terminals "marred" the Mall and other downtown sites. Union (for the union of the various lines) Station opened on October 27, 1907, as the Baltimore and Ohio Railroad's *Pittsburgh Express* pulled into the station. A showcase terminal, designed by Daniel Burnham of Chicago, it was heralded as the "great and impressive vestibule" of the nation's capital; its boosters called it the finest railroad station in the world. The main halls of the station were inspired by the Baths of Diocletian in ancient Rome. The station was designed to handle Inauguration Day crowds of up to 100,000 people. According to some claims, 100,000 were on the concourse when Woodrow Wilson returned from the Paris Peace Conference in 1918.

On an average day in 1932, Union Station was used by 32,000 passengers, and its around-the-clock use during World War II is part of its lore. It also featured a private waiting room for the President.

On January 15, 1953, the Pennsylvania Railroad's 16-car *Federal Express* from Boston crashed into the concourse after brake failure. The concourse floor caved in, and the engine and two cars fell through. There were no deaths, as the engineer had signaled ahead, giving the stationmaster a few moments to clear the area. More than 80 people were injured. Had the concourse not

The Old Baltimore and Ohio Station. Between 1852 and 1907, the Baltimore and Ohio railroad station—replete with clock and bell tower—was located about at the point on Union Station Plaza where New Jersey and Louisiana Avenues intersect today. Abraham Lincoln's funeral train departed from here on its ceremonial journey back to Illinois in April 1865. This photograph shows the station in the 1890s. It was razed in 1907 when Union Station went into operation.

Celluloid Palace. This 1922 photograph shows a motion picture theater, the Apollo, which once stood at 624-634 H Street NE. It is one of many stunningly attractive movie theaters that are no longer in existence.

collapsed, the train would have smashed into the commuter-filled waiting room.

As the nation's rail system began to falter in the 1950s and 1960s, the station slipped into decline. An attempt was made to give the place new life by transforming it into the National Visitors' Center, which opened on July 4, 1976. The Visitors' Center featured an ill-advised and poorly executed 10-minute slide show that, when it was working, was presented in a large sunken area of the station's floor. Known as the Primary Audio-Visual Experience, or PAVE, most people referred to it as "the pit." The Visitors' Center attracted few visitors after the Bicentennial summer and was closed in 1978.

The building declined rapidly from inadequate maintenance. After the roof leaked, causing plaster to fall and toadstools to grow inside, the main building was sealed up in 1981. The railroad station continued to function at a position at the rear of the building, accessible through plywood passageways. Union Station had become a mammoth white elephant, leaving officials with two options: demolish or redevelop. Congress set up a public/private partnership to save it, establishing the Union Station Redevelopment Corporation, which then engaged LaSalle Partners of Chicago to lead the redevelopment. Upon reopening in September 1988 after a 181-million-dollar renovation, the new station featured more than 120 restaurants and shops, a nine-screen movie complex, and facilities for the eight million passengers who ride trains in and out of Washington each year. A rousing success with residents and visitors, the revitalized Union Station boasts average daily attendance between 70,000 and 75,000 and total annual sales exceeding 100 million dollars.

② Northeast corner of North Capitol Street and Massachusetts Avenue NE

THE OLD CITY POST OFFICE—Formerly the city's main post office (from 1914 until 1986 when that function was relocated to 900 Brentwood Road NE). Designed by Daniel Burnham's firm as a beaux arts companion to neighboring Union Station, this building became the site in 1993 of the National Postal Museum, a joint project of the Smithsonian and the U.S. Postal Service. The building's 200-million-dollar restoration and redevelopment, designed by Shalom Baranes Associates of Washington, also allowed extensive space for government offices in addition to retail activities and a branch post office.

During the years it served as the Washington City Post Office it was regarded as the model for all future post offices because of its modern mail-handling equipment. The system relied on conveyor belts (one through an underground tunnel for bringing the enormous amount of government mail from the Government Printing Office directly into the post office), bucket lifts, gravity chutes, and a miniature trolley system to carry small amounts of mail, or even single important letters, from one section of the workroom floor to another.

③ West side of North Capitol Street between G and H Streets NW

GPO—These immense redbrick buildings comprise the Government Printing Office (known locally as the GPO), an agency established in 1861. When the building at the G Street corner was completed in 1903, it was considered the largest printing plant in the world and is still listed in the *Guiness Book of World Records* as such. The GPO prints *The Congressional Record and Federal Register*.

④ 201 I Street NW, southeast corner of New Jersey Avenue and I Street

MOUNT JULEP—The residence of Stephen A. Douglas, senator from Illinois and candidate for the presidency in 1860, was once on this site. Known as the "Little Giant," Douglas moved here in 1857. The house became known as "Mount Julep" because of Douglas's role as provider of good food and drink. This house and three attached to it (see next entry) were known as Douglas or Minnesota Row. The last of the units fell in 1965. Today this site and the following one are covered by the northern leg of I-395.

⑤ 205 I Street NW

GRANT'S HOME—This site, together with those at Nos. 201 and 203 I Street, was used as a hospital during the Civil War. Number 205 was given to Gen. Ulysses S. Grant and his wife by admirers after the war. The Grants lived in the house from 1865 to 1869, when they moved to the White House after his election to the presidency. Number 203 was presented to Grant's war colleague, Gen. William T. Sherman.

⑥ 615 New York Avenue NW

THE LAST BLACKSMITH—Site of G. Herbert Ofenstein's blacksmith shop, the city's last, which closed January 30, 1959. The shop had been on the site since 1860. According to the chronicler of the Columbia Historical Society, Ofenstein had worked there 56 years without a vacation and was known for having shod 225 horses in one day "back in 1910." Principal clients were horses used by the fire and police departments.

In recent decades the site has been the parking lot for A.V. Ristorante Italiano, a venerable Washington eatery.

BENNING ROAD NE. This has been the traditional staging area for the circus when it arrives in town by rail. Over the years there have been many newspaper photographs of grand processions of elephants marching down this road to the circus site, which is usually at the intersection of 15th and H Streets NE. Lifelong District resident, Francis W. Brown, when 89 years young, recalled in a letter written in 1992: "Here the 'Big Tent' of Barnum and Bailey was raised annually. We regularly watched the roustabouts hammer the stakes in the ground."

7 East side of 5th Street between K and L Streets NW

HOUSE OF WAX—In 1872 Board of Public Works member, Alexander R. "Boss" Shepherd, directed the forced eviction of vendors from the market space on Mount Vernon Square. Incensed, the vendors incorporated and erected a block-long market building at this nearby Fifth Street location. The building had an enormous iron-framed, 324-foot arched roof rising 85 feet above the 284 market stalls. After the addition of a second floor in 1891 provided a 5,000-seat auditorium, its name was changed to Convention Hall, although the market continued to operate on the first floor. During the 1920s the upper space was converted and billed as "The World's Largest One Floor Bowling Alley." Fire destroyed the upper portions of the building in 1946. It continued to operate as a market on the ground floor until the 1960s, when it became the home of the National Historical Wax Museum. The museum boasted 75 large-scale tableaus reproducing scenes from American history. The figures, despite the name of the museum, were made of vinyl. The building has since been torn down.

8 1205 M Street NW

WHITMAN HOUSE—Site of one of the cheap boarding houses where poet Walt Whitman lived while in the city. During the Civil War, Whitman worked in various temporary hospitals around the city nursing the Union wounded. Today it is the site of the Claridge Towers apartments.

9 Intersection of Florida Avenue and M Street NE

GALLAUDET UNIVERSITY (established in 1857 as the Columbia Institution for the Deaf, Dumb and Blind, Gallaudet College became a university in 1986)—Named for Thomas Hopkins Gallaudet, pioneer educator of the deaf, Gallaudet is said to be the only liberal arts college in the world for the hearing-impaired. It is located in a parklike setting once called Kendall Green, formerly the Amos Kendall estate. Kendall was President Andrew Jackson's postmaster general and political advisor. In addition to founding the college, Kendall allowed Samuel F.B. Morse the use of a cottage on the estate in which to develop the telegraph and became Morse's business manager. On the grounds is Daniel Chester French's bronze sculpture group showing Gallaudet teaching a deaf child by making the letter "A" with his right hand.

An interesting first that emerged from Gallaudet was the football huddle. Devised by the college's star quarterback, Paul Hubbard, who led the team from 1892 to 1895, it was intended to shield the deaf team's hand signals from the opposition. The practice spread when Hubbard took the huddle with him to the Kansas School for the Deaf, where he went to teach and coach. Before long, other schools in the Midwest—not just those for the hearing-impaired—were using it.

⑩ 2530 Bladensburg Road NE

FREEDOM IN A CAST—Sculptor Clark Mills, responsible for the statues of Andrew Jackson (in Lafayette Square) and George Washington (in Washington Circle) among others, lived and worked on a farm just east of Bladensburg Road about 1 1/2 miles north of its intersection with Benning Road NE. Mills' foundry was an unusual two-story octagonal building. In it he cast the colossal statue of "Freedom" now on the Capitol dome, after the original plaster by William Crawford. The building was demolished about 1900.

⑪ Fort Lincoln New Town, off Bladensburg Road near the district line NE

REFORMING DELINQUENTS—The site of a Civil War fort defending Washington, this location became the National Training School for Boys and is now a housing development. The *WPA Guide to Washington D.C.* described the school in the 1930s as "a federally operated rehabilitation school for boys from any part of the United States who have violated Federal laws." When the British attacked Washington in 1814, the Battle of Bladensburg (August 25, 1814) swirled nearby. Commodore Joshua Barney had scuttled his boats to prevent their capture, and marched his sailors and marines to join the ground forces assembling at Bladensburg to defend the capital. The forces were routed but Barney and his men stood their ground, firing their battery until captured. Breastworks from Fort Lincoln's Civil War era can be seen at nearby Fort Lincoln Cemetery.

⑫ 3701 Benning Road NE

A-BOMB PARTS—This was the site during World War II of the Capital Tool and Manufacturing Co., a machine shop run by the Dorr family that became the scene of intense activity for a year while developing components for the atom bomb. The highly secret project was reported in the *Washington Times-Herald* (August 10, 1945), where Joseph Dorr was then employed as a master pressman. The article quoted a War Department spokesperson's opinion that "it has taken thousands of people like the Dorrs and their relatives to shape the pattern of peace."

Women's Dorm. Over 30 temporary buildings were erected on this site in front of Union Station to house government workers during the World War I era. One group of these buildings, the Union Plaza Dormitories, was built between 1918-1920, specifically for 2,000 female government workers. The dorms featured maid service and a spacious dining room serving two meals a day. These "Government Hotels" were razed starting in July 1931, to clear the area for today's Union Station Plaza. Directly in front of Union Station is the Columbus Memorial Fountain by Lorado Taft.

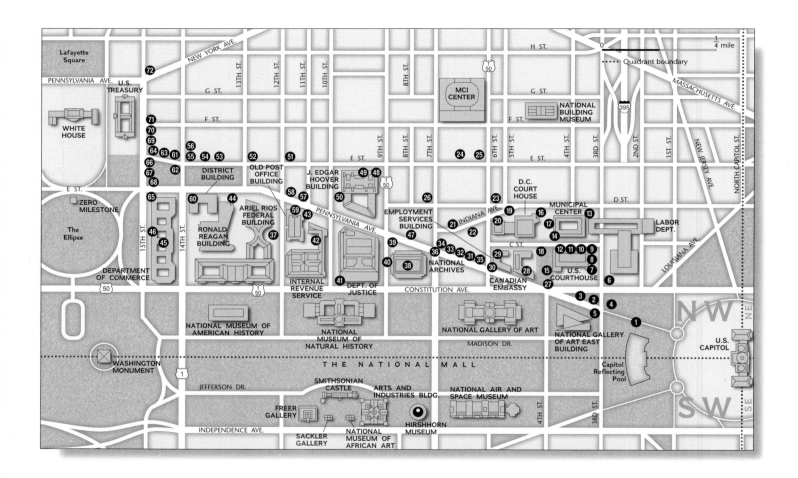

Old Pennsylvania Avenue—America's Main Street

① Intersection of Pennsylvania Avenue and 2nd Street NW

JEFFERSON TO THE RESCUE—President Thomas Jefferson was said to have directed the rescue of a number of men caught in a flood of Tiber Creek, which crossed Pennsylvania Avenue at this site until covered over in the late 19th century. Writer James Croggon noted that initially Pennsylvania Avenue ran right through the stream and that a small footbridge was erected for pedestrians. When a sudden flood prevented Jefferson from riding through to the Capitol for his second inaugural in 1805, he dismounted, crossed the footbridge, and walked the rest of the way.

Later an arched bridge over the creek at this location was a major attraction for local anglers. Writing in 1919 in the *Times-Herald,* Captain J. Walter Mitchell, who had fished here 50 years earlier, commented, "Most of the boys of old Washington who were wont to line the balustrade of the bridge and with hook and line yank the festive 'catties,' eels, and roach fish from the creek flowing placidly below, are now in the great beyond."

For 15 years after its arrival in 1835, the Baltimore and Ohio Railroad, the first to reach the city, terminated at what was then the northwest corner of Pennsylvania Avenue and Second Street. Today this site is just north of the reflecting pool at the foot of Capitol Hill. The depot was later relocated to New Jersey Avenue and C Street NW.

Klan Women. Part of a massive August 8, 1925, Ku Klux Klan demonstration in which some 50,000 members of "The Invisible Empire" marched up Pennsylvania Avenue. The exact reason for the show of strength remains unclear. The Klan members displayed American flags and departed from their usual public practice by throwing aside their hoods and allowing their faces to be seen. *The City of Magnificent Intentions,* a D.C. history textbook, suggests that the Klan was trying to soften its image of violent and racist behavior. The size of the march apparently took Washington by surprise. H.L. Mencken is quoted as writing in *The New York Sun* that the showing was "grander and gaudier by far than anything the Wizards had prophesied." The *Baltimore Afro-American,* meanwhile, described the event as the "greatest demonstration of intolerance ever held in a land dedicated to tolerance."

STREET LORE

PENNSYLVANIA AVENUE. Washington's main street was named after Pennsylvania when that state lost its bid to have the nation's capital located in Philadelphia. It was a consolation prize. In 1800, when the federal government moved to Washington, the boulevard existed as little more than a name and a line on a map. One congressman was appalled to note that this supposed great avenue was, in reality, "a deep morass covered with elder bushes."

The first president to have an inaugural parade on Pennsylvania Avenue was Thomas Jefferson, and the only president to walk back down the avenue after his inauguration was Jimmy Carter in 1977.

There have been many parades on the avenue, but the longest of them all began on May 23, 1865, when over 200,000 troops returning from the Civil War marched in the Grand Review of the Union Armies. For two days they marched in ranks of up to 60 abreast. The Army of the Potomac marched all day on the 23rd, followed the next day by William Tecumseh Sherman's Army of the West. The sprightly pace of Sherman's troops, lean and tough from their southern campaign to the sea, made them the favorites of the grateful crowd.

The area at the foot of Capitol Hill, now the site of the East Wing of the National Gallery of Art and park areas adjacent to Pennsylvania Avenue, was once a thriving commercial neighborhood, part of a section called "Hash Row" in the 19th century because of the large number of boarding houses, hotels, and bars, including the following four places.

2 Northwest corner of Pennsylvania Avenue and 3rd Street NW

GADSBY'S—Among the hotels that once stood where Constitution and Pennsylvania Avenues now merge were Gadsby's in the 1830s and 1840s, the Washington House, run by Amanda Beveridge and her family from the late 1850s to 1881, and the Vendome in the 1920s. Boarders included future President James Buchanan, and Hanibal Hamlin and Henry Wilson, vice presidents to Lincoln and Grant, respectively.

3 339 Pennsylvania Avenue NW

JACKSON HALL—Erected in 1845, approximately where the monument to Civil War Gen. George Gordon Meade is now located, Jackson Hall was the home of the *Congressional Globe*, precursor of *The Congressional Record*, and between 1878 and 1882 site of the newly established *Washington Post*. Its meeting halls were used for many Democratic Party functions, including President Zachary Taylor's inaugural ball in 1849, held to benefit the poor.

4 Northeast corner of Pennsylvania Avenue and 3rd Street NW

ST. CHARLES HOTEL—The St. Charles was erected here in 1820. A temporary residence for many congressmen before the Civil War, it later became a favorite hotel for visiting American Indian delegations conducting business with government agencies. After about 1900, it became the Capital Hotel. When the building was razed to build a filling station in the 1920s, remains of a pre-Civil War slave pen were uncovered in the basement. Today a grassy park with gardens rests on what was one of the busiest sections of Pennsylvania Avenue in the 19th century.

❺ Southwest corner of Pennsylvania Avenue and 3rd Street NW

MADES HOTEL—During the post-Civil War period, Mades Hotel was the first tavern reached by those traveling from Capitol Hill along Pennsylvania Avenue to the executive offices across town. According to writer George Rothwell Brown, it was noted for fried chicken, game and frogs. The owner of property where gold was discovered in California, John A. Sutter, died here in 1880 while lobbying for financial relief from Congress, his lands having been jumped in the frenzied gold rush of the late 1840s.

Construction of the Frances Perkins Department of Labor Building and the inner leg of I-395 in the late 1960s required the elimination of parts of Second, Third, and C Streets between Constitution Avenue and D Street NW. The following three sites were once located in this area.

❻ 219 3rd Street NW

DUELIST—Now the site of the Department of Labor, this was once the boarding house residence of Congressman Jonathan Cilley of Maine, who became the first (and only) House member killed in a duel when shot by Representative William J. Graves of Kentucky on February 24, 1838. Cilley had served less than a year and found himself challenged after his remarks during congressional debate were held to be an affront to Graves's allies. The duel was fought

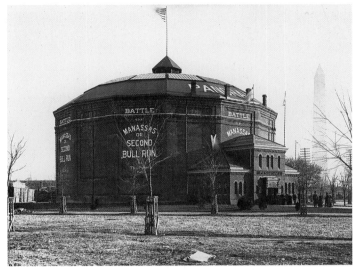

Early Cyclorama. On the east side of 15th Street between E Street and Constitution Avenue NW was the site from 1885 to 1918 of the Manassas Panorama Building. The 16-sided building was erected to present a large-scale mural of the Second Battle of Manassas, and it was subsequently used to exhibit murals of other Civil War battles as well. World War I temporary buildings replaced the Panorama in 1918. Part of the Department of Commerce building covers the site today.

Northwest Corner of 2nd Street and Pennsylvania Avenue NW. This photograph graphically underscores the degree to which Pennsylvania Avenue has changed over the course of the 20th century.

with rifles at Bladensburg, Maryland. Cilley's death, after the third exchange, caused a national furor against dueling in the District and led to anti-dueling legislation a year later, after ex-President Andrew Jackson charged that "Cilley was sacrificed." Jackson challenged Congress "to wipe out the stain of the blood of the murdered Cilley from its walls." Graves vigorously argued the moral virtues of dueling in defense of honor and principle, and opposed the anti-dueling bill, stating that "it requires a higher order of courage to refuse than to fight a duel." Congress thought otherwise and passed the bill.

7 224 3rd Street NW

BOARDING HOUSE—One of the most notable boarding houses in this area during the 19th century was operated on the site of today's E. Barrett Prettyman Courthouse by the Beveridge family from about 1880 to 1909. For over 50 years, the Beveridges specialized in catering to the needs of visiting American Indian delegations at this establishment, known as the "Indian House," and in a building on the northwest corner of Pennsylvania Avenue and Third Street NW, known as Washington House. Their rooming houses accommodated Geronimo, Red Cloud, White Feather, Crazy Horse, and other famous chiefs. In *Diplomats in Buckskin* (1981), historian Herman J. Viola quotes Benjamin Beveridge as claiming in 1906 to have met more Indians "of different tribes, I reckon, than any man in the United States, and I've never been a hundred miles from Washington." The housing of the Indian delegations was a steady business, paid for by the government. Service included room and board, medical care, and facilitating business arrangements. A scandal caused the Beveridges a temporary setback in 1873. They lost their lucrative business with the Bureau of Indian Affairs when Benjamin was found to have falsified invoices to the bureau to cover payments to prostitutes.

8 **226 3rd Street NW**

FILLMORE RESIDENCE—As U.S. Representative and Senator, respectively, Millard Fillmore and John C. Calhoun resided in a house once standing on this site while attending sessions of Congress. In 1850, Fillmore succeeded to the presidency upon the death of Zachary Taylor. As President he dispatched the naval expedition under Commodore Matthew Perry that opened up commerce with Japan in 1853. South Carolinian Calhoun led Southern states-rights advocates for over 30 years in efforts to limit federal interference with the practice of slavery.

Accompanying construction in the 1930s of the Federal Triangle complex, the area between Judiciary Square and Pennsylvania Avenue NW was developed for court buildings and new municipal offices for the District of Columbia. Several blocks of residential and commercial buildings were displaced, including those once occupying the following four sites.

9 **308 C Street NW**

KEY LOCALE—Francis Scott Key, author of "The Star-Spangled Banner," moved to a residence here in 1833 to seek respite from the construction noise on the Chesapeake and Ohio Canal then being extended behind his house in Georgetown. He lived here until his death in 1843.

10 **312 C Street NW**

CLAY RESIDENCE—Henry Clay resided in a house on this site, then known as Mrs. Dilly's boarding house. Clay served Kentucky in Washington for more than 40 years, as U.S. Representative and

Senator, and was defeated three times as a candidate for president. Noted for his eloquence and ceaseless efforts to preserve the Union, Clay played key roles in the Missouri Compromise in 1820 and the Compromise of 1850, each an attempt to reconcile differences over the extension of slavery into western territories seeking statehood. Although successful in forging political compromises, Clay was decidedly uncompromising in his personal principles, stating, according to the *Oxford Companion to American History,* that he'd "rather be right than be President" when told that his public position opposing abolition of slavery would cost him votes.

11 **326 C Street NW**

ELOPEMENT SITE—Gen. John C. Frémont, called "the Pathfinder" after his exploits in the West, was boarding here as a lieutenant in 1841 when he eloped with Jessie Benton, resident of nearby 334 C Street NW and daughter of Senator Thomas Hart Benton of Missouri, one of the nation's most powerful lawmakers. Mrs. Benton supposedly opposed the match on the grounds that Jessie was only 16 and couldn't endure the rigors of a military marriage. In 1856 Fremont became the first Republican candidate for the presidency, losing to James Buchanan. The Frémonts later lived at 318 C Street NW.

12 **334 C Street NW**

BENTON HOME—Thomas Hart Benton, Senator from Missouri and champion of exploration of the West, construction of a railroad to the Pacific, and preservation of the Union, lived in a house on this site. After his pro-Union sentiments cost him his seat in 1850, he wrote his famous political memoirs and 15-volume "abridgement" of congressional debates since 1789, completing it on his deathbed here in 1858. Writer James Betts recounted in 1879 a conversation with an "Irish bookseller" named Shillington who had supplied Benton with news articles and back copies of the *Congressional Globe*. "He knew that he had but a week or two to live, and he was running a race with death to get the book finished; for he believed that it was the vital thing to keep the country together."

---

13 Southwest corner of D and 3rd Streets NW

BLAGDEN ROW—The Municipal Center of the District of Columbia, which has occupied this site since the 1930s, and the Labor Department cover one of the most elegant early residential areas of the District, the former Indiana Avenue. A five-building complex of connected four-story row houses, Blagden Row, dating from 1852, occupied 310-318 Indiana Avenue. Chief Justice Roger Brooke Taney lived at No. 318. One of seven justices appointed by Andrew Jackson to the Supreme Court, Taney presided as Chief Justice for 28 years. When Taney died in 1864, President Lincoln and his Cabinet attended funeral services at the house.

Another prominent resident nearby at 324 Indiana Avenue was Adm. Robley D. Evans, popularly known as "Fighting Bob." He perfected the long-distance signal lamp in 1876 and was influential in getting the U.S. Navy to build warships of steel rather than wood.

John Marshall Place once extended from Pennsylvania Avenue to D Street NW, beginning opposite where today's Fourth Street meets Pennsylvania Avenue. The following five sites are today covered by John Marshall Park and, between C and D Streets NW, by the D.C. Municipal Center and court buildings.

14 Former northeast corner of C Street and John Marshall Place NW

ADAMS CHRONICLED—Site of a residence of John Quincy Adams. One of this man's unique achievements was that he was elected to the House of Representatives two years after leaving the White House. He served with distinction in Congress from 1831 to 1848.

15 Former 213 John Marshall Place NW

PIERCE SITE—Before he became President, Franklin Pierce was a boarder in the house formerly on this site.

16 Former southwest corner of John Marshall Place (extended) and D Street NW (opposite Old City Hall)

FREEMASON'S HALL—Erected here in 1826 to accommodate five "lodges," or chapters, of the Masonic Order in Washington. Combining the notions of professional practice and fraternalism harking back to the Middle Ages, the Masonic Order claimed the most prominent of American leaders among its members. Inaugural balls for Andrew Jackson (1833) and William Henry Harrison (1841) were held there (see also Dance Theater, p. 43, and Carusi's, p. 58). A prominent site for social and political events during the mid-19th century, the building later housed lawyers practicing at the nearby courts until razed in the 1930s.

17 Former John Marshall Place, between C and D Streets NW

FIRST PRESBYTERIAN—The First Presbyterian Church was erected here in 1827 and attended by Presidents Andrew Jackson, James A. Polk, Franklin Pierce, and Grover Cleveland. Church members provided a "female charity school" in the early 1840s, prior to the development of a comprehensive city public school system after 1860. Shortly after the Civil War, church membership was split when a charitable group of prominent Republican women gained use of the church for a lecture by black orator and civil rights champion Frederick Douglass to benefit destitute black women and children. The city's other lecture halls had denied them access. Douglass was at the time on a speaking tour in support of black suffrage. Byron Sunderland, pastor for 33 years, served from 1867 to 1869 as the second president of the newly established theological seminary for Negro men known as Howard University, organizing the law, medical, agriculture, military, and commercial schools. The church was demolished in the 1930s.

⓲ Former southwest corner of C Street and John Marshall Place NW

METROPOLITAN MEMORIAL METHODIST EPISCOPAL CHURCH—Built at a then-substantial cost of $250,000, when this neighborhood was among the most fashionable residential areas in the city, the Metropolitan Memorial Methodist Episcopal Church was completed on this site in 1869. According to historian James M. Goode, the building was a prime local example of Gothic Revival church architecture; its 240-foot spire was the tallest private structure in the city in the 1870s. Parishioners prior to its demolition in the 1930s included Presidents Grant, McKinley, and Coolidge, Chief Justice Salmon P. Chase, and many prominent federal and local officials. Goode notes that plaques and busts commemorating many of these figures earned the church the nickname the "Westminster Abbey of American Methodism."

⓳ Indiana Avenue, opposite 5th Street NW

DANCE THEATER—On this site the "new" Washington Theatre was constructed after the former Washington Theatre at 11th and C Streets NW burned in 1820. The building was renamed

Traffic Control. This photograph from 1915 was taken at the corner of Pennsylvania Avenue and 14th Street NW. It shows a Haynes automobile and one of the manually operated semaphore traffic signals common in the city until 1925 and the advent of electric traffic lights. The umbrella protected the officer from rain and sun. A former traffic officer, Joseph V. Osterman, told the authors the streetcar owners paid half the salaries of the semaphore operators because the officers helped keep the streetcars on schedule. The structure in the background is the venerable Willard Hotel.

JOHN MARSHALL PLACE AND PARK. What is now 4th Street NW once was called 4 1/2 Street from the Old City Hall south. The two blocks between Judiciary Square (D Street NW) and Pennsylvania Avenue were lined with residences, churches, and public buildings, all now removed. The name of the street was changed to John Marshall Place in the 20th century in honor of the nation's third chief justice, who served from 1801 to 1835. He once lived in a rooming house at a site indicated by a plaque at the Pennsylvania Avenue end of the walk along the east side of what has become John Marshall Park since the street was removed in the late 1970s. Today in the park one finds there a sculpture of two chess players by Lloyd Lille and a copy of John Marshall's sundial.

the American Theatre (also known as the Washington Assembly Rooms) and was adapted to host one of President William Henry Harrison's three inaugural balls in 1841. The three events occurred because of disagreements among Harrison's supporters over ticket prices.

The $10 dollar private event was held on this site on March 4, 1841, while a public event called the People's Tippecanoe Inaugural was held at Carusi's Assembly Rooms (see also Carusi's, p. 58) the same night for $5 a ticket. Harrison attended the latter. The third ball was held on March 9 at Freemason's Hall (see also Freemason's Hall, p. 42).

20 500 Indiana Avenue NW, in front of the D.C. Courthouse

HOLE IN THE GROUND—Here on December 9, 1969, ground was broken for the new Metro subway system. Symbolic shovelfuls of earth were turned with a gilded spade by officials of local jurisdictions, both states, and the U.S. Department of Transportation. Work began the next day when bulldozers filled the ceremonial hole and commenced digging across the street.

21 637 Indiana Avenue NW

ELEVATING HISTORY—Litwin's is a furniture and antiques store that has been in the family since 1912. Its freight elevator, operated by hoisting a rope hand-over-hand, is quite possibly the oldest of its type still operating in the District. Smithsonian curator emeritus Robert M. Vogel says the elevator dates from the 1880s. Owner Fred Litwin says the elevator is still being used to move furniture from floor to floor, and it continues to meet District of Columbia safety and licensing requirements.

22 South side of Indiana Avenue between 6th and 7th Streets NW

SEATON HOTEL—The Seaton Hotel was located here, a six-story building used for a time as the city post office and converted in the 1880s into the Central Union Mission. The mission was described by Charles M. Pepper in 1900 as a multi-denominational service agency stressing self help and providing the destitute with food and lodging in return for work. "A genuine tramp has no standing in the Mission. If he is hungry, he must either saw wood for his meal or move along." The mission had a 1,200-seat auditorium, dining room, chapel, bunks for 85, and two horse-drawn "Gospel Wagons" plying the streets to serve and convert the needy. The site is now occupied by a luxury apartment building.

23 Northeast corner of 6th and D Streets NW

RINGS A BELL—Once the site of the First Unitarian Church, dedicated on June 9, 1822. Many important figures worshiped here, including John Quincy Adams. Designed by Charles Bulfinch, the building stood for 55 years. It had the first church bell in the new City of Washington, cast in Paul Revere's foundry in 1822.

24 623-627 E Street NW

MUSICAL LANDMARK—Buildings in which the Columbia Record Company was born. In 1889 a group of court reporters formed the Columbia Phonographic Company to take dictation of the human voice. The fledgling firm in 1890 produced the world's first musical recordings—phonographic cylinders containing the marches of the U.S. Marine Band—despite the fact that the phonograph's inventor, Thomas Edison, didn't think music could be satisfactorily reproduced. In 1893, the company became the first to record the female voice when it recorded songs by Susan Davenport. After releasing her first group of songs, including

Old Louisiana. The south side of Louisiana Avenue between 4 1/2 and 6th Streets as it looked in 1927. It has since been renamed Indiana Avenue. George Manthos, who lived in the quarters above Manthos Brothers Confectionery on the left, has identified other locations in the image: "Two doors down, the two buildings that look alike, contained the Marine Reserve Center in the late 1930s and until World War II. This reserve unit was sent to Iceland in early 1941," he writes, adding, "Next to the Reserve Center, the tall building was the D.C. Police Headquarters until they built the new one on the SW corner of Indiana and John Marshall Place."

Map on page 36

Down the Avenue. View from the Treasury Department stairs looking down Pennsylvania Avenue toward the Capitol as it looked in 1927. Then, as now, the Occidental was an avenue landmark. The large building in the middle of the photograph is the Raleigh Hotel.

renditions of "Daddy Won't You Buy Me a Bow Wow" and "Ta Ra Ra Boom Der E," she was never heard from again. The company moved to 919 Pennsylvania Avenue NW in 1893 and later to Bridgeport Connecticut, and finally evolved into Columbia Records. The building still stands on this spot.

25 Northwest corner of 6th and E Streets NW

CHASE HOUSE—Salmon P. Chase resided in a house at this location. Rival to Lincoln within the Republican Party, Chase served loyally in Lincoln's wartime Cabinet as Secretary of the Treasury, earning appointment as Chief Justice of the United States, where he served from 1864 until 1873. He moved in 1869, and the house was used for a boarding house, among other purposes, until purchased and razed by the Hecht Company in 1936, to become a parking garage. Today the site is occupied by the headquarters of the American Association of Retired Persons (AARP).

26 Northwest corner of 7th and D Streets NW

THE *NATIONAL INTELLIGENCER*—For much of its history the *National Intelligencer* was located on this site, now 400 Seventh Street. Beginning as a tri-weekly in 1800, the paper became a daily in 1814 and served as the main city paper and a leading one in the nation until 1870. It was published by Joseph Gales, Jr., and his brother-in-law William Winston Seaton from 1812 to 1865, during which time each served as mayor of Washington. According to Fred A. Emery's article "Washington Newspapers" in the *Records of the Columbia Historical Society* (1937), the two men were the "first official reporters of Congress" and had privileged access to the House and Senate debates. Many stories about Congress first published in the *National Intelligencer* were recirculated in other papers nationwide.

British Adm. Sir George Cockburn ordered the building demolished during the attack on Washington in August 1814, a reprisal for Gales's editorial comments about him. Other private buildings were spared, but the admiral allegedly said he did not want Gales to feel slighted after learning the British had burned the President's house. Contemporary Washingtonian Margaret Bayard Smith noted that the admiral agreed not to burn the building for fear others on the block would also catch fire, but instead ordered it torn down and the papers burned in the street.

Later this corner was the site of Alexander Gardner's photographic gallery. Gardner worked for Mathew Brady and took many of the Civil War battlefield photographs published by Brady.

27 4th Street and Pennsylvania Avenue NW

FIRST CHINATOWN—This intersection was once the heart of Chinatown. In 1935 when the government began acquiring the land on which Chinatown was situated, the elders of the community hired a real estate agent to buy property a few blocks north on H Street NW. To the astonishment of the city, Chinatown packed up and moved en masse to the new area.

28 501 Pennsylvania Avenue NW

CANADIAN EMBASSY—Pierre Charles L'Enfant's original plan for the District envisioned embassies flanking the Mall, but not until the Canadian government began building its embassy here in 1986 did one appear in the area. At one time this was the site of Mrs. Peyton's boarding house, where such politically disparate luminaries as John C. Calhoun, Henry Clay, Robert Y. Hayne, Henry A. Wise, and Henry Wilson resided. Wilson was a strong abolitionist and senator from Massachusetts who introduced an early bill in Congress for emancipation in the District. He became

STREET LORE

PENNSYLVANIA AVENUE. In their 1965 book *Washington: Magnificent Capital,* A. Robert Smith and Eric Sevareid aptly described the evolution of the avenue: "By mid-twentieth century Pennsylvania Avenue had lost its social magnetism. The Federal Triangle, the great wedge of government buildings, had cleaned up the appearance of the south side but deadened it after twilight. Harvey's restaurant had moved to Connecticut Avenue, leaving the Occidental the only recommendable dining room on the entire avenue. The *Star* and the *Post* had built modern publishing plants elsewhere. New hotels farther uptown had eclipsed those that remained on the avenue. And commercial sin had been outlawed. The old promenade was dying and no one seemed to care."

But help was on the way. The Pennsylvania Avenue Development Corporation was created by Congress in 1972, to guide the preservation and development of the Pennsylvania Avenue area and surrounding city blocks. PADC followed a series of commissions and councils dating from the early 1960s that grew out of President Kennedy's observation of the deterioration of the area during his inaugural ride down the avenue.

THE FIRST AVENUES. "No American had an avenue as his address until after the founding of Washington", wrote George Stewart In *Names on the Land* (1945), his classic work on American place names. Before the City of Washington was laid out with its broad avenues named for the states, the word "avenue" was used only as a French or British designation for a tree-bordered approach to a country house.

Grant's vice president in 1873 and is considered one of the founders of the Republican party. Calhoun and Hayne were South Carolinians and rabid states' righters; Henry Clay was the Great Compromiser who sought to mediate between the two sides.

㉙ North side of the 500 block of Pennsylvania Avenue NW

BONUS ARMY ENCAMPMENT—This is where the ragtag "Bonus Army" gathered in 1932 after arriving in the city to demand bonus money the participants felt they were owed for their service in World War I. Some 20,000 jobless World War I veterans converged in June 1932 to lobby for a cash bonus approved by Congress in 1924, but not to be paid until 1945. Most camped along the Anacostia River, but others occupied vacant lots and buildings along Pennsylvania Avenue near the present site of the National Gallery of Art.

While many departed after Congress adjourned on July 16, about 10,000 remained. Food supplies were exhausted. Despite the enlightened actions of District police superintendent Pelham D. Glassford to defuse the situation, tensions mounted as federal and District authorities demanded the veterans leave town and threatened forcible eviction.

Fighting broke out between city police and the protesters on July 28 and federal troops attacked, led by Army Chief of Staff Gen. Douglas MacArthur and his subordinate, Maj. Dwight D. Eisenhower. In an April 25, 1971, *Washington Post* article, reporter Paul Hodge reconstructed the scene: "Gen. MacArthur changed into his full-dress uniform, mounted his horse, and led 800 soldiers down Pennsylvania Avenue. Soldiers threw tear gas...the cavalry followed, flags flying and sabers drawn, with tanks under the command of Maj. Eisenhower rumbling behind."

According to historian Constance McLaughlin Green, the forces included six Whippet tanks with hooded machine guns. Once veterans along the avenue and on the Mall were routed by tear gas and their makeshift dwellings crushed and burned, the forces turned on the main encampment, "Camp Marks," along the Anacostia River. Smoke from the destruction lingered for two days. The losses were 2 veterans and 2 babies dead, 3 babies abandoned, and 66 veterans and police injured. Hodge reported that Gov. Albert C. Ritchie of Maryland spoke for many in decrying the use of force and the sight of "men driven into the night at the point of the bayonet. To an uninformed and unwarned public the whole thing came as a shock."

In 1864 Walt Whitman lived in this block—one of his many Washington locations—and prior to that it was the site of a popular gambling palace known as Pendleton's Palace of Fortune.

30 Northeast corner of Pennsylvania Avenue and 6th Street NW

NATIONAL HOTEL—Formed from six row houses built in 1816, the 200-room National Hotel was for many years after it opened in 1826 one of the largest in the nation. Elevated to four stories in 1844 and renovated in 1857, the hotel was a perennial favorite. It was severely damaged in an October 1921 fire and converted in 1931 into a National Guard Armory. It fell to the wrecker's ball in 1942.

Andrew Jackson was a guest here when he took the oath of office in 1829 and Henry Clay died in the hotel on June 29, 1852. Mathew Brady lived here during most of his Washington years. In 1857, while staying at the National during his inaugural celebration, President James Buchanan fell victim to an illness that many ascribed to poisoning but was later determined to be due to bad sewers. The alleged poisoning—which took the life of Buchanan's nephew—was attributed to abolitionists by some Southerners and referred to as "Buchanan's mysterious sickness" for many years to come. John Wilkes Booth stayed at the National on April 13, 1865, the night before he shot Lincoln; from his room he watched the massive celebration on Pennsylvania Avenue of Lee's surrender.

31 Former 615 Pennsylvania Avenue NW

DEBUT OF AN ANTHEM—About 1805 Solomon Myer opened the Pennsylvania House here, next to William Duane's bookstore on the corner of Sixth Street. Myer's establishment was supplied by water piped from a prized spring two blocks away near C and Fifth Streets. It later became the McKeown Hotel, where "The Star-Spangled Banner" was first sung in the District, shortly after being penned by Francis Scott Key and set to music. According to the *National Intelligencer* of December 14, 1814, the occasion was a ceremony for retiring Secretary of the Navy William Jones. A boun-

Major Fire. Spectacular fire of May 9, 1861, next door to the old Willard Hotel being extinguished by Col. E. E. Ellsworth's New York Fire Zouaves, a unit of 1,100 men that was one of the first to sign up to defend the Union. The Zouaves, named for and dressed like the French Zouaves of the Crimean War, playfully attacked the fire like a troop of acrobats. Having saved the hotel, the Zouaves were treated handsomely by the Willard brothers.

WATCH YOUR QUADRANT. A few old—but still relevant a century later—lines from the turn-of-the-century book *Around the Capital:* "Washingtonians will tell you that the system of dividing the city into the four sections of the compass is a beautiful one—when you understand it; but the difficulty is understanding it. If you are so constituted as to be able to see a joke in everything, it is very amusing to find that upon arriving in the city, and wishing to locate an address given you, and after spending considerable time in reaching the street and number, you discover yourself miles from your destination because you failed to notice the talismanic N.W. or S.W. attached to the end of your address. If you are humorously inclined you will laugh at your predicament—but the chances are very great the other way."

tiful dinner was served and ended with the presentation of some 25 toasts. Key's "very beautiful and touching, lines...were sung with great effect by several of the guests." (That is, one imagines, by those still able to stand.)

Two buildings at 601 and 633 Pennsylvania Avenue today cover the block between Sixth and Seventh Streets that held many famous hotels and businesses over the years.

32 **North side of Pennsylvania Avenue between 6th and 7th Streets NW**

HOTEL ROW—For over a century this entire block was the site of many famous hotels succeeding the Pennsylvania House and McKeown's Hotel. In 1820 the Indian Queen was established here and extended along the block by Jesse Brown. The Indian Queen, according to *Rider's Washington*, "remained for many years Washington's leading hotel kept by Jesse Brown, the 'Prince of Landlords,' who wearing a large white apron, personally presided at table, on which decanters of brandy and whiskey were served without extra charge."

Brown's hotel was the site where President John Tyler took the oath of office in 1841. In his *Washington, Outside and Inside* (1873), George Alfred Townsend notes that this was the first hotel in the city to establish a "bridal chamber."

After the hotel became the Metropolitan in 1851, exiled Hungarian patriot Lajos Kossuth and his entourage were entertained here in 1852 and, according to *Washington, Outside and Inside*, "Kossuth's compatriots went to bed with their boots and hats on after getting very drunk...." Charles F. Crisp resided in the Metropolitan while speaker of the House, as did many other members of Congress. The Metropolitan was replaced in 1935 by an office building complex at 601 Pennsylvania Avenue NW.

33 633 Pennsylvania Avenue NW

MR. LINCOLN'S CAMERA MAN—Serving today as the Sears Roebuck and Company's governmental affairs office, this complex combines the twin-towered Central National Bank building erected in 1888, and the double building which included the Brady National Photographic Gallery from 1858 into the early 1870s. Mathew Brady, "Mr. Lincoln's camera man," photographed almost all of the notables of his era in this building. His reception area was on the first floor and his studios and processing areas were on the upper floors. He lost the studio when he fell into financial trouble, declaring bankruptcy in 1873. (An earlier depictor of presidents, portrait painter Gilbert Stuart, also had his studio on the north side of Pennsylvania Avenue between Sixth and Seventh Streets NW from 1803 to 1806, close to, if not on, the very spot of Brady's studio 60 years later.)

The building was later the site of Zadoc D. Gilman's ornate drug store, known for decades as Gilman's. In the late 1960s the drug store had deteriorated and was remodeled as a camera store.

From the early 1940s into the 1980s the Central National Bank structure, also known as the Apex building, housed a popular discount liquor store—an ironic neighbor to Temperance Fountain out front.

34 Northeast corner of Pennsylvania Avenue and 7th Street NW

TEMPERANCE FOUNTAIN—One of a number of water fountains built by a teetotaling dentist, Dr. Henry Cogswell, as an alternative to hard liquor. This example, topped by a water crane representing the purity of water, was erected about 1880.

Photographer's View. This 1865 photograph by Mathew Brady was taken out of his studio window at 633 Pennsylvania Avenue. The large ornate building is Center Market. While at this address, Brady photographed the likes of Walt Whitman, Robert E. Lee, and Abraham Lincoln. It was said that Brady's nondescript three-story brick building attracted more prominent people than any other place in Washington save for the White House itself.

Great Flood. Floodwaters covered much of downtown Washington in February 1881, as shown in this view down 7th Street toward Pennsylvania Avenue.

It should be noted that during much of the 19th century the city's red-light district began at this point and stretched along Pennsylvania Avenue to 15th Street.

35 Northwest corner of Pennsylvania Avenue and 6th Street NW

AURORA BOOKSTORE—Site of one of the city's earliest bookstores (1801-07), operated by William Duane, who was the editor of the *Philadelphia Aurora* newspaper.

36 Pennsylvania Avenue and 7th Street NW

HIGH WATER MARK—On June 1, 1889, the Potomac rose from the same storm that caused the tragic flood that destroyed Johnstown, Pennsylvania, the day before and killed more than 2,000. The residents of Washington were so morbidly fascinated with the horror of Johnstown that they seemed genuinely surprised when the Potomac transformed Washington into what one reporter termed a "wet and bedraggled imitation of Venice," with more than two feet of water at this site. Nobody died as a result of the Potomac flood in Washington, but it turned the city upside down. Boats navigated Pennsylvania Avenue for days, and a "canal culture" emerged as much business was conducted from second-story windows with people in boats.

Consisting of 70 acres of bureaucrats, the Federal Triangle complex of federal offices today covers the next ten sites. The base of the triangle is 15th Street NW, its sides are Pennsylvania and Constitution Avenues, and it reaches its apex just beyond the Federal Trade Commission near Sixth Street NW, where the two avenues intersect. Taken for granted today, the

Federal Triangle was considered a public works marvel when construction occurred in the 1920s and 1930s. In a special guidebook prepared for the third Roosevelt inauguration in January 1941, the complex was described as the "largest single enterprise of the kind ever carried out by any nation in the history of the world." Its buildings contained the Federal Trade Commission, the National Archives, the Department of Justice, the Post Office Department, the Department of Commerce, the Department of Labor, the Government Auditorium, and the Interstate Commerce Commission. It was initially left unfinished; the structure intended for the north side at Pennsylvania Avenue and 14th Street, which would have displaced the District Building, was not built. Instead the area east of the District Building and the vast space behind it—first planned to be a grand plaza opening on 14th Street—became the city's largest parking lot for the next half century.

The completion in 1998 of the 3.1 million-square-foot Ronald Reagan Building and International Trade Center, covered eleven acres of the original Federal Triangle site. Promotional material on the building describes it as larger than any federal building but the Pentagon and having more square feet than the Empire State Building. Consisting of ten stories above ground and five below, the building contains sufficient concrete to pave a two-lane 106-mile highway, and its exterior includes 42,000 slabs of limestone from Indiana. But the greatest superlatives are its costs. As the building neared completion the Washington Post analyzed the massive project (November 16-17, 1997) and noted that the tab, including projected long term financing costs on an 818-million-dollar mortgage, stood at 1.9 billion dollars.

In a Washington Post article (May 24, 1998), architecture critic Benjamin Forgey noted a yet unrealized possibility that courtyards, walkways, and public amenities within the overall

Center Market. The National Archives covers the site of the old Center Market, located in various structures between 7th and 9th Streets on the south side of Pennsylvania Avenue NW and the Mall from 1801 to 1931. This 1920s photograph shows market stalls across from the National Museum of Natural History grounds, shortly before the buildings were razed to construct the Justice Department and National Archives, as part of the Federal Triangle project to provide government offices and beautify the city.

Map on page 36

Enormous Flag. Parade staged sometime before 1931, when Harvey's restaurant (in the right background) was still on the south side of Pennsylvania Avenue NW opposite 11th Street. The site is now occupied by the Internal Revenue Service building.

Federal Triangle complex could be connected and promoted as a "Federal Walkway," serving as both a center for public activities and a link between the city's commercial core and the museums and life of the National Mall. This prospect would draw on existing but unimplemented plans. It also would convert the barrier of buildings between the city and the Mall—which has a modern-day effect equivalent to that of the squalid 19th-century canal on the site of today's Constitution Avenue that caused the Mall and Southwest Washington to be referred to as "the Island"—into a bridge between two vital and interdependent areas of the capital city. The public spaces and facilities of the Reagan Building significantly advance this goal.

37 Area from the old canal—which is now Constitution Avenue—north along the Ellipse almost to Pennsylvania Avenue NW

MURDER BAY— Before and during the Civil War, freed slaves from Virginia and poor whites poured into what was certainly the city's worst slum known as Murder Bay. Some moved on, but many died here in squalid poverty. At what may have been its worst in 1867, police superintendent Major Richards wrote of the area: "Here, crime, filth and poverty seem to vie with each other in a career of degradation and death....Whole families are crowded into mere apologies for shanties which are without light or ventilation. During storms of rain or snow their roof's [sic] afford but slight protection, while from beneath a few rough boards used for floors, the miasmatic effluvia from the most disgustingly filthy and stagnant water renders the atmosphere within these hovels stifling and sickening in the extreme. Their rooms are usually not more than six or eight feet square, and not a window or even an opening (except a floor) for the admission of light. Some of the rooms are entirely surrounded by other rooms so that no light at all reaches where persons spend their nights and days. In a space of about fifty yards square I found about a hundred families composed of about three to five persons each living in shanties one story in height except in a few instances where tenements are actually built on top of others."

During the Civil War this area earned the name "Hooker's Division" when Gen. Joseph Hooker mandated that the city's prostitutes be concentrated there, according to news stories at the time. The coincidence of the general's name being the same as the slang word for a prostitute undoubtedly popularized the area's nickname, which persisted, along with the bawdy houses, until construction of the Federal Triangle began in the 1920s. The area was also home to a racially and ethnically mixed working class, but by 1900, virtually all the residences in the area were brothels. Archaeological finds on the Reagan Building site revealed the differing lifestyles of the residents: cheap buttons from the homes of the working poor; jewelry, light fixtures, and bones from expensive steaks from the sites of the brothels.

38 The block bounded by 7th and 9th Streets (8th Street ends at this point) and Constitution and Pennsylvania Avenues NW

WINDOWLESS TREASURE HOUSE—The National Archives was built between 1931 and 1937 to house U.S. government documents, including the most important ones of all: the Constitution, the Bill of Rights, and the Declaration of Independence. When new, the building attracted much comment because this immense structure lacked outside windows. Preservation and display of the nation's precious formative documents is a constant concern. A 4.8-million-dollar project to design and build new display cases,

Globe Theater. This photograph taken from the corner of Pennsylvania Avenue and 11th Street NW, shows the southeast corner of D and 11th Streets NW. The glass street sign in the center right was once the standard for the city.

Harvey's Corner. The southeast corner of Pennsylvania Avenue and 11th Street NW was home to Harvey's restaurant from just before the Civil War until 1932. Every President from Grant through Franklin D. Roosevelt dined here. It was famous for its oysters and during the Civil War 50-foot high piles of oyster shells were disgorged on to Pennsylvania Avenue. Reader Robert M. Morris pointed out to the authors that the marchers in the foreground are the Washington High School Cadet Corps. The Corps marched in Presidential inaugural parades. Morris himself marched in Woodrow Wilson's second inaugural parade in 1917.

a new vault, and a monitoring system—replacing units from 1952 that are beginning to deteriorate—will take place between 2001 and 2003.

The National Archives covers the site of the old Center Market that occupied this part of the south side of Pennsylvania Avenue from 1801 until it was demolished in 1931. The city's 19th-century commercial center formed around the market. According to Jason Baum in The *Washington Post* on March 9, 1990, more than 140 businesses operated in or near the market by 1870. Daniel Webster, a gourmet with his own chef, was often seen marketing here. But for all its color, the market had its drawbacks. It was located next to the open sewer that was the Washington Canal. The canal not only gave off a terrible smell but occasionally overflowed. In 1872 the canal was filled in and a massive brick two-block-long market building was erected, eventually expanding to accommodate 1,000 vendors and 30 produce wagons by 1890.

Longtime District resident Francis W. Brown told the authors he remembers the large ballroom on the second floor of the market being used variously for a skating rink, professional wrestling matches, "chicken shows," and, from 1920 to 1924, as the home court for The George Washington University basketball team.

39 SE Corner, 9th Street and Pennsylvania Avenue NW

FDR MEMORIAL—Placed in front of the National Archives, the Franklin D. Roosevelt Memorial is a simple granite block, dedicated in 1965, etched with these words: "In Memory of FRANKLIN DELANO ROOSEVELT, 1882-1945."

One day in 1941 President Roosevelt summoned his friend Supreme Court Justice Felix Frankfurter to his office. "I am likely to shuffle off long before you kick the bucket," said Roosevelt, according to the justice. "If they are to put up any memorial to me,

I should like it to be placed in the center of that green plot in front of the Archives building. I should like it to consist of a block about the size of this," he said, pointing to his desk. Just the same, a half century later his admirers built the 48-million-dollar memorial to him described in Chapter 5 (see FDR Memorial Number 2, p. 102).

⓺ 9th Street between Constitution and Pennsylvania Avenues NW

OPERA HOUSE—The landmark Ford's Opera House formerly located on this site was purchased by the federal government in 1931, to be razed for the Federal Triangle project. Earlier it was the site of Wall's Opera House and, during the 1870s and 1880s, the Bijou Theatre. *Keim's Hand-book of Washington* (1884) described Ford's as one of the "best places of amusement in the city....Here the standard comedies and tragedies and plays of the day are performed by excellent stock companies during the winter season, varied at intervals by Italian, German, or English opera, and the presence of theatrical 'stars.'" It was managed by the same family that ran Ford's Theatre.

⓻ Northeast corner of 10th Street and Constitution Avenue NW

WASHINGTON GAS WORKS—Where the Justice Department now stands was the site of the original Washington Gas Works, established in 1848 by the Washington Gas Light Company. According to *Growing With Washington,* the company's history, the firm was chartered by Congress after James Crutchett received a $17,500 appropriation in 1847 to demonstrate the use of gas for lighting by illuminating the Capitol grounds. Tubes carried the gas from an improvised plant outside, through the Capitol building, and up to an enormous gas lantern mounted on an 80-foot tripod on top of the dome. The light not only illuminated the grounds but was visible for many miles down the Potomac. The government was

Sinful Section. Looking toward the Mall and the Smithsonian from the Treasury Department, this 1860s photograph shows the red-light district called Murder Bay later replaced by the Federal Triangle complex of government office buildings. Building materials for completion of the Treasury Building line 15th Street in the foreground.

Map on page 36

Market Square. Looking down Pennsylvania Avenue toward the Capitol. The large building with the two turrets on the right is the Center Market, built in 1871 after a fire destroyed the previous building. The new market covered an area of three acres between 7th and 9th Streets NW and featured a large refrigeration system for perishables.

the initial client when the company was formed, then stores and hotels along Pennsylvania Avenue in 1850, and finally the general public in 1851. A new gas plant was constructed on the Mall in 1852.

42 Site of the Internal Revenue Service, formerly the northeast corner of 11th and C Streets NW

CARUSI'S (Harrison's Last Dance)—Theaters and public halls operated on this site beginning in 1805, the most prominent by the Carusi family during the 19th century. Carusi's Assembly Rooms replaced the Washington Theatre, which burned in 1821 after having been the first theater erected in the city. Its opening show in 1805 was a popular farce entitled "Wives As They Were and Maids As They Are." The Carusis operated a dancing academy and provided a site for the inaugural balls of every president from John Quincy Adams (1825) through James Buchanan (1857), with the exception of Tyler and Fillmore, who succeeded presidents who died in office. One of the deceased luminaries was William Henry Harrison, who met his maker a month after his inaugural ball here on March 4, 1841. Franklin Pierce's inaugural ball was to have been held at Carusi's, but was canceled because of the death of his young son in January 1853. Boston mayor and future Harvard president Josiah Quincy reported in 1826 that he saw the waltz introduced into society for the first time at a ball at Carusi's. After its glory years, the building in 1872 was transformed into a burlesque hall (known as the Washington Theater Comique) when upscale attractions moved elsewhere. The building was razed in the 1930s for the Federal Triangle project.

43 South side of Pennsylvania Avenue NW opposite 11th Street

HARVEY'S—Now the site of the Internal Revenue Service, from 1858 to 1931 this was the location of Harvey's restaurant. It moved from this spot in 1931 to 1107 Connecticut Avenue NW to make way for the Federal Triangle project. In 1975 it was forced to move again, this time because of construction of the Farragut North Metro station. The new location was at 1001 18th Street NW.

Owner George Harvey is credited with creating a new dish in 1862—steamed oysters. Patrons had become impatient waiting for the oysters to be roasted, according to Robert Kimmel in *Mr. Lincoln's Washington,* and Harvey responded by steaming them. Oysters were so extremely popular that during the Civil War Harvey's advertised to delighted Washingtonians that its own little pung boats were daily running the Confederate blockade of the Potomac River to bring in fresh oysters.

In a 1977 review of the restaurant, *Washington Post* dining critic Phyllis C. Richman took note of Harvey's remarkable longevity. "In 1874, the Washington city directory listed but thirty restaurants. By 1877, the number jumped to over 200. Only one of them has survived to this day...Harvey's...." Alas, Harvey's, no longer owned by the family, closed its doors in 1991.

44 South side of Pennsylvania Avenue between 13th and 13 1/2 Streets NW

FIRST LIBRARY—Washington's first library was established on this site in 1812. Wilhelmus Bryan wrote that it was open two days a week, for two hours, and lent to shareholders only. By 1815 it held over 900 volumes and published a catalog. The site is now the location of the Ronald Reagan Building and International Trade Center.

45 The block bounded by 14th and 15th Streets and Constitution and Pennsylvania Avenues NW

COMMERCE DEPARTMENT—When it opened it was said to have floor space equivalent to the land of a good-size farm. The

Center Market. The city's main market was located where the National Archives is today, spreading throughout the adjacent streets.

Map on page 36

Early *Post*. This image was taken at 10th and D streets NW during the celebration of the Garfield inaugural in 1881. At that time, the building to the right was the home of the *Washington Post*. After the building pictured was burned in an 1885 fire, the *Post* building was rebuilt on the spot with two more stories.

building stands on 15,000 pilings driven into the soft bed of Tiber Creek. When completed in 1932 at a cost of 17.5 million dollars, it was seen as a visible symbol of the growing power and cost of the federal government. George Rothwell Brown noted in 1933 that the new complex "is flung across several squares in a neighborhood once a part of one of the most notorious 'red light' districts in the world." Today it also contains what is said to be the nation's oldest public aquarium, established on another site in 1873. The aquarium entrance is on 14th Street NW between Constitution and Pennsylvania Avenues.

46 East side of 15th Street between E Street and Constitution Avenue NW

PANORAMA—Where part of the Commerce Building is located today was the site from 1885 to 1918 of the Manassas Panorama Building, a 16-sided building erected to present a large-scale mural of the Second Battle of Manassas, and subsequently used to exhibit murals of other Civil War battles. According to historian James M. Goode, the owners also presented vaudeville shows, demonstrations of Edison's phonograph, and Civil War lectures. The building was converted in 1903 into the city's first major automobile garage, and replaced by World War I temporary buildings in 1918.

---

47 Market Square, on the north side of Pennsylvania Avenue between 7th and 9th Streets NW, immediately north of the National Archives

U.S. NAVY MEMORIAL—Funded through private donations, this commemoration of Navy men and women was dedicated on October 13, 1987. The "Lone Sailor" bronze statue was designed by sculptor Stanley Bleifeld. The memorial includes an amphitheater for public concerts by the Navy Band and other groups. Behind the memorial is the recent Market Square development—which architecture critic Benjamin Forgey notes is a "nonmarket unsquare" by function and shape—employing massive neoclassical architectural motifs to reflect the Federal Triangle buildings in the vicinity.

The following three sites are covered today by the J. Edgar Hoover FBI Building, which occupies the block bounded by Pennsylvania Avenue, Ninth, Tenth and E Streets NW. The building was dedicated on September 30, 1975, after being completed at a cost of 126.1 million dollars. It was given its new official name on May 4, 1972, two days after the death of Hoover, the FBI's first director. Although the immensely popular FBI tours draw more than half a million people a year, the building itself has its share of detractors. Preservationist and historian James M. Goode calls it the "city's best example of Brutalism—a phase of the International Style of architecture. Its forbidding and fortress-like, overpowering features make it one of the most unpopular buildings among local residents."

48 914 E Street NW

MARINI'S HALL—On this site stood Old Temperance Hall, later known as Marini's Hall. Local historian Washington Topham mentions in the *Records of the Columbia Historical Society* that the building was completed in the early 1840s and served as headquarters for various temperance organizations of the city. During the Civil War it was an armory. Then it became Marini's Assembly Rooms and Fashionable Dancing Academy. E.E. Barton's *Historical and Commercial Sketches of Washington and Environs* provided an account of Marini's in 1884: The 40-by-150-foot ballroom, flanked by "dressing and reception rooms for ladies and gentlemen," was

Thespian House. The new National Theatre was the fifth on its Pennsylvania Avenue site when completed in 1885 and the first not to be destroyed by fire. Its prominent facade and ornate interior proclaimed the District's cultural aspirations. In 1922 it was razed to make way for the current building.

a "model of neatness and beauty." Marini's was "patronized by the elite of the city, for indulging in what has aptly been called the 'poetry of motion.'" The ballroom, with its 650-seat capacity, was also used for concerts. It was razed on February 2, 1935.

49 916 E Street NW

SPY NEST?—Site of a boarding house where an Englishman named George Downing was arrested in 1898, as the nation prepared for war with Spain. The city underwent a scare when rumors circulated that the city was loaded with spies. An extensive manhunt brought the police, Secret Service, and military to this address, where Downing was found with "incriminating" documents. Before he was brought to trial, Downing, who had served in the U.S. Navy as a petty officer in the Washington barracks, hanged himself in his jail cell. He was the only spy arrested in the roundup.

50 Northeast corner of 10th and D Streets NW

PETER FORCE HOME—On this site was the home of Peter Force, a printer and historian who compiled the *American Archives*, documenting early affairs of the federal government, and who sold an invaluable collection of over 50,000 works to the Library of Congress. Philp's *Washington Described* (ca 1861) called Force's holdings the world's "most complete library upon American history." Force also served as mayor of Washington from 1836 to 1840.

The Washington Gas Light Company constructed a building on this site (413 10th Street NW) in 1866 to house its main office. Next on the site was the Hutchins building, named after *Washington Post* founder Stilson Hutchins. The *Post* was located here from 1880 to 1889. According to *Rider's Washington*, the city's first experimental electrical generating plant was set up in the building in

Rum Row. The Imperial Hotel and the old National Theatre fit in with the saloons of E Street NW between 13th and 14th Streets NW. On February 10, 1881, this block was subjected to what George Rothwell Brown described as "one of the most spectacular raids in the history of the city" when four police detachments not only rounded up gambling equipment but some of the city's most influential public figures.

1881 for electrical lighting along Pennsylvania Avenue to mark the reunion of veterans of the Army of the Cumberland.

---

51 Northeast corner of E and 12th Streets NW

WHISTLER'S HOUSE—James McNeill Whistler once lived in a house that was on this site. Whistler took up painting in Paris after failing chemistry and leaving the United States Military Academy in 1854. He eventually became one of America's best known painters, although he lived as an expatriate in England. One of his most famous works, "Arrangement in Grey and Black," located in the Louvre, was a portrait of his mother.

52 Northeast corner of 13th and E Streets NW

MOVIE PALACE—The restored Warner Theater brings to modern Washingtonians the glory days of the American theater. It first operated as the Earle Theater in 1924. In a letter to the *Washington Post* (October 3, 1992), Henry H. Brylawski, descendent of the family that built the original theater, noted that investors at the time named it after Governor Earle of Pennsylvania, but it was renamed the Warner in 1947 when Harry Warner of Warner Brothers became a controlling investor. During its heyday it was a center for live stage, featuring America's favorite entertainers, and a premiere movie palace. It declined in the 1980s and closed in 1989. Following a 10-million-dollar renovation funded by Kaempfer Company developers, and guided by Shalom Baranes Associates architects Gary Martinez and Patrick Burkhart, the Warner reopened in 1992. It is incorporated into a block-long office building designed by James Ingo Freed. Because the theater entrance faces Freedom Plaza, the developer succeeded in securing the prestigious address of 1299 Pennsylvania Avenue for the complex. Brylawski credited the building's sensitive restoration to

Snowscape. E Street between 13th and 14th Streets at the turn of the century. The *Washington Post* building is third from the left and the National Theatre, farther down the block, sports two towers. At the time of this photograph the two buildings were relatively new. The paper stayed at this location until 1950.

Map on page 36

Shoomaker's. The E Street saloon, which 1920s journalist George Rothwell Brown called "a rendezvous unique in the annals of Washington."

the developer/architect team but also to its designation as a historic landmark, thus providing protection and incentives for its preservation and continued public role.

The J.W. Marriott Hotel, National Place, National Theatre, and the 1301 Pennsylvania Avenue NW office building sit upon the four sites described below.

53 Formerly E Street, now Pennsylvania Avenue, between 13th and 14th Streets NW

NATIONAL THEATRE—The current National Theatre occupies the sixth building erected here since 1835 for theatrical performances. An alternate inaugural ball for President James K. Polk was held here on March 5, 1845, by Democrats protesting the official ball organized by local Whigs. The event was marked by high spirits but poor organization; most attendees failed to leave with their own wraps. After performances resumed the next night, a fire started that destroyed the theater. A temporary building was erected for a performance by singer Jenny Lind in 1850 and then replaced by a new National Theatre, which housed performances by Charlotte Cushman and Edwin Thomas Booth (brother of John Wilkes Booth) before it too burned in 1857. Grover's Theater opened on the site in 1862, and after remodeling became the National Theatre in 1864, presenting Joseph Jefferson and other notables before burning again and reopening in 1874. That building burned in 1885 and was replaced by an ornate five-story structure, which was replaced in 1922. This building survives with various improvements, the latest completed between 1982 and 1984.

Like other public facilities in Washington, the National Theatre was segregated prior to the 1950s. According to *The Guide to Black*

Washington, blacks were restricted to the balcony from 1835 to 1873. After 1873 they were refused admission altogether until the theater was integrated in 1952, four years after President Truman's Advisory Committee on Civil Rights issued a report condemning segregation in the District.

54 Former 1337 E Street NW

THE *POST* BUILDING—Directly opposite the main entrance to the District Building, a plaque on the wall of 1331 Pennsylvania marks the former site of the fourth home of the *Washington Post,* occupied from 1893 to 1950, when it moved to 1150 15th Street NW. The old *Post* building was an elaborate and imposing affair described as being in the "Gashouse Gothic" style.

55 Northeast corner of Pennsylvania Avenue and 14th Street NW

NEWSPAPER AND RUM ROWS—Now occupied by the J.W. Marriott Hotel, this corner once served as the intersection of "Newspaper Row" and "Rum Row." Along 14th Street were the offices of the *New York Herald, New York Times, New York World, Philadelphia Public Ledger, Boston Transcript,* and *Cincinnati Gazette.*

After the Civil War, the Western Union telegraph office was located around the corner on what was then called E Street. Also there, in the 1890s, and also serving newspapermen of the day, was Rum Row, a string of watering holes along Pennsylvania Avenue that began at 14th Street and ran eastward. It included Tim Sullivan's popular bar and the Lawrence Hotel, which sported a beer garden and Washington's first cabaret. George Rothwell Brown recounted that Colonel Joseph Rickey, a St. Louis lobbyist and drinkmeister at nearby Shoomaker's Tavern, was the originator of the "Whiskey Rickey," composed of whiskey, Apollinaris water, and lime juice, later made with gin and called the "Gin Rickey."

Changing Downtown. A view from the Washington Monument about 1900 shows the Federal Triangle area when it was still a section of two- and three-story commercial, residential, and light-industrial structures, including the Pepco powerhouse at the lower left, next to a lumber yard on what is now the site of the Departmental Auditorium across from the National Museum of American History. At left center the new *Evening Star* and Post Office Department buildings, completed in 1898 and 1899 respectively, announce a new scale of public architecture for the 20th-century city.

Map on page 36

Old Willard. This 1870s photo shows the 1858 extension of the Willard Hotel on the southwest corner of 14th and F Streets NW. Below to the left is part of the original hotel, which also faced on Pennsylvania Avenue. Willard's Hall, the Greek temple structure to the right, served successively as the F Street Presbyterian Church, a theater operated by the Willards, and the site in 1861 of an unsuccessful last-minute effort of Northern and Southern officials to negotiate away the impending Civil War. Both sites are now covered by the modern Willard Hotel.

For much of the 20th century, the building at the intersection of Pennsylvania Avenue and 14th Street, taking in Newspaper Row and part of Rum Row, was occupied by Bassin's Restaurant, a downtown magnet for those in search of an economical meal, including tourists, office workers, and reporters from the adjacent National Press Building. Bassin's opened the city's first sidewalk café here in 1961, winning the city's approval despite predictions of dire consequences, including the attraction of ladies of the night. None of the forecasts came to pass.

In the late 1970s and early 1980s, the buildings on the site were razed as part of the Pennsylvania Avenue redevelopment, including those formerly housing Bassin's and the *Washington Post* building on E Street.

56 Northeast corner of 14th and E Streets NW

POLITICAL SALOON—Former site of Dennis Mullany's Saloon, which George Rothwell Brown described as a rallying center for Irish Americans and others favoring the Boers in their war against the British in South Africa in the 1890s. Later the bar was a hangout for a group of politicians and journalists called the "Brain Trust," which decided to promote Woodrow Wilson for the presidency. Wilson was eventually nominated and served two terms.

57 Northwest corner of 11th Street and Pennsylvania Avenue NW

STAR CORNER—The *Evening Star* building was erected on this site in 1898. It is regarded as a prime Washington example of the beaux arts style. *Washington Post* architecture critic Benjamin Forgey viewed the rehabilitation of this exuberant turn-of-the-century building—a "splendid splinter," he termed it—as a testament to the work of the Pennsylvania Avenue Development Corporation. In this case, the bold, upright facade expressing the civic confidence of 1890s Washington, D.C., was saved and joined with new wings to the west and north that complement the original.

The *Star* was one of four newspapers in the city when established in a print shop at Eighth and D Streets NW, on December 16, 1852. From 1854 to 1881 it occupied engraver William A. Stone's building on the southwest corner of Pennsylvania Avenue and 11th Street. It then moved across Pennsylvania Avenue, occupying various buildings there until the "splendid splinter" was constructed in 1898. Although a hundred papers had already failed in Washington's early history, the *Star* survived for 129 years. A *Star* handbill, at its inception, pledged to give the "most reliable Washington News, fearlessly expressing all the Corruptions of Government, and every attempt to defraud the public Treasury...."

58 Northeast corner of Pennsylvania Avenue and 12th Street NW

KIRKWOOD HOUSE—Now the site of an office building at 1111 Pennsylvania Avenue, beginning in the 1820s it was the location of many important hotels, including the Fountain Inn, Fuller's, and the Irving, the name of which was changed to the Kirkwood House after a senator died there of smallpox in 1853. Vice President Andrew Johnson was living at Kirkwood's when Lincoln was shot at the nearby Ford's Theatre on the night of April 14, 1865. The conspirators were unsuccessful in their attempt also to kill Johnson, and he was sworn in as president at the Kirkwood the next morning, immediately following Lincoln's death. The Kirkwood was replaced by Alexander R. "Boss" Shepherd's Centennial office building, which was turned into the Raleigh Hotel in 1893. With additions in 1905 and 1911, the Raleigh became one of the city's most prominent hotels until razed in 1966 to make way for the present building.

After the War. The famous Wartime Information Center as it looked after World War II and was used as a center to aid veterans.

Old Pennsylvania Avenue—America's Main Street 67

Lots of Artists. The Corcoran Building, demolished in 1917 to make way for the Hotel Washington, housed the studios of many local artists.

59 South side of Pennsylvania Avenue between 11th and 12th Streets NW

THE OLD POST OFFICE—This Romanesque Revival structure, built between 1892 and 1899 and nicknamed "Old Tooth" because of its tower, is the tallest building in the city. It was designed by Willoughby J. Edbrooke. When it originally opened it was the first major steel-frame building in the city and boasted the largest uninterrupted enclosed space—a 99-by-184-foot interior court—of any building in Washington.

Slated for demolition from 1928 to 1975 because it did not fit the neoclassic lines and uniform height restriction of the Federal Triangle, local preservationists fought long, hard, and successfully to save it. Restoration began in 1978. The building now houses an array of shops and restaurants as well as the offices of the National Endowments for the Arts and Humanities and the Institute for Museum and Library Services.

60 Southeast corner of 14th Street and Pennsylvania Avenue NW

THE DISTRICT BUILDING—Washington's city hall, completed in 1908. Earlier it was the location of Washington and Allison Nailor's Livery Stables. Then, in 1892, with cable streetcars replacing horse cars, it became the site of the power house for the Washington and Georgetown railway, later known as Capitol Traction. The block-long brick building was supposedly fireproof. Nevertheless, in one hour on September 29, 1897, it succumbed to a spectacular fire. George Rothwell Brown reported that the only remaining wall sported the sign "Absolutely Fireproof." The building's immense chimney stood for five years as a testament to the disaster, until dynamited on September 4, 1902.

The District Building's design resulted from a competition whose guidelines specified a "classical design in the manner of the

English Renaissance." The sculptured figures across the front represent "Sculpture" (with mallet, presumably portraying the Italian sculptor Adolfo de Nesti), "Painting" (palette), "Architecture" (Ionic capital), "Music" (harp), "Commerce" (winged globe), "Engineering" (surveying instrument), "Agriculture" (grain), "Statesmanship" (eagle), and just over the main entrance, the District coat of arms flanked by "Justice" (scales) and "Law" (scroll).

For years a statue of Alexander R. "Boss" Shepherd stood in front of the building at Pennsylvania Avenue and 14th Street. In 1980, during the administration of Mayor Marion Barry, it was removed without explanation. The work, by Ulric Stonewall Jackson Dunbar, was the city's first outdoor statue in honor of a native Washingtonian and was dedicated on May 3, 1909. As head of a massive public works program in the 1870s, Shepherd both transformed and bankrupted the city. He was controversial in his own time and since. Historian Constance McLaughlin Green describes Shepherd's statue as the "one example in America of a politician portrayed with his hand behind him." As of this writing in 1999, the statue stands in an automobile impoundment lot across the Anacostia River, with Boss Shepherd looking toward Maryland. Efforts are continuing by the Association of Oldest Inhabitants of the District of Columbia to return the statue to an appropriate display site in the District.

In 1977, the District Building as well as the Islamic Center (2551 Massachusetts Avenue NW) and the headquarters of B'nai B'rith (1640 Rhode Island Avenue NW) were taken over by Hanafi Muslims. The act was an attempt by the sect to avenge the 1973 murders of Hanafis. Future Mayor Marion Barry, then a city councilman, was wounded, one reporter was killed, and 124 hostages were held at the three sites for 39 hours.

Prior to 1908, Washington's city hall was located at Fifth Street and Indiana Avenue NW.

Inaugural Throng. Theodore Roosevelt's inaugural parade of 1905 from the Treasury Department showing the old Corcoran Building on the right and Rhodes Tavern, the three-story building to the left, both at the corner of 15th and F Streets NW. The parade included Roosevelt's beloved Rough Riders and an African-American Cavalry unit.

Map on page 36

61 Northwest corner of 14th Street and Pennsylvania Avenue NW

THE WILLARD—The present Willard Hotel, constructed in 1901, occupies the site of an earlier building that has come to be known as the "old" Willard Hotel, the one where Presidents Zachary Taylor, Millard Fillmore, and James Buchanan resided, and where Abraham Lincoln stayed prior to his inauguration in 1861. Charles Dickens stopped there in 1842.

Nathaniel Hawthorne, who worked in the city as a bureaucrat and was later assigned to cover the Civil War for the *Atlantic Monthly,* used the earlier incarnation of this building as his headquarters. He wrote that the "hotel may be much more justly called the center of Washington and the Union than either the Capitol, the White House or the State Department," and described its character as a watering hole. "You adopt the universal habit of the place, and call for a mint-julep, a whiskey-skin, a gin-cocktail, a brandy smash or a glass of pure old Rye, for the conviviality of Washington sets in at an early hour and, so far as I have had the opportunity to observe, never terminates at any hour...."

In 1861 Julia Ward Howe wrote "The Battle Hymn of the Republic" at the hotel. According to a history of the Willard, Howe was awakened by Union soldiers singing "John Brown's Body," the tribute to abolitionist Brown and his raid on Harpers Ferry in 1859. She composed new words to the tune, writing them down on Willard stationery.

Thomas R. Marshall, Calvin Coolidge, and Charles G. Dawes, Vice Presidents to Wilson, Harding, and Coolidge respectively, lived at the Willard. The Coolidges—the Vice President and wife, Grace—occupied an $8-a-day suite in the hotel from 1921 until 1923.

It was at the Willard in August 1963 that the Rev. Martin Luther King, Jr., wrote his "I Have a Dream" speech, which he delivered from the Lincoln Memorial. Eventually, financial troubles caused the closing of the hotel. It remained boarded up for 15 years. During the years it was closed there were many legal skirmishes over its future, and on several occasions it appeared as if it would be torn down. It was saved through the efforts of the Pennsylvania Avenue Development Corporation and in 1986 was reborn as a fully restored, elegant hotel.

Also on this spot, at the F Street NW entrance to the present hotel, was Willard Hall, where Jenny Lind appeared in 1851 under the managerial eye of P.T. Barnum. She stayed at the old Willard Hotel.

62 Pennsylvania Avenue between 14th and 15th Streets NW, across from the Willard Hotel

WORLD WAR II CENTER—The site of the Wartime Information Center, built in 36 days in 1942 to provide information to thousands of servicemen and women pouring into the city during the war. It cost $530,000 to build and was torn down at the end of the war. A man who worked here at the end of the war recalls that the men's room of the center was well-known as a prime source of World War II graffiti.

63 Former 1423 Pennsylvania Avenue NW (now covered by the Willard complex)

1,000 SANDWICHES—Once the site of Childs Restaurant, which was paid an unusual visit by one of Washington's wealthiest women, Evalyn Walsh McLean, owner of the Hope Diamond.

Appalled by the condition of the Bonus Army in June 1932, Mrs. McLean was walking among them when, as she reported in her autobiography, *Father Struck it Rich*, she turned to the chief of police after he announced he was going to get coffee for them and said, "All right, I am going to Childs." As she retold it, "It was two o'clock [in the morning]...a man came up to take my order, 'Do you serve sandwiches? I want a thousand,' I said. 'And a thousand packages of cigarettes....I want them right away. I haven't got a nickel with me, but you can trust me. I am Mrs. McLean." The sandwiches and cigarettes were delivered.

After this McLean obtained a tent for the marchers to use as their headquarters and bought cots for the women and children to sleep on. She was most upset by the hunger among the marchers and went as far as calling Vice President Charles Curtis to demand that something be done.

64 **North side of Pennsylvania Avenue between 14th and 15th Streets NW**

HOTEL WASHINGTON—William Lovell built a tavern on the site of the present-day hotel in 1800, the first of many hotels built here. In the 1920s the "new" Hotel Washington charged $5 for a single and $8 for a double, with bath. Suites were $20 and up.

The present hotel is the oldest continuously operating hotel in the city. A frieze on the building's facade depicts presidents of the United States, appropriate for a hotel that has been a preferred vantage point for inaugural parades for most of the 20th century.

65 **Southeast corner of 15th Street and Pennsylvania Avenue NW**

ENEMY B&B—On this site was Mrs. Suter's boarding house, where British Adm. Sir George Cockburn stopped at the time of his capture of Washington in August 1814. Cockburn had been sent to this side of the Atlantic to harass the American Navy.

66 **Corner of 15th Street and Pennsylvania Avenue NW**

EUREKA!—On the evening of October 15, 1881, the first electric street light in the District of Columbia was turned on at this spot.

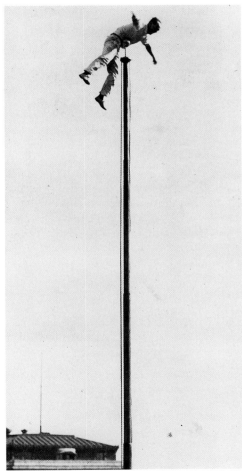

Human Fly. John Reynolds, who called himself the "human fly", on the flag pole of the old *Times-Herald* Building on E Street between 13th and 14th Streets NW. The stunt took place in 1924 and typified the wacky view of the city portrayed in the photographs of the National Photo Company.

Map on page 36

It was reported at the time that "all Washington" came downtown that night to see this modern miracle.

67 405 15th Street NW

WHEELMEN—The Capitol Bicycle Club was organized on the site of what is now Pershing Park, on January 31, 1879, reflecting the widespread popularity of bicycling in that era. When the club celebrated its 50th anniversary in 1929, 60 of its charter members were in attendance.

68 North corner of 15th and E Streets NW

OPERA HOUSE—Albaugh's Grand Opera House was opened on what is now the site of Pershing Park in 1884, operated by John W. Albaugh of Baltimore. Poli's Theater succeeded Albaugh's and the building also served as the Washington Light Infantry Armory and headquarters of the Quartermaster Corps. It was razed in November 1930.

69 535 15th Street NW

WHITMAN'S LAST WASHINGTON ADDRESS—A long-gone house between E and F Streets across from the Treasury Department was the site of Walt Whitman's crippling stroke in 1873. The poet had an attic room in the building. After his stroke he moved in with his brother in Camden, New Jersey. In *Reveille in Washington* (1941), Margaret Leech writes, "The deep admiration for Lincoln, which Whitman expressed in his poems, created the impression that they had been friends, but Whitman never met the President, and knew him only as a passerby in the Washington streets."

70 South corner of 15th and F Streets NW

FROM TREASURY TO ART—Banker and founder of the Corcoran Gallery of Art William W. Corcoran built a five-story office building (one of the city's largest at the time) here in 1847 to lease to the nearby Treasury Department. In 1875 Corcoran replaced the building with a six-story structure double the size, stretching to Pennsylvania Avenue. James M. Goode noted in *Capital Losses* that this building became the center for local artists' studios and art classes for two generations of Washington art students. The Hotel Washington was constructed on the site in 1917.

71 North corner of 15th and F Streets NW

RHODES TAVERN—William Rhodes operated a tavern and hotel on this site in 1801 that served as a polling place and early community center. Leaders met here to organize the city's central market, street improvements, the Washington Theatre, and various community endeavors.

British officers dined here in August 1814, ordering that the candles be doused so they could sup by the light of the blazing President's House and Treasury Building.

In the heart of the original financial community, the building held the offices of the Bank of the Metropolis beginning in 1815. The National Press Club had its headquarters here from 1909 to 1914. Its history was at the heart of a long and bitter struggle between preservationists and developer Oliver Carr, who wanted to demolish the building so he could proceed with construction of the Metropolitan Square project. In 1984, the city finally allowed Carr to tear down what had been Rhodes Tavern. Interestingly, the 130-foot building erected on the site overlooked the White House and its grounds, prompting a nervous Secret Service to install vision-blocking screens at the executive mansion.

⑫ 721 15th Street NW

BRITISH OBSERVER—Charles Dickens, when in Washington in 1842, resided in a house on this spot, covered since 1880 by The National Savings and Trust Company building (now Crestar). After visiting the more established cities of Boston, New York, and Philadelphia, he found the nation's capital far from complete. In his *American Notes for General Circulation* (1892), he wrote: "It is sometimes called the City of Magnificent Distances, but it might with greater propriety be termed the City of Magnificent Intentions...Spacious avenues, that begin in nothing, and lead nowhere; streets, mile-long, that only want houses, roads and inhabitants; public buildings that need but a public to be complete." But he saved his best shot for the chewers. "As Washington may be called the head-quarters [sic] of tobacco-tinctured saliva...the prevalence of these two odious practices of chewing and expectorating...soon became most offensive and sickening....In public buildings, visitors are implored...to squirt the essence of their quids, or 'plugs,' as I have heard them called by gentlemen learned in this kind of sweetmeat, into the national spittoons, and not about the bases of the marble columns."

Powerhouse. A Pepco powerhouse and its giant stack dominated the intersection of 14th Street and Constitution Avenue NW adjacent to the Mall until cleared to make way for the Federal Triangle government complexes in the 1930s.

Map on page 36

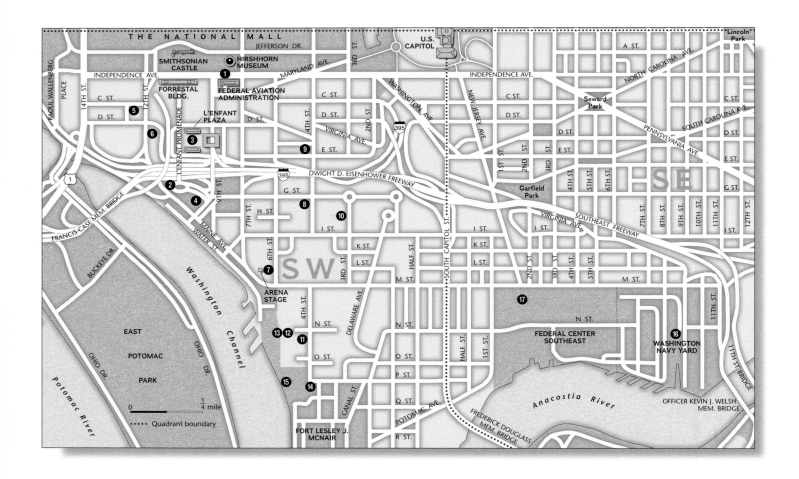

THE NATIONAL MALL

Lincoln Park

JEFFERSON DR.

SMITHSONIAN CASTLE

HIRSHHORN MUSEUM

A ST.

U.S. CAPITOL

INDEPENDENCE AVE.

MARYLAND AVE.

NORTH CAROLINA AVE.

INDEPENDENCE AVE.

FORRESTAL BLDG.

FEDERAL AVIATION ADMINISTRATION

Seward Park

PENNSYLVANIA AVE.

SOUTH CAROLINA AVE.

C ST.

C ST.

C ST.

C ST.

D ST.

D ST.

D ST.

D ST.

D ST.

L'ENFANT PLAZA

E ST.

E ST.

SE

VIRGINIA AVE.

DWIGHT D. EISENHOWER FREEWAY

G ST.

Garfield Park

G ST.

SOUTHEAST FREEWAY

VIRGINIA AVE.

7TH ST.

H ST.

I ST.

I ST.

I ST.

I ST.

K ST.

K ST.

SW

L ST.

L ST.

M ST.

M ST.

M ST.

ARENA STAGE

N ST.

N ST.

N ST.

FEDERAL CENTER SOUTHEAST

WASHINGTON NAVY YARD

O ST.

O ST.

EAST POTOMAC PARK

Washington Channel

P ST.

Anacostia River

OFFICER KEVIN J. WELSH MEM. BRIDGE

Potomac River

Q ST.

FREDERICK DOUGLASS MEM. BRIDGE

0   ¼ mile

Quadrant boundary

FORT LESLEY J. MCNAIR

R ST.

RAOUL WALLENBERG PLACE

14TH ST.

12TH ST.

L'ENFANT PROMENADE

9TH ST.

MAINE AVE.

WATER ST.

6TH ST.

4TH ST.

BUCKEYE DR.

OHIO DR.

OHIO DR.

FRANCIS CASE MEM. BRIDGE

1

CANAL ST.

DELAWARE AVE.

3RD ST.

HALF ST.

SOUTH CAPITOL ST.

POTOMAC AVE.

NEW JERSEY AVE.

WASHINGTON AVE.

3RD ST.

2ND ST.

4TH ST.

1ST ST.

2ND ST.

3RD ST.

1ST ST.

2ND ST.

3RD ST.

4TH ST.

5TH ST.

6TH ST.

7TH ST.

8TH ST.

9TH ST.

10TH ST.

11TH ST.

12TH ST.

11TH ST.

11TH ST. BRIDGE

Half St.

1ST ST.

395

395

74

Southwest Washington and the Navy Yard

1 **Now the site of the Federal Aviation Administration building on Independence Avenue between 7th and 9th Streets SW, formerly 8th and B (now Independence Avenue) Streets SW**

PLACE OF INFAMY—Robey's Slave Pen operated here when the slave trade was still permitted in the District prior to its abolition in 1850.

2 **Part of a totally redeveloped area, once bounded by 10th, 11th, E, and G Streets SW, now covered by L'Enfant Plaza and highway interchanges**

CAL'S MARKET—In one of his final acts as President, Calvin Coolidge authorized a farmers' produce market for this site on March 2, 1929. It was still active in the 1950s. While the site was transformed by urban renewal in the 1960s, a small vegetable market remains as part of the nearby Maine Avenue Fish Market. The transformation symbolizes the vast changes that have occurred in this part of the city.

3 **L'Enfant Plaza, formerly 85 E Street SW (between 9th and 10th Streets SW)**

UNDERGROUND RAILROAD STATION—The east end of the L'Enfant Plaza complex rests on the site of the home of Anthony Bowen, a free black community leader who operated a school for black children and, according to *The Guide to Black Washington*, started the first YMCA in the world for "colored men and boys"

Riv Vu. This 1849 lithograph by E. Weber and Company shows the view from the Capitol terrace toward the Potomac, including Southwest, Long Bridge (now the 14th Street Bridge), and, at right center, the canal that extended down the Mall and then cut across it (near where the National Gallery of Art is today) on its route to the Anacostia River. The Washington Monument is fancifully depicted as a completed structure replete with a columned base that appeared in early plans and models.

SOUTHWEST. Beginning in the early 1950s with the annihilation of 5,700—mostly slum—dwellings, Southwest Washington went through dramatic change. Not only was a large part of the area razed and rebuilt, but the old building lot system was abandoned to permit open spaces, apartment towers, and town house clusters. Today the residential mix of the area ranges from posh upper-income to public housing, extremes often only a few doors apart.

Before the area was razed, it was largely populated by poor African Americans. Over half of their dwellings lacked bathrooms, and more than 70 percent were without central heating.

The new Southwest was the first part of the city to offer high-quality housing to both blacks and whites. However, many of the more than 15,000 people displaced were poor who relocated to other parts of the city. Many residents and small business owners did not want to leave.

in 1853. Bowen also ran an underground railroad station to help convey fleeing slaves to safety in the North. In 1863 he assisted President Abraham Lincoln in recruiting blacks from Washington to serve in the Union Army unit called the First U.S. Colored Troops.

④ 926 G Street SW

BOSS' HOUSE—Probable site of the birthplace of Alexander R. "Boss" Shepherd, whose dramatic improvements and public works programs paved the way for the modern city. Although he served as governor of the Territory of Columbia in 1873-74, Shepherd's real impact on the city came from his direction of the Board of Public Works from 1871 to 1874. Shepherd oversaw the installation of 123 miles of sewers, 133 miles of water mains and pipes, 3,000 street lamps, more than 180 miles of streets and sidewalks, and the planting of more than 25,000 trees along the city's streets. According to Eugene L. Meyer in an article in the Washington *Post Magazine* on April 28, 1991, improvements "appeared with uncanny frequency in areas where Shepherd and friends had invested. Assessments were uneven and cost overruns frequent."

Buildings on this site were cleared in the early 1960s.

⑤ Southeast corner of 13th and C Streets SW

PIONEER ROMANTIC WRITER—Novelist E.D.E.N. Southworth lived in a house on this site and taught evening school classes attended by Rear Adm. Robley D. Evans, who developed the steel navy. Southworth (1819-99) penned novels with names like *The Missing Bride* and *The Hidden Hand* that were the rage of Victorian America and are all but forgotten today. She later moved to Georgetown.

Since 1932 the site has been unromantically occupied by the GSA central heating and refrigeration plant.

6 Southeast corner of 12th Street and Maryland Avenue SW

ROBERT BRENT HOME—Robert Brent was the first mayor of Washington, appointed by the President to ten annual terms from 1802 to 1812. He presided over a city that Benjamin Henry Latrobe described in 1806 as abounding "in cases of extreme poverty and distress....Workmen...are to be found in extreme indigence scattered in wretched huts over the waste the law calls the American metropolis....There are a higher order of beings quite as wretched and almost as poor, though as yet not so ragged...master tradesmen, chiefly building artisans. Above these again are others who brought larger fortunes to this great vortex that swallowed everything...thrown into it...nothing but the grave will set them free." This bleak picture was part of Latrobe's plea for improved and dependable financing for construction of public buildings under his direction as superintendent of public buildings.

During Brent's administration the city imposed taxes, established markets, began a rudimentary fire control system, and opened two public schools paid for by public subscription.

7 6th and M streets SW (although the address is often given as 6th Street and Maine Avenue SW)

MODERN THEATER—The Arena Stage repertory group broke local precedent when it opened to integrated audiences in 1951. Among its other achievements was a Tony award, the first one awarded to a theater company outside New York City. Its prior locations were the Hippodrome (1951-55), at Ninth Street and New York Avenue NW—according to historian Constance McLaughlin Green, "an old burlesque house opposite the [old Carnegie] Public Library"—and, beginning in 1955, in Foggy Bottom in the old Heurich Brewery. It opened at its present building in 1961. Six years later the Arena premiered Howard Sackler's *The Great White*

Shame of the City. This 1942 photograph by African-American author and photographer Gordon Parks was one of a number that he and others took to demonstrate living conditions in the city. The original caption on this image: "Back houses in the Negro districts."

Map on page 74

Resting Up. Columbus Scriber, a free black, photographed in front of his business establishment at 119 E Street SW in 1863.

Hope, which won a Pulitzer Prize for the playwright and also launched the careers of James Earl Jones and Jane Alexander. In 1971 it added a second stage, the Kreeger Theater. As this book goes to press in 1999, the Arena is enjoying one of its most successful seasons while contemplating a relocation, possibly to the emerging downtown arts and cultural area along Seventh Street north of Pennsylvania Avenue.

4th and 7th Streets SW

8 JOLSON'S NEIGHBORHOOD—During the late 19th century (when today's 4th Street was named 4 1/2 Street in Southwest), these streets were lined with small shops and were centers of a Jewish immigrant community. A synagogue of the Talmud Torah Congregation opened in 1906 under the direction of Rabbi Moses Yoelson. One of his sons was singing star Al Jolson. Historian Keith Melder's essay "Southwest Washington" in *Washington at Home* (1988)mentions that Jolson attributed his later success in part to the fact that while a youth in Southwest Washington he had "traveled with a 'tough gang' and learned Afro-American dialects."

4th Street SW

9 OLD 4 1/2—Then called 4 1/2 Street, by 1900 this street was a dividing line between white residents on the east and blacks on the west. When renamed 4th Street between the world wars, both groups joined together and persuaded the city to widen and repair the street, add modern paving, and improve lighting. Community activist Harry Wender reported that the neighborhood commemorated its victory by holding the "biggest celebration in the history of the city" and that "it was the first time that Negroes and whites paraded together in the history of Washington."

10 Former 825 3rd Street SW

LONG GONE—The two-story row house and the street that existed here were among those first demolished by the government in the early 1950s to make way for the new Southwest. It became emblematic of the structures that were being destroyed. Here is how the house was described on the eve of its demolition in the *Evening Star:* "It had no central heat. The only running water came from a single cold water faucet protruding from a kitchen wall. Toilet facilities were in an outhouse, backed against the dwelling in a rubble-littered yard. For this, the family was charged $61 a month rent, not counting coal and wood for the two pot-bellied stoves used for heat and cooking."

On the site today is a town house development erected in the 1960s.

11 1315-1321 4th Street SW

LAST VESTIGE—Wheat Row, constructed in 1794-95, is one of the earliest row house complexes surviving in the city and the result of an early development scheme advanced by speculator James Greenleaf. According to Diane Maddex in *Historic Buildings of Washington, D.C.,* Greenleaf was permitted to purchase at bargain rates 3,000 city lots for resale. In return he was to erect ten houses a year for seven years and lend the government $2,200 each month to complete public buildings. At one time, he controlled more than a third of the buildings for sale in the city. Unfortunately there was insufficient demand for lots, and Greenleaf's syndicate went bankrupt in 1797. Named after an early resident of No. 1315, John Wheat, this block is one of the few examples of pre-1960 architecture to survive the massive urban renewal—or as some termed it then, "urban removal"—clearances of the late 1950s.

12 470 N Street SW

SPECULATOR—A mansion on this site was occupied by Capt. William Mayne Duncanson after his arrival in Washington, D.C., with fellow real estate speculator and developer Thomas Law in 1794. Duncanson met heavy losses in his ventures. In the 20th century the mansion was used for the Washington Sanitarium, a home for the indigent elderly, and as the Barney Neighborhood House. It was saved from demolition and is now incorporated into the Harbour Square residential complex.

13 500 N Street SW

HUMPHREY CALLED IT HOME—The Harbour Square cooperative apartment building was the Washington home of Senator, Vice President and presidential candidate Hubert Horatio Humphrey from 1966 to his death in 1978.

14 4th and P Streets SW

FORT LESLEY J. McNAIR—The home of the National Defense University (formerly called the Army War College), this strategically located point has been associated with military purposes since the origins of the city. An early speculative real estate venture by James Greenleaf failed to take but gave the site the name Greenleaf's Point. Washington's first newspaper, a weekly called *Impartial Observer and Washington Advertiser,* was published here for a year beginning in 1795. The area was the site of a federal arsenal after 1804, destroyed by the British in the War of 1812 and rebuilt. In 1864, when 21 women working in the arsenal room were killed in an explosion, President Lincoln attended their funeral and led the procession to Congressional Cemetery.

Navy Yard. This 1870s photograph shows the Navy Yard in its post-Civil War glory, complete with displays of armaments and ships.

A federally constructed penitentiary for the District of Columbia, built here in the 1830s, was taken over by the Army as part of the arsenal for the Civil War and then appropriated as the site of the trial of the Lincoln conspirators in 1865. George Atzerodt, Davy Herold, Lewis Paine, and Mary Surratt were hanged in the yard on July 9, 1865. A tennis court now occupies the site of the scaffold.

The imposing redbrick beaux arts War College building was added to the site in 1903. The post itself has had several names. For a while it was Fort Humphreys; in 1938 it became the Army War College and later still Fort McNair. The grounds are open to the public.

🄖 4th and P Streets SW, in Washington Channel Park next to Fort McNair

MEMORIAL TO *TITANIC* MEN—Gertrude Vanderbilt Whitney sculptured this striking monument to the men who gave their lives so that women and children could escape the doomed *Titanic*. The stone bench that surrounds the draped granite figure at the center of the memorial was designed by Henry Bacon, designer of the Lincoln Memorial.

🄗 M Street between 1st and 11th Streets SE

THE NAVY YARD—Established in 1799, it's the nation's oldest naval facility, built on land originally reserved by George Washington for federal use. Beginning in 1803, Benjamin Henry Latrobe worked to give order and design to the ramshackle set of buildings at the original yard. His design for the main gate, still standing at Eighth and M Streets SE, was mocked in a poem. Latrobe sued and the offending poet, Dr. William Thornton, was ordered to pay a penny. The poem:

This Dutch man in taste, this monument builder
This planner of grand steps and walls
This falling arch-maker, this blunder-proof gilder,
Himself an architect calls.

At the time, Latrobe was changing Thornton's designs for the Capitol and the two were locked in a public dispute.

Gunboats built here participated in the defense of Washington during the War of 1812, but they failed to stave off the enemy. The buildings of the yard were set on fire on August 24, 1814, to keep them from falling to the advancing British forces, who added their own torches to the conflagration. The fire spared three buildings, but they were pillaged by Washingtonians who even took the door locks. The yard was rebuilt and later became the site of the Naval Gun Factory. Established in 1886, the ordinance production facility turned out warship guns until it closed in 1961.

On November 12, 1912, the first airplane was successfully catapulted from this site, establishing a principle that would be employed in aircraft carrier takeoffs.

The Navy Yard employed 22,300 persons during World War II, including many industrial production workers. The 14- and 16-inch battleship guns used as recently as the Persian Gulf war of 1991 were manufactured here.

Since production ended in 1961, the Yard has been used as an administrative and supply center, while offering a number of public attractions. Today the Navy Museum occupies the former breech mechanism shop, a 600-foot-long building once part of the Naval Gun Factory. Exhibits detail the history and traditions of the U.S. Navy. The Marine Corps Historical Center, located in Building 58, houses archives and museum collections presenting the history of the Marine Corps. Building 70, the former Experimental Model Basin used for testing scale models of ships, is now the Cold War Museum for the United States Navy, and the first component is an exhibit on the Korean War. As of this writing, the destroyer U.S.S. *Barry* is at anchor here and is open to tourists. The ship was decommissioned in 1982 after seeing service during the Cuban missile crisis and the Vietnam War.

The commandant's house has been occupied by many distinguished officers, including Thomas Tingey, Isaac Hull, Hiram Paulding, and John A. Dahlgren, who commanded the facility during the Civil War. During the war his son Ulric Dahlgren lost a leg pursuing Lee's forces after Gettysburg. The leg, according to a plaque at the site, was brought back and built into the wall of a foundry under construction. Ulric Dahlgren came back to duty on crutches and was killed in an attempt to release Union prisoners in Richmond.

⑰ South end of New Jersey Avenue SE, between M and N Streets SE

SUGAR REFINERY—This was the site of Thomas Law's sugar refinery, the first manufactory in the city, built in 1797. At that time a ferry across the Eastern Branch, now called the Anacostia River, departed from a nearby wharf. Joseph Wheat and Elizabeth Leslie operated taverns here as well, according to historian W. B. Bryan. The site is currently occupied by the Washington Navy Yard.

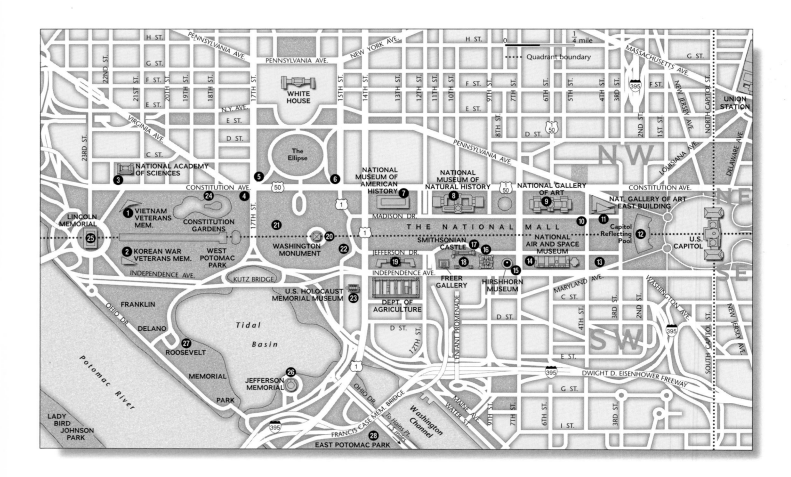

Along the Mall

① West Potomac Park opposite 21st Street NW

58,000 NAMES—Dedicated in 1982, the Vietnam Veterans Memorial generated controversy because of its severe abstract design by architect Maya Ying Lin. Yet this poignant memorial, a polished black granite wall inscribed with the names of more than 58,000 dead, has become one of the most revered and popular commemorative sites in the city, with over 25 million visitors in the first decade following its completion. Two sculptures nearby are associated with the same war: a sculpture entitled "Three Servicemen," by Frederick E. Hart, added in 1984, and the Vietnam Women's Memorial, designed by Glenna Goodacre, dedicated in 1993 to the 265,000 women who served in the conflict.

② West Potomac Park opposite the Vietnam Veterans Memorial

WAR MEMORIALS AND PROTEST—On this spot is the Korean Veterans Memorial, created by sculptor Frank Gaylord, and muralist Louis Nelson, and dedicated in 1995. Close by is the District of Columbia World War Memorial, marking the service of 26,000 Washingtonians who served in World War I, designed by Frederick Brooke, Horace W. Peaslee, and Nathan C. Wyeth and dedicated on Armistice Day 1931 by President Herbert Hoover. A memorable event occurred in this vicinity following the assassination on April 4, 1968, in Memphis, Tennessee, of revered civil rights leader Dr. Martin Luther King, Jr. Dr. Ralph Abernathy, King's successor as head of the Southern Christian Leadership Council, continued with King's planned march on Washington to

Temporary Bridges. Bridges or gangways were constructed during World War II to connect Navy temporary buildings, or "tempos," on the Mall. As seen in this photograph, they also bridged the Reflecting Pool leading to the Lincoln Memorial. While the bridges were removed soon after the war, the last of the "tempos" survived on Constitution Avenue NW until 1973.

Carp Pools. These ponds were formed at the corner of 17th Street and what is now Constitution Avenue as the area was reclaimed from the Potomac in the late 19th century. The U.S. Fish Commission once used the ponds to propagate European carp for distribution.

demonstrate for government anti-poverty programs. King had planned a peaceful but sustained encampment in the city as part of what was termed a Poor People's Campaign, to call attention to the needs of the poor. According to *City of Magnificent Intentions,* at the peak of the 42-day encampment (marred by 28 days of rain), about 2,400 people camped here in plywood shanties in a complex called "Resurrection City." Despite the high state of tension accompanying the event, many organizations and individuals provided sympathetic support.

③ Near northwest corner of 22nd Street and Constitution Avenue NW

EINSTEIN MEMORIAL—Here, on the grounds of the National Academy of Sciences, is a 21-foot-high sculpture of Albert Einstein. He is shown contemplating 3,000 stars in the universe (stainless steel studs embedded in black granite) and holding a paper with his famous mathematical formulas. The work was completed in 1979 by sculptor Robert Berks. Small children seem captivated by it and often climb onto the statue's lap.

④ Southwest corner of 17th Street and Constitution Avenue NW

ON THE TOWPATH—This small stone house was erected alongside the canal about 1835, for the lockkeeper who allowed barges to transfer between the Chesapeake and Ohio Canal extension from Georgetown and the Washington City Canal.

⑤ Northeast corner of 17th Street and Constitution Avenue NW

BULFINCH GATEHOUSE—One of four gatehouses for the north and south entries to the Capitol grounds, designed by Charles Bulfinch, the architect who completed construction of the Capitol in the 1820s. This gatehouse and a twin at the northwest corner of 15th Street and Constitution Avenue NW were relocated about 1874 during the landscaping of the Capitol grounds by Frederick Law Olmsted, best known for his design of New York City's Central Park.

❻ Northwest corner of 15th Street and Constitution Avenue NW

FLOOD MARKER—A historic marker on a gatehouse building here reads: "Erected about 1828 under the direction of Charles Bulfinch, Architect of the Capitol, this gatehouse stood until 1874 with another [now at 17th and Constitution] at the west entrance to the Capitol grounds." A line incised into the sandstone about three feet above ground level is labeled "High Water Mark February 12, 1881." Heavy rains and a rapid thaw caused chunks of ice to jam against Long Bridge, forcing floodwaters into the city, covering Pennsylvania Avenue and the Mall as far as the base of Capitol Hill.

❼ South side of Constitution Avenue between 12th and 14th Streets NW

NATIONAL MUSEUM OF AMERICAN HISTORY—Government temporary buildings erected here in the 1940s and 1950s were removed to make way for the Smithsonian's National Museum of History and Technology, which opened in 1964. The museum, renamed to the National Museum of American History in 1982, exhibits collections broadly documenting American history as well as the national numismatic collection (money). Known for the First Ladies' Gowns, the gigantic flag that inspired "The Star-Spangled Banner," and pioneering examples of American technology, the museum presents a variety of exhibits and public programs interpreting the American experience.

The single item with perhaps the most intriguing past is the large

STREET LORE

CONSTITUTION AVENUE. When it was first created by filling in the City Canal, this was known as B Street. It was given its new name in 1931. Author E.J. Applewhite informs us in his book, *Washington Itself*, that the names Memorial and Jefferson were considered but finally rejected. Only Franklin D. Roosevelt broke with tradition and held his inaugural parades along this avenue rather than the traditional Pennsylvania Avenue.

marble statue of a seated and bare-chested George Washington, draped in a toga that has fallen to his waist. This was the first memorial to Washington authorized and acquired by Congress. In 1842 it was completed by American sculptor Horatio Greenough and placed in the Capitol's Rotunda. B.B. French, clerk of the Senate, took keen interest in its installation and reported observers' comments in his journal. "One gentleman remarked [they should] put a pair of runners under it, and place a whip in the right hand...." Another said Washington "was about to give us a tune...his fiddle in his hand, all ready." One commented the founding father "had just come out of a bath and was preparing to be bled." Onlookers were shocked by Washington's semi-nudity and found the former president's depiction wearing sandals to be "ridiculous." It seemed that Greenough's attempt to depict Washington in the garb of a classical leader didn't square with the public's need to revere him as an American hero.

Eventually the statue's seven-ton weight proved too heavy for the Rotunda's floor, and it had to be moved outside. For many years it rested in front of the Capitol, until it was moved into the Smithsonian's Arts and Industries Building in 1908 where it was exhibited with other national treasures. Special construction underpins the sculpture in its current site in front of an escalator bank, where it is likely to remain.

❽ 10th Street and Constitution Avenue NW

NATIONAL MUSEUM OF NATURAL HISTORY—When completed in 1910, this building was the second largest in the city after the Capitol, providing more than ten acres of floor space. It was the first classical building constructed along the Mall within the 19th-century Smithsonian Park or Smithsonian Pleasure Grounds, the area between 9th and 12th Streets set aside when the Smithsonian was established in 1846. Additional wings were added to the east and west in the 1960s. Ellis L. Yochelson's 1985 history of the building recounts that exhibitions included dinosaur skeletons, animal specimens gathered in Africa by President Theodore Roosevelt specifically for the new museum, and a host of natural history specimens of all types. These were juxtaposed with the Smithsonian's collections of painting, sculpture and ethnography, and, after World War I, contemporary military memorabilia. In 1918 the museum was closed and turned over to some 3,000 clerks, who typed and filed for the Bureau of War Risk Insurance. Many of the collections were later transferred as other museum buildings were constructed for the Smithsonian beginning in the 1960s. Building expansion, new exhibitions, and an IMAX Theater are transforming this museum as the book goes to print.

The National Gallery building and its East Wing cover the sites described in the following three entries. The National Gallery of Art, a monumental classical building that occupies Constitution Avenue between Fourth and Seventh Streets NW, was donated to the United States by Andrew W. Mellon along with an art collection, in order to provide the nation's capital with an art museum of international stature. It was opened in 1941 by President Franklin D. Roosevelt "for the benefit of all Americans." Designed by John Russell Pope, architect of the National Archives and the Jefferson Memorial, the building responded to the desire of federal planners to line the Mall with classical structures and to continue the architectural style of the nearby Federal Triangle buildings. The Gallery's pamphlet on the building explains that the massive marble structure is situated on once swampy ground far above bedrock. It sits on a reinforced concrete platform supported by 6,800 40-foot-deep steel and concrete piles. The original totally integrated air conditioning system is still in use today. The artwork is lit primarily by natural light entering through skylights and diffused through the ceilings of the galleries, augmented by floodlights. The Gallery's East Wing, also a gift of the Mellon family and designed by I.M. Pei and Partners, was opened in 1978 on the trapezoidal block to the east of the original building. Until the 1930s, Sixth Street extended across the Mall and Missouri Avenue ran parallel to Pennsylvania Avenue between Third and Sixth Streets NW, forming a boundary between the city and the Mall.

⑨ Southwest corner of 6th Street and Constitution Avenue NW

INFAMOUS RAILROAD STATION—Constructed in 1873 to serve points south of the city (complementing the Baltimore and Ohio Railroad terminal at New Jersey Avenue and C Street NW, which led to the north and west), the Baltimore and Potomac Railroad station and its tracks across the Mall on Sixth Street were eventually seen as a nuisance and visual blight. Also known as the Sixth Street Depot, it is best remembered as the site where President James A. Garfield was shot on July 2, 1881. Charles Guiteau, a disturbed federal office-seeker, fired two bullets at Garfield as the President was being escorted to the train that was to take him to his 25th reunion at Williams College in Massachusetts. One bullet struck him in the back, the other grazed his arm. He died from his wounds two months later in a cottage on the New Jersey shore. According to *Keim's Hand-book of Washington* (1884), a gigantic silver star in the floor and an inscription painted on the wall marked the spot of the shooting. The terminal and tracks were removed from the Mall and merged into the new Union Station, which opened in 1907.

Adjoining this site was the location of an abortive attempt to build a civic center and auditorium to honor George Washington and the veterans of World War I. Launched by civic boosters before the war, the project had enlisted federal backers by the time

Work in Progress. Site on the Mall where the National Gallery of Art would open in 1941. At the time this picture was taken in the 1930s, the site contained an immense area known as the "wood yard," where large numbers of men were paid by the hour to saw wood in the open air. Locally, newspaper photographs of the wood yard activity served as visible reminders of the Depression. The grand marble steps to nowhere were intended for a civic center and auditorium that would honor the first president and veterans of World War I but were never built.

Map on page 82

CANAL LORE

CANALS. Canals were a central feature of mid-19th-century Washington. The most important of these still remains, the nearly 185-mile Chesapeake and Ohio Canal connecting Georgetown with Cumberland, Maryland. Intended to stimulate trade and commerce with the trans-Allegheny West when it opened in the 1830s, its impact was blunted by competition from railroads. But for many decades it served effectively to bring products and raw materials into the city.

The Georgetown terminus was located where Rock Creek joins the Potomac near the Kennedy Center. In 1833, a 1 1/4-mile canal was built from Rock Creek to what is now 17th Street and Constitution Avenue NW, to connect the C&O Canal with the Washington City Canal, which led from that point down what is now Constitution Avenue past the Central Market at Eighth Street before crossing the Mall in front of the Capitol. The canal then forked, with branches emptying into the Anacostia River (then called the Eastern Branch) near present-day Fort McNair and the Navy Yard. These canals cut off the Mall and Southwest sections of the city, and the area between the canal and the riverfront became known as the Island. The

continued on next page

President Warren G. Harding dedicated its cornerstone in 1921. However, the George Washington Victory Memorial Building never gained sufficient funding beyond that pledged by its principal backer, Mrs. Susan Whitney Dimock, and its foundations were removed in 1937 to make way for the National Gallery of Art, which opened on March 17, 1941.

During the Depression the foundations of the ill-fated memorial contained an immense wood yard where large numbers of men were given work sawing wood in the open air. Local newspaper pictures of the wood yard were as common a symbol of the Depression as pictures of apple vendors in other cities.

10 **Near the southwest corner of Madison Drive and 4th Street NW**

NATIONAL GRANGE—A plaque on a stone block here commemorates the founding of "The National Grange of the patrons of Husbandry...organized on December 4, 1867 in the office of the Superintendent of the Propagating Gardens of the Department of Agriculture." The Grange movement began in the Midwest as a means of advancing the interests of farmers and developed into a powerful lobby advocating regulation of the railroads and other economic reforms in the post-Civil War period.

11 **Former site along Madison Drive between 3rd and 4th Streets NW**

PROPAGATING GARDENS—According to *Keim's* 1884 handbook, propagating gardens were planted in this area by the government in 1858 to test sorghum and Chinese sugarcane, as part of a program to develop improved agricultural specimens for distribution to farmers. The gardens were relocated to the southwest end of the Mall after the Agriculture Department building was constructed near 14th Street NW in 1868.

Area between 1st and 3rd Streets and Maryland and Pennsylvania Avenues SW

CONGRESS'S FLORIST—The United States Botanic Garden building now on Independence Avenue opposite Washington Street SW is a survivor of a more extensive 19th-century complex of gardens and greenhouses. Tradition held that this once-marshy area at the foot of Capitol Hill served as the early execution ground of the city, but the site is better known as the location of the Botanic Garden since 1820. The botanical activities were begun by a congressionally chartered society, and after 1850 were supported by government appropriations. In that year, greenhouses located at the southwest corner of Seventh and G Streets NW were relocated here in order to permit the extension of the Patent Office building. Gardens eventually extended over 10 acres and contained 15 conservatories, including one for classes and lectures. Various conservatories were kept at different temperatures to house exotic plants from Africa, South America, and the Pacific. The establishment was administered by Congress's Joint Committee on the Library, which allowed members of Congress to obtain plants and flowers from the gardens for their offices.

For many years after the Civil War, Scottish immigrant William R. Smith both tended plants and amassed a famous collection of the writings of his countryman Robert Burns. (According to writer George Rothwell Brown, the collection was important enough to be purchased by Andrew Carnegie for the Washington chapter of the Scottish Rite Masons.) These extensive grounds were reduced in scope to the present complex along Independence Avenue in the early 20th century. Its grand "crystal palace" conservatory was the largest aluminum structure of its day when completed in 1933, but deterioration caused the removal of the central Palm House structure in 1992, and the overall physical plant is now being renovated. Reopening is planned for late 2000, when the

CANAL LORE

continued from previous page

Washington City Canal was more of a nuisance than a spur to local commerce; as the city grew, the canal became an open sewer, which backed into the city from tidal flows. Massive public works programs begun by Alexander R. "Boss" Shepherd in the 1870s filled in the canal to form what is now Constitution Avenue. Covered channels of the old canal system are currently used for portions of the city's sewer system.

An extension of the C&O Canal at Georgetown, completed in 1843, crossed the Potomac and carried cargo 7 miles to Alexandria. Canal boats traveled in a water-filled wooden trough supported by eight masonry piers. Remains of the Aqueduct Bridge can still be seen just upstream of Key Bridge. According to Thomas F. Hahn's *Towpath Guide,* the bridge was converted during the Civil War from canal to a double-decked vehicular bridge. After the war one level remained in use for wagons and the canal level was restored. The excess water from the canals powered a number of mills in Georgetown and along the route to Alexandria during the mid-19th century.

Map on page 82

Armory Square Hospital. Chapel and other buildings of the Armory Square Hospital, which was part of an extensive Civil War medical facility on the Mall between 5th and 7th Streets NW. The complex was named for the District's armory, erected in 1856 where the National Air and Space Museum stands today. The hospital's location near the steamboat landings of Southwest Washington permitted quick transfer of the wounded from the battlefields of Virginia. Since many died here, the chapel was an important part of the installation. This photograph, taken just after the Civil War, shows the completed Capitol dome in the background.

site will be linked to the National Garden being developed between the conservatory and Third Street with funds contributed by private donors.

13 Maryland Avenue between 3rd and 4th Streets SW

GAS HOUSE—The newly established Washington Gas Light Company built a gas plant here in 1851. The cluster of buildings and a spherically domed storage tank occupied the site for more than 50 years. Now the last building site on the National Mall, this location is designated for the Smithsonian's National Museum of the American Indian, slated to open in late 2002. Historical and archaeological research performed by John Milner Associates has revealed that this once marshy site partly traversed by Tiber Creek had a varied urban history during the 19th and early 20th centuries when this portion of the Mall was turned over to the city and contained a mix of residential, commercial, and light industrial structures. Findings included 400 pounds of oyster shells, marking a onetime oyster house. Among other businesses there were a foundry, a stone yard, and in the 1860s, one of the swankiest parlors of prostitution in the city, run by Mary Ann Hall, who was a substantial property owner in the area. The abstract of the archaeological report notes evidence of a high quantity of porcelain and consumption of "champagne and a wide range of foods." In later decades the site was occupied by bawdy houses and working-class residences and, between 1880 and 1900, "dwellings facing Louse Alley (later named Armory Place)." The area was razed in the 1930s and held temporary buildings during and after World War II.

⓮ North side of Independence Avenue opposite 6th Street SW (current site of the National Air and Space Museum)

SOMETHING FISHY—In 1856, when Sixth Street continued across the Mall, the District of Columbia Armory was constructed on this site, centered approximately on the spot where the Wright brothers' flyer hangs today in the National Air and Space Museum. When the armory was demolished on January 19, 1964, the *Washington Post* observed that the 107-year-old building had served as an armory, hospital, museum warehouse, aquarium, motion picture studio, office building, library, and finally a paint shop for government building maintenance. During the Civil War, the building and grounds housed Armory Square Hospital, with hospital tents spread across the Mall.

After the 1876 Centennial Exposition in Philadelphia, the armory building stored 50 freight-carloads of exhibits during construction of the Smithsonian's Arts and Industries Building, completed in 1881. Smithsonian collections and staff continued to occupy the building along with the U.S. Fish Commission during the 1880s. The Smithsonian's 1883 annual report described a fish hatchery in the lower story for "shad, salmon, and other food-fishes," with offices, laboratories, and storage above and in adjacent sheds. A railroad siding from the nearby Baltimore and Potomac Railroad (which crossed the Mall on Sixth Street) was used for shipments distributing fish, as well as loading and unloading Smithsonian collections. The Fish Commission's breeding ponds and aquaria soon became popular visitor attractions. Dozens of uses of the building by various government offices followed the Fish Commission's relocation to the Commerce Department in the late 1920s.

The National Air and Space Museum opened on this site in 1976. It is now one of the city's leading tourist attractions and the most visited museum in the world.

⓯ Northwest corner of 7th Street and Independence Avenue SW

FROM "GREWSOME" TO ARTISTIC—The Hirshhorn Museum and Sculpture Garden occupies the former site of the Army Medical Museum, a morbid but popular attraction that existed here from 1887 to 1968 and housed a variety of dental and anatomical collections as well as an extensive library. The museum had relocated from Ford's Theatre, which had ceased operation as a theater after Lincoln's assassination in 1865. According to Rand McNally & Company's 1902 guide, the museum's 25,000 specimens comprised a "grewsome [sic] array of preserved flesh and bones, affected by wounds or disease" that shocked the tourist but intrigued the surgeon. Walter Reed worked there in the 1890s shortly before his discoveries that helped wipe out yellow fever. In the 1930s visitors could see a world-renowned collection of gunshot wounds preserved in alcohol, vertebrae from John Wilkes Booth and British Gen. Edward Braddock (d.1755, a casualty of the French and Indian War), and World War I memorabilia. As the building overflowed after World War II, some exhibits moved to an annex across Independence Avenue. In 1968, prior to preparing the site for the Hirshhorn, the museum collections were relocated to Walter Reed Army Medical Hospital.

⓰ South side of the Mall, next to the Smithsonian Castle between 9th and 10th Streets SW

WHAT A BARGAIN—The National Museum Building was erected as an annex to the Smithsonian Castle to accommodate the burgeoning collections from the Philadelphia Centennial Exposition in 1876 and others gathered by many government agencies, including the U.S. Geological Survey, the U.S. Signal Service, and the U.S. Fish Commission. According to James M. Goode's essay in *1876, A Centennial Exhibition,* the 2 1/4-acre structure took only 15

Golf at the Point. Miniature golf as it was played at Hains Point ca 1930. The government opened a "Tourist Camp" here during the 1920s to accommodate the postwar boom in motoring vacations. Tens of thousands of visitors camped here annually, parking next to their tents.

months and $310,000 to complete, an all-time bargain for a government building at a cost of less than $3 per square foot. The building was completed just in time for President James A. Garfield's inaugural ball on March 4, 1881. Although soon over-crowded, its exhibitions were a great public success. Introduced by Caspar Buberl's allegorical group above the main entrance, representing Columbia as the patroness of Science and Industry, the "U.S. National Museum" exhibited industrial, technical, and ethnographic collections reflecting contemporary notions of human progress and celebrating American resources. Rand McNally & Company's 1902 guidebook claimed that "it would be quite impossible to mention in detail one in a hundred of the objects of artistic, historic, and scientific value in this overflowing museum." Today it is known as the Arts and Industries Building of the Smithsonian Institution.

Designed and built by Adolph Cluss in partnership with Paul Schulze, the building is one of several in the city by Cluss, including the prize-winning Franklin School and Eastern Market.

Cluss, in fact, is worth a slight digression. According to Diana McLellan, writing in the Washington Star of April 7, 1975, Cluss was closely associated with revolutionary political thinker Karl Marx before emigrating from Germany about 1850. In the late 1840s, he was a member of Marx's Communist Correspondents' Committee and head of a branch of the League of Communists in Maintz. In Washington, Cluss married and directed his reformist zeal into innovative designs for many of the capital city's schools, churches, markets, and museums. He died in 1905.

🔟 South side of the Mall, SW, Smithsonian Institution building

THE CASTLE—The Smithsonian Institution was created by Congress in 1846 in response to the bequest to the United States by Englishman James Smithson of $508,000 to "found at

Washington, under the name of the Smithsonian Institution, an establishment for the increase and diffusion of knowledge..." New York architect James Renwick, Jr., introduced a romantic Norman castle design to the otherwise classical complex of public buildings in Washington, signifying the institution's educational purpose. When completed in 1856, the building contained a lecture hall, museum, art gallery, library, laboratories, offices, and living quarters. Joseph Henry, the Smithsonian's first secretary, resided there until his death in 1878, although he bitterly resented the $250,000 cost of the structure. Instruments in the building's towers were used to monitor the weather, and the institution's systematic reports on weather conditions were a precursor of the U.S. Weather Bureau. Here, also, Secretary Samuel Pierpont Langley carried on his investigations in aerodynamics, ultimately resulting in his successful demonstration of an unmanned flying machine over the Potomac River in 1896.

Just inside the main entrance is the mortuary chapel of James Smithson, created in 1904 to receive Smithson's remains when his tomb was relocated from the San Benigno Cemetery in Genoa, Italy. When informed the previous year that Italian authorities had expropriated the cemetery, the Smithsonian sent Dr. Alexander Graham Bell, a member of its board of regents, to bring Smithson's body to the United States. According to the Smithsonian's 1905 annual report, medical experts found the remains "to be in a remarkable state of preservation," and the full board of regents looked on as the examined remains "were placed within the tomb, which was then sealed," on March 6, 1905. In 1973 a Smithsonian team led by Dr. J. Lawrence Angel examined the remains again and was able to determine that Smithson had been about five feet six inches tall, smoked a pipe, and, judging by the development of his upper body, may have been an avid fencer.

Mighty Flood. The February 1881 flood covered downtown Pennsylvania Avenue and moved up the low-lying portions of the Mall to the base of Capitol Hill. Here, the humble stone shaft in right center has been identified by historian Silvio Bedini as the "Capitol Stone, erected in 1804 to mark where the north-south meridian line from the rear door of the White House intersected an [east-west] line through the west end of the Capitol." By 1881 the obelisks marking the north-south line, on Meridian Hill, and the Jefferson Stone behind the White House, had been removed, and within a decade of this photo, the Capitol stone met its demise as well.

Map on page 82

NATIONAL MALL. Although Pierre Charles L'Enfant laid plans for the Mall, it wasn't until the mid-19th century that it was first landscaped. L'Enfant's plan envisioned the Mall as a Grand Avenue, 400 feet in breadth and about a mile in length, with gardens ending in a slope from the houses on each side. By houses he seems to have meant a mix of public and recreational buildings and diplomatic residences. L'Enfant's approach was elegant and formal, accenting broad vistas between monumental structures.

The first landscaper of the Mall, however, was Andrew Jackson Downing, who envisioned a quite different sort of Mall, one featuring a variety of winding carriage drives and special gardens, a "public museum of living trees and shrubs." Before he could complete his work, Downing died in 1852 in a steamboat explosion, but his plans continued to guide the landscaping of the Mall.

Then, in the 20th century, the Mall was straightened out by the classicists. In 1901, the chairman of the Senate Committee on the District of Columbia, James McMillan, commissioned a grand scheme for the development of Washington's monumental core

continued on next page

In front of the Castle stands the statue of Joseph Henry, completed by sculptor William Wetmore Story in 1883. Recognizing Henry's pioneering discoveries in the field of electromagnetism, Story cast a copy of Henry's electromagnet into the monument's pedestal. In 1965 the statue, which originally faced the building, was ordered turned by then-Secretary S. Dillon Ripley to face the Mall and symbolize the expanding scope of the institution and present a more welcoming appearance to its visitors.

Today the Castle is the headquarters building of the Smithsonian Institution. Its distinctive profile serves as one of the symbols of the institution, and makes it one of the most recognizable buildings in the city.

18 **Between the Smithsonian Castle and Independence Avenue SW**

DEPARTMENT OF LIVING ANIMALS—Today the Enid A. Haupt Garden occupies the site; in 1887 the city's first zoo was established here by William Temple Hornaday, the Smithsonian's chief taxidermist. As frontiersmen and recreational hunters slaughtered bison in the West, Hornaday rushed to Montana to collect skins to mount. He became a conservationist instead, returning with live animals and establishing the "Department of Living Animals" on the Mall. The animals were a treat to the public as well as an aid to the taxidermists, who used them as guides for mounting specimens. According to "From Bison to Biopark, 100 Years of the National Zoo," the facility soon "contained a variety of North American animals including mule deer, prairie dogs, badgers, lynx, and a few exotic pets, such as a cockatoo." Within two years Congress authorized creation of the National Zoo in Rock Creek Park.

South side of the Mall between 12th and 14th Streets SW

DEPARTMENT OF AGRICULTURE—This sector of the Mall has been assigned to the Agriculture Department since soon after its establishment in 1862. During the Civil War, the area held live-stock and supply yards to support Union troops. Next, following many early 19th-century proposals to use the Mall for agricultural purposes, the department erected greenhouses and carried out plant propagation experiments. The grounds became a showplace for both popular and exotic plants. A fashionable mansard-roofed administration building was constructed in 1868, aligned with the Smithsonian Castle. An herbarium and agricultural museum were established, including specimens turned over by Smithsonian Secretary Joseph Henry that had been collected by government expeditions and deposited at the Smithsonian, but not yet mounted and exhibited there. After the 1876 Centennial Exhibition in Philadelphia, numerous foreign governments donated agricultural specimens, requiring additional buildings for exhibitions.

The present beaux arts white marble departmental building was constructed behind the older building, which was later removed. After President Theodore Roosevelt thwarted plans to build in the center of the Mall, the wings of the existing building were erected between 1904 and 1908. When Secretary of Agriculture James Wilson was denied full funding for the entire building, he is said to have retorted that he would "build two wings to his bird—and later Congress would supply the body." As Wilson predicted, the central block was erected between 1928 and 1930.

The only site on the Mall used exclusively for offices, the Agriculture Department building rarely attracts notice. One flurry of excitement occurred in 1977 when a group of playful employees dedicated a new cafeteria with a plaque honoring Alferd Packer, a Coloradan guide convicted of cannibalizing five prospectors in

MALL LORE

continued from previous page

based on the principles of the 1791 L'Enfant plan. The design, drawn up by a group of nationally known architects and artists headed by Daniel Burnham, proposed to replace the 19th-century landscape and structures on the Mall (including the Baltimore and Potomac Railroad station and the Smithsonian Castle) with formally arranged classical-style public buildings and vistas emphasizing key monuments. Although the Smithsonian Castle was retained, the Mall, the central downtown core, and the principal axes of the city south from the White House and west from the Capitol were subsequently developed in accordance with the McMillan Plan.

The Constitution Gardens area, installed in 1982 north of the Reflecting Pool between 17th and 20th Streets NW, restores some of the feeling Downing sought to achieve and offers a counterpoint to the formality and monumentality of the rest of the Mall. Constitution Gardens honors the 56 signers of the Declaration of Independence. They are recognized on a memorial island where 56 stones, each inscribed with a different signature, are arranged in groups for each of the original states.

Cleaning the Monument. During the New Deal years of 1934 and 1935, the Works Progress Administration created a major project—critics called it "make work"—to clean the monument. It involved the creation of the highest tubular steel scaffold ever erected—necessary because the monument is the tallest masonry structure in the world. The scaffolding took eight weeks to erect, about as long as the cleaning itself. While the scaffolding was up, someone climbed it and stole the monument's platinum-tipped lightning rods. The most recent refurbishing began in 1998 and by the spring of 1999 the structure was fully scaffolded and artfully lit, giving it the look of an immense piece of modern sculpture.

1874. The tongue-in-cheek naming was intended to be critical of the quality of food being served, and the plaque was removed by the building manager. *Washington Post* reporter Joseph P. Mastrangelo noted on August 9, 1977, that the sign's removal was opposed by the "Friends of Alferd F. Packer," whose membership card bears a photograph of Packer captioned, "I never met a meal I didn't like." A story that often accompanies the tale includes this rebuke to Packer from the judge who sentenced him: "Packer, there are seven Democrats in the county and you 'et five of them."

A much more serious event centered on the building in February 1979 when the department was the target of a massive demonstration for higher farm prices by the American Agriculture Movement. Thousands of farmers with hundreds of tractors and other vehicles (estimates went as high as 2,000) converged on Washington from across the country. On February 6, 1979, during the morning rush hour, they entered the city on major traffic arteries. The *Washington Post* described the resulting traffic jam as "perhaps the worst in Washington history." Police confined the tractors to the Mall by penning them behind a barricade of city buses and garbage trucks, setting up a siege that was to last for weeks.

When snow fell and temperatures plunged, the Agriculture Department opened some offices as sleeping quarters to farmers encamped on the Mall. According to the *Post,* the farmers made use of the federal long-distance telephone system and ran up significant bills before the department rethought the situation and closed its doors to non-employees at night.

On February 19, an 18-inch snowstorm paralyzed the city. Police allowed some tractors to leave the Mall to assist in digging out hospitals, police stations, and the loading dock of the *Washington Post.* Further goodwill was generated for the farmers as the occupation became something of a tourist attraction in its own right; on weekends, parents brought their children to the Mall to see the spectacle and to be given tractor rides by obliging farmers. Nevertheless, the disruption of traffic and extensive damage to the Mall caused widespread criticism of the event.

⑳ Near the center of the Mall, almost midway between the U.S. Capitol and the Lincoln Memorial

TALLEST MASONRY STRUCTURE IN THE WORLD—The Washington Monument rises 555 feet 5 1/8 inches, weighs 81,120 tons, and contains a 50-flight iron stairway (no longer in use) of 900 steps. The L'Enfant plan assigned a site on the Mall for the placement of the "equestrian figure of George Washington, a monument voted in 1783 by the late Continental Congress." Despite L'Enfant's plan and strong sentiment to honor Washington after his death in 1799, Congress failed on several occasions to fund the monument, and the Washington National Monument Society was formed in 1833 to raise private subscriptions for the purpose. By 1848, the society had collected $230,000 and work began.

Many proposals were made as to the exact nature and form of the memorial. The equestrian statue proposed in 1783 would have marked Washington's achievements in the Revolutionary War. After his death in 1799, proposals called for a mausoleum in the form of a pyramid "one hundred feet square at the base and of a proportionate height," according to a 1903 federal history of the monument and the society. Congress refused to fund the proposal. Proposals over the next three decades foundered over money or the refusal of Washington's descendants and Virginia officials to allow the body to be removed from its crypt at Mount Vernon.

The centennial of Washington's birth in 1832 awakened new interest in the matter and led to the proposal to commission a

Monumental Stump. Started in 1848 with money from private subscribers, construction of the Washington Monument stopped in 1854 in the face of political controversy and inadequate funding. The federal government resumed construction in 1876. This 1860s photograph taken near what is the Ellipse area today shows the extent of the Potomac's intrusion into the city.

At the Top. In this photograph by the late Joe Roberts, workers adjust lightning rods at the top of the Washington Monument while it was being cleaned in the mid-1930s.

monumental statue of a seated figure of Washington. Sculptor Horatio Greenough created the statue and it was placed in the Capitol in 1842 (see National Museum of American History, p. 85).

But according to an essay by architectural historian Pamela Scott in the 1989 book, *Robert Mills, Architect,* the Washington Monument Society was not satisfied with the Greenough statue and set out to erect a monument "whose dimensions and magnificence...will be without parallel in the world." To assure broad public support for the monument, the society limited individual contributions to one dollar per individual, a self-defeating policy that was changed in 1845. In that year the society selected Robert Mills's design for a 600-foot obelisk rising above a circular colonnaded base 250 feet in diameter and 100 feet high intended as a pantheon to celebrate American heroes. The colonnade was dropped and minor modifications were made in the monument's height and the shape of the pyramid at the top.

The cornerstone was laid on July 4, 1848, with the same ceremonial Masonic trowel that Washington had used to lay the cornerstone of the Capitol in 1793. Several writers have insisted that a freshman representative from Illinois named Abraham Lincoln was at the dedication. The ceremony was witnessed by about 20,000 onlookers and a 40-year-old live American eagle perched on a ceremonial arch, the same eagle that had similarly observed Lafayette's triumphal parade through Alexandria 24 years earlier. A time capsule placed in the cornerstone contains statistics on Washington, D.C., the United States, the Washington family, American coins and currency, the Bible, about 60 news papers, reports of government agencies, and the initial "Programme of Organization of the Smithsonian Institution."

Blocks of stone were donated by various nations, states, cities, and organizations, most inscribed with mottoes and slogans. Indiana's reflected pre-Civil War sectional tensions: "Indiana.

Knows No North, No South, Nothing but the Union." New York City's Eureka Lodge 177 of the International Order of Odd Fellows simply wrote: "Excelsior." The Templars of Honor and Temperance declared: "We will not make, buy, sell or use as a beverage, any spirituous or malt liquors, Wine, Cider, or any other Alcoholic Liquor...." Another read: "From the Citizens of the United States of America Residing in Foo Chow Foo, China. February 22, 1857."

The shaft rose slowly and in 1854 (at a height of 153 feet) work stopped. Money was scarce and controversy ensued. A massive stone donated by Pope Pius IX enraged a band of anti-Catholics who stole the stone, broke it into pieces, and threw them into the Potomac.

Work resumed in 1880 when Congress came up with enough money to finish the job. The monument opened in 1888 complete with a steam elevator to the top, its towering cage a tour de force of the art of iron construction.

During the New Deal years of 1934 and 1935, the Works Progress Administration cleaned the monument. In 1964 it was cleaned again, but this time instead of surrounding the entire structure with scaffolding, a doughnut device was placed over the top from which electrically driven cables and platforms were suspended, allowing workers to scale the monument in the fashion of high-rise building window washers.

㉑ The grounds of the Washington Monument

KINGS OF CLOUT—Over the years the grounds of the Washington Monument have provided space for all sorts of celebrations and demonstrations.

The grounds have also been used as a recreational center. In the 1860s an odd form of baseball was played here. Capt. J. Walter Mitchell wrote about this "Washington game" in the *Times Herald* in 1919:

"When the first rules were written it was permissible for a batter to make as many home runs as possible before the ball was returned to the home plate. It is recorded that Babcock, the catapult of the original Nationals, knocked the ball so far on one occasion that he made three home runs in succession." This special home run rule was dropped as scores topped the 100 mark. The final score of one game played in 1866 was Washington 102 and Richmond 87. Today the grounds are still a popular site for softball games, and dozens can be observed in progress on summer evenings.

㉒ Between the Washington Monument and Independence Avenue SW

PROPAGATION—Before reclamation projects of the 1880s and 1890s, the Potomac River reached to where Independence Avenue now passes the Tidal Basin. For many years in the second half of the 19th century, an eight-acre area between the river and the Washington Monument was devoted to the Agriculture Department's propagating garden and nursery, earlier located on the Mall at 4 1/2 Street, near the site of the present National Gallery of Art. According to *Keim's* 1884 Washington guidebook, in 1872 alone some 20,000 "papers of flower seeds were collected and cured," and with some 10,000 surplus plants, "consisting of roses, chrysanthemums, verbenas, geraniums, begonias and other hot-house annuals and shrubs...were distributed to members of Congress, and others notified by circular letter that such stock was ready."

㉓ 100 Raoul Wallenberg Place and 14th Street near Independence Avenue SW

HOLOCAUST MEMORIAL—The United States Holocaust Memorial Museum occupies this site next to the Bureau of Engraving and Printing stretching between 14th Street and Raoul Wallenberg Place, formerly 15th Street. Chartered by Congress in

1980, the museum opened in 1993 and has become one of the most heavily visited of any Washington museum. The building, designed by James Ingo Freed, provides a dignified setting for exhibitions, programs, and research to assure the public's continuing education about the tragedy of the Nazi atrocities toward Jews and other victims from 1933-1945 and to stimulate visitors to consider their responsibilities as world citizens.

㉔ The Mall along Constitution Avenue between 17th and 21st Streets NW

TEMPOS—For decades this area was covered with temporary wood and stucco frame buildings—"tempos"—built to accommodate the rapid expansion of government offices during World War I. Additional tempos were erected during the early days of World War II. They were built on other parts of the Mall but dominated the area between 17th and 21st Streets like no other. Although they were slated for demolition in 1946, it was 27 years before the last of the 50 Mall tempos was removed. For many years an oft-heard comment was that there were few things in Washington more permanent than a temporary building.

They had letter and number names. Building E (on the other end of the Mall at Sixth Street NW) was one of the last to go; Building V was more elaborate than buildings U and W since it served as the headquarters for the Department of the Navy. It was referred to as "Main Navy."

Perhaps the best known tempo was Building Four, the one that experienced a near-tragedy. The building took up the entire block bounded by C, D, 20th, and 21st Streets NW. On August 29, 1930, this aging tempo burned in a matter of minutes—the classic tinder-box fire. It began less than an hour after the 500-odd government employees who worked there left for the day. Twenty-six firefighters were injured battling the blaze.

㉕ At the west end of the Mall, the circle on 23rd Street between Independence and Constitution Avenues NW

LINCOLN MEMORIAL—The proposal to build the Lincoln Memorial on land reclaimed from the Potomac provoked vigorous opposition from formidable Speaker of the House Joe Cannon of Illinois during debates in 1902 and 1903. "I'll never let a memorial to Abraham Lincoln be erected in that god-damned swamp," he vowed. Cannon preferred a site in Virginia, but those who insisted that Virginia was an inappropriate site for the "preserver of the Union" prevailed.

The monument sits on fill consisting in part of the original sandstone columns used in 1836 to build the 15th Street colonnade of the Treasury Department building. (The columns were replaced with granite in 1907.) A cavernous area 165 feet long, 60 feet wide, and 60 feet high beneath the memorial was later found to have developed stalactites and stalagmites.

The structure was designed by Henry Bacon, the statue by Daniel Chester French. Both were completed in 1922. French had a son who was deaf and the sculptor was familiar with sign language, so Lincoln's left hand, resting on the arm of the chair, is shaped in the sign for "A" while his right hand makes an "L."

On Easter Sunday 1939, some 75,000 people massed here to hear a recital by African-American Marian Anderson, who sang from the steps. Her appearance there was the result of action by the Daughters of the American Revolution. The organization had refused to rent Constitution Hall (it invoked a "white performers only" clause in its contract) and Anderson had been denied the use of a then-segregated "white" high school. Secretary of the Interior Harold Ickes made the memorial available for the concert. The event was sponsored by Chief Justice Charles Evans Hughes and a committee headed by First Lady Eleanor Roosevelt, who resigned as a D.A.R. member when Anderson was refused permission to sing. The Anderson incident focused national attention on discrimination in the nation's capital and the nation as a whole. Yet at the same concert, prominent members of the Washington black community were forced to sit in a segregated section. (This was par for the course at that time. At the dedication of the Lincoln Memorial on Memorial Day 1922, blacks were also relegated to a segregated position across the road. Chief Justice Taft provided the defense that the Jim Crow arrangement was not "officially sanctioned" by the federal government.)

In 1952 Anderson sang from the Lincoln Memorial steps again, to mark the 1939 decision to use the symbolic site. A mural in the Interior Department building (on C Street between 18th and 19th Streets NW) depicts the Easter Sunday concert.

㉖ At the Tidal Basin SW

JEFFERSON MEMORIAL—Until displaced by landscaping projects after 1925, a popular public beach for white bathers was located here. Swimming and other recreational facilities in the District were segregated. Although the National Park Service began to open up its local picnic, golf, and tennis courts about 1940, equal access to the District's recreational facilities did not occur until the late 1950s.

Planners and architects argued for a decade over locations and designs for the Jefferson Memorial. Finally, despite impassioned pleas from those wishing to save displaced cherry trees, the memorial was constructed on this site from 1939 to 1942. The domed building was designed by John Russell Pope, architect of the National Gallery of Art and the National Archives, and echoed the rotunda design of Jefferson's library at the University of Virginia, based in turn on Rome's Pantheon.

Map on page 82

TREE LORE

CHERRY TREES. Early in the 20th century, the Japanese government made a gift of 3,000 white Yoshino cherry trees to the United States. They were shipped in 1912 and planted around the Tidal Basin. By early 1999, only 125 of the original trees—with a life expectancy of about 45 years—survived. As the old trees died, they have been replaced by stock from commercial growers. In 1997 the National Arboretum began a program of growing a new generation of saplings from the original stock.

In early April 1999, four of the flowering Yoshino cherry trees and five cedar trees were destroyed by three beavers who were eventually trapped and moved to an undisclosed location. This drama of discovery and capture was played out against the background of the Cherry Blossom Festival, and the large crowds got even larger. The beavers became, as a National Park Service ecologist put it, "celebrities," and their exploits created something of a frenzy until they were taken into custody (or the Federal Beaver Protection Program, as some quipped).

Summer of '23. This large float sat in the Tidal Basin, off a public "whites only" beach constructed in 1917. Closed in 1925 to make way for beautification projects, the bathhouse and beach stood at about the spot where the Jefferson Memorial is today. The Lincoln Memorial is visible to the left of the float.

27 West side of the Tidal Basin, midway between the Lincoln Memorial and the Jefferson Memorial SW

FDR MEMORIAL NUMBER 2—This highly successful and popular memorial, completed in 1997, could be termed the memorial Franklin Delano Roosevelt did not want but got anyway. Half a century after his expressed preference for a simple block of stone the size of his desk, later placed in front of the National Archives (see FDR Memorial, p. 56), the power of his deeds moved followers and planners to disregard his request to keep any memorial simple. The result, placed on a site planners originally named in 1901 as a key location for a public memorial, is a series of granite stone settings integrating water elements, the natural environment (including some 350 mature trees transported to the site), and texts drawn from Roosevelt's major public addresses, carved into the stone. The memorial covers over seven acres and cost 48 million dollars. The ensemble is both educational and recreational and has become a major attraction for visitors to the Tidal Basin.

28 East Potomac Park SW

HAINS POINT—This artificial peninsula is named after Army Corps of Engineers Maj. Gen. Peter C. Hains, who supervised the reclamation of the Potomac flats between 1882 and 1890. The flats consisted of about 300 acres of sediment that had piled up over the years. After a devastating flood in February 1881 that spread up the Mall to the foot of Capitol Hill, Congress decided to dredge the river's channel and elevate the flats well above normal water level. The resulting land mass would create a buffer against floods and serve as a recreational center.

The government operated a "tourist camp" here during the 1920s to accommodate the postwar boom in motoring vacations. Tens of thousands of tourists camped here annually, parking next to their tents. According to the 1927 *Book of Washington,* campers were charged "50 cents for the first night or four nights for $1, including a tent, two beds and mattresses." The 60-acre camp, just south of the railroad bridge, included bath and wash facilities, commissary, and filling station, and abutted a golf course, tennis courts, ball fields, and the Potomac Speedway. A longtime Washingtonian noted in 1922 that "where ducks used to feed, is now the beautiful Speedway, one of the busiest places on warm evenings, with the purring motor cars and the awful odor of gasoline," the same odor rising from "gasoline launches" in the harbor.

A favorite attraction of present-day Hains Point is the large sculpture by J. Seward Johnson, Jr., of a partially reclining man entitled "The Awakening." It was placed there "temporarily" after an International Sculpture Conference meeting in 1980. The looming figure seems to be emerging from the earth, and has a particularly eerie presence at night.

World Cruiser. Inveterate explorer and traveler Francis H. Buzzacott is shown in 1929 en route through Washington, D.C., as part of a 500,000-mile tour of the world in a customized land cruiser complete with refrigerator, gas stove, and shower bath.

Southwest Waterfront and Hains Point. The Southwest waterfront is seen here in 1885 during dredging operations to create Hains Point and East Potomac Park, across from the waterfront. This artificial peninsula was named after the supervising engineer, Maj. Gen. Peter C. Hains. This image, which takes in much of the old Southwest, underscores how vulnerable the area was to flooding. The large structures near the shore are icehouses, a reminder of Washington before air-conditioning and electrical refrigeration.

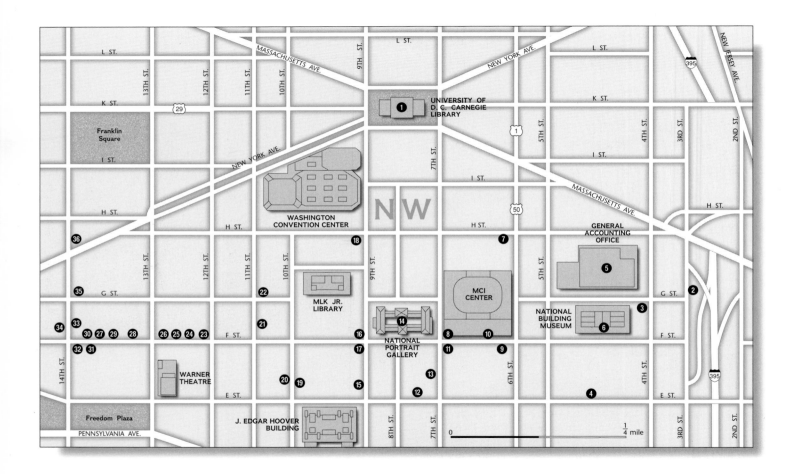

UNIVERSITY OF
D. C. CARNEGIE
LIBRARY

1

L ST.

L ST.

MASSACHUSETTS AVE.

NEW YORK AVE.

K ST.

K ST.

29

Franklin
Square

I ST.

NEW YORK AVE.

I ST.

I ST.

1

NW

MASSACHUSETTS AVE.

H ST.

H ST.

H ST.

WASHINGTON
CONVENTION CENTER

50

GENERAL
ACCOUNTING
OFFICE

36

18

7

5

2

G ST.

35

G ST.

22

MCI
CENTER

3

G ST.

MLK JR.
LIBRARY

NATIONAL
BUILDING
MUSEUM

34

33

21

6

F ST.

30 **27** **29** **28**

26 **25** **24** **23**

F ST.

16

8

10

F ST.

32 **31**

14

17

11

9

NATIONAL
PORTRAIT
GALLERY

WARNER
THEATRE

13

20 **19**

15

12

4

E ST.

E ST.

E ST.

Freedom Plaza

J. EDGAR HOOVER
BUILDING

PENNSYLVANIA AVE.

0   ¼ mile

13TH ST.

12TH ST.

11TH ST.

10TH ST.

9TH ST.

7TH ST.

5TH ST.

4TH ST.

3RD ST.

2ND ST.

14TH ST.

8TH ST.

6TH ST.

NEW JERSEY AVE.

395

395

1

The Old Downtown

① New York Avenue between 7th and 9th Streets NW

THE OLD CARNEGIE LIBRARY—The building now occupying Mount Vernon Square was given by Andrew Carnegie and served as the city's main public library from 1903 to the late 1960s. In 1999, The Historical Society of Washington, D.C. received funding to convert the building into the City Museum of Washington, D.C. It occupies the site of the original Northern Liberty Market, established on the open square in 1845, and the Northern Liberty Fire Company. The market building was along the Seventh Street side, the firehouse centered at the Eighth Street intersection to the south. Six people were killed here and 21 wounded during election riots in 1857. A nativist party opposing foreign immigrants and Catholics, the Know-Nothings had narrowly lost the 1856 mayoral race and now sought victory. "Plug uglies," or firehouse gangs, from Baltimore joined local Know-Nothing supporters in mounting a cannon in front of the polls. When District Mayor William B. Magruder asked President James Buchanan for help, Marines marched from the Marine Barracks and fired when the crowd failed to disperse.

More violence struck at 8 p.m. on September 3, 1872, when zealous demolition crews dispatched by Alexander R. "Boss" Shepherd began to raze the sprawling market building complex while it was still occupied by vendors refusing to move. Historian James M. Goode notes in *Capital Losses* that several people were killed by falling debris while Shepherd wined and dined the District judges—who might otherwise have issued an injunction—at his country estate five miles away.

Ornate Theater. The Lust Company's Leader Theater at 507 9th Street NW was a popular attraction in the 1920s.

JUDICIARY SQUARE. The 19 acres bounded by Fourth and Fifth Streets between D and G Streets NW were destined to accommodate civic functions. Possibly intended by Pierre Charles L'Enfant as the site of the Supreme Court, the area became instead the city's municipal center and the location of various lesser federal and local courts. About midway between the Capitol and the executive buildings near the White House, the section surrounding the square contained prominent residences and numerous hotels and businesses during the 19th century, before shifting to predominantly governmental and legal functions in the 20th. It is said that the city's last public whipping post was located on the square.

James Croggon, in the *Washington Star* of February 23, 1913, wrote of a stream that began in springs at about Fifth and L Streets NW and ran south through Judiciary Square to join Tiber Creek near First and C Streets. The stream provided a convenient sewer for residents of the square, the nearby city jail, and the hospital. It drained a sizable area, often overflowed and, Croggon added, "indeed, in Fifth Street sixty years ago the water was often deep enough for canoeing."

continued on next page

② 701 3rd Street NW

JEWISH HISTORY IN WASHINGTON—This building—though not at this site—was the first synagogue built in Washington. It was erected at 600 Fifth Street NW in 1876—President Ulysses S. Grant attended the dedication—by the congregation of Adas Israel, which had been meeting at homes and store fronts since its founding in the late 1860s. In 1908 Adas Israel moved to a new building.

According to Julian Feldman, executive director of the Jewish Historical Society, the first floor of the old structure was used for various retail purposes including a restaurant, and the second floor sanctuary was rented out to St. Sophia Greek Orthodox Church and eventually the Evangelical Church of God, while retail activities continued on the first floor. In 1969 the old building was threatened with demolition as the area underwent redevelopment. The District government, which had taken title to the property, negotiated an agreement with the Jewish Historical Society of Greater Washington under which the society moved the building to its present site and under a 99-year lease maintains it as a national trust. The society operates the Lillian and Albert Small Jewish Museum in the building, where visitors are able to view exhibits and documents portraying the history of Washington's Jewish community.

Although Adas Israel was the first congregation in the city to build its own synagogue, it was not the District's first Jewish congregation. That distinction belongs to the Washington Hebrew Congregation, which came into being in 1852 but was housed for many years in a structure that was intended for, but never occupied by, a Methodist church. At its inception the Washington Hebrew Congregation was traditionally Orthodox; in the 1860s, it began to liberalize its practices. Women were allowed to sit with men and some English was introduced into the liturgy. Not all congregants were pleased. "The straw that broke the camel's back," says

Feldman, was the use of an organ during services. About 35 families left Washington Hebrew Congregation to form Adas Israel, where they prayed in a more traditional setting.

Today Washington Hebrew Congregation is a Reform synagogue and remains the largest Jewish congregation in the city. Adas Israel, the second largest, is a Conservative synagogue.

❸ Southwest corner of 4th and G Streets NW

THE OLD JAILHOUSE—The new "fireproof" city jail, built on this site about 1840 by architect Robert Mills for $38,000, provided separate cells for criminals and debtors, reflecting liberal penal theories of the time. Mills reported in 1842 that the iron bars were placed inside the windows on the front of the building in order to avoid the "painful appearance of a prison house." The jail was also the site of executions until 1875, when a new jail was erected near 19th Street and Independence Avenue SE.

❹ North side of E Street, centered between 4th and 5th Streets NW

HOSPITAL SITE—Directly behind old City Hall was the City Hospital, dating from the 1840s. The hospital was operated in a converted jail, initially by the medical faculty of Columbian College (predecessor of The George Washington University) and later by the Sisters of Charity.

At the outset of the Civil War, the building was adapted into a military hospital. On the morning of November 4, 1861, it burned to the ground. All but one of the patients were saved, even though it took an hour before a single alarm was sounded and an hour after that for the first fire engine to arrive.

The Judiciary Square Hospital rose in its place and housed Civil War wounded. Abraham Lincoln often visited.

STREET LORE

continued from previous page

In the center of Judiciary Square today, above the Metro entrance, is the new National Law Enforcement Officers Memorial, dedicated to officers who have died in the line of duty. It was designed by architect Davis Buckley. New names are added to the memorial's wall as the list grows. The total had reached over 14,500 by May 1999.

Growing City. Viewed from the Capitol in the 1880s, downtown Washington was a densely packed mix of residential, commercial and government buildings. Aided by the rapidly expanding electric streetcar lines, the population was about to leap across the city's original boundary of Florida Avenue into the elevated regions of the District and Maryland suburbs, in the background.

❺ The block bounded by G, H, 4th, and 5th Streets NW

WATCHDOG—When the General Accounting Office building was dedicated by President Truman in 1951, the Pentagon was the only building in the metropolitan area that was larger. The GAO serves as Congress' formal investigating arm.

❻ F and G Streets between 4th and 5th Streets NW

MEIGS' RED BARN—Designed to offer light and air to clerks processing military pensions, this immense structure, known for years as the Pension Building, now celebrates the nation's building and construction heritage. For many years the open square was used for stonecutting and support of construction during the erection of nearby federal offices, including the Patent Office and General Post Office buildings at Seventh and E and F Streets NW. The U.S. Pension Bureau erected its office building here between 1882 and 1887, at a cost of $886,614. Designed and built by Army engineer Gen. Montgomery C. Meigs, it was planned as a high-tech Italian Renaissance-style structure, with the latest in skylighting, ventilation, and fireproofing. It was an architectural tour de force, with 75-foot-high walls, colossal columns containing 70,000 bricks each, an iron roof, double-glazed windows, highly functional interior spaces, and an extensive wraparound terra-cotta frieze featuring the different branches of the military services. Derisively called "Meigs' Red Barn," the massive structure used 15,000,000 bricks. Gen. Philip Sheridan quipped that the only thing wrong with it was that it couldn't be burned down!

The Pension Building's great hall has been a favorite inaugural ball site for over a century. A gigantic tarpaulin was stretched across its top when Grover Cleveland's first inaugural ball took place in 1885, since the building still lacked a roof. When canaries were released during the ball, the result was grotesque rather than festive. The birds flew up to the tarpaulin, froze to death in the frigid air, and plummeted to the dance floor.

Today the building serves as the National Building Museum, opened in 1985 to educate the public about the building arts.

❼ 604 H Street NW

TREASON'S NEST—Currently Go-Lo's Restaurant in the heart of Chinatown, it was the Surratt House during the Civil War, a boarding house that once dominated this street. It figured in the plotting of the Lincoln assassination—typically described as the "nest where the egg of treason was hatched"—and Mary Surratt, the woman who ran the boarding house, was hanged as a co-conspirator. She is buried in Mount Olivet Cemetery on Bladensburg Road NE. The building has been described as a typical example of a pre-Civil War downtown residence.

The MCI Center, a downtown sports arena seating 20,000, opened in 1997, covers the following three historic sites, and breathes new vitality into an area long the center of the commercial life of the city. A prime example of public-private partnership, the Center cost over 200 million dollars, financed chiefly by real estate and sports magnate Abe Pollin, owner of the NBA's Washington Wizards. In addition to the Wizards, the arena is the home of the NHL's Washington Capitals and the WNBA's Mystics. Discovery Channel built and operates a three-level destination theme store in the arena containing interactive exhibits, an 80-seat HDTV theater, and a 15-minute film that orients visitors on the history of the capital and its neighborhoods. Over 2.5 million patrons attended sports events, concerts, and other activities at the Center during its first year of operation.

Laying the Tracks. Electric streetcar lines being installed in 1896 at the corner of Fifth Street and Indiana Avenue NW, at Judiciary Square. As no overhead lines were allowed within city limits, various attempts were made in the 1890s to provide power from below the car, including compressed air and electrical contacts on the surface—which toppled more than one unfortunate mis-stepping horse. According to local historian Robert A. Truax, the most successful system is seen here, where a "plow" beneath the streetcar contacted the central power rail. Cars passing out of the city crossed over pits where a worker quickly removed the plow as the trolley was raised to contact electric power lines overhead and reversed the process on incoming cars (the car would slide slowly into the plow). With the turn of a switch, the car would continue after only a moment's delay.

Map on page 106

Monumental Building. Column for north wing of the General Post Office being hoisted in about 1865. Patent agent offices in the background at the southeast corner of 7th and F Streets NW reflect the proximity of the Patent Office. In the 1990s, the 7th Street corridor reestablished itself—this time as a center for sports, entertainment, and the arts—with the MCI Center and other developments surrounding the Gallery Place Metro station spearheading the revival.

8 East side of 7th Street NW just above the intersection with F Street

ABOLITIONIST PRESS—The American and Foreign Anti-Slavery Society established the *National Era* newspaper on this site opposite the Patent Office in 1847.

In April 1848 the *Era*'s abolitionist editor, Gamaliel Bailey, refused to close his press when faced by a mob angered by an unsuccessful attempt to help a number of black slaves of prominent city citizens escape on a ship named the *Pearl*.

An anti-slavery story by Harriet Beecher Stowe, later published in book form as *Uncle Tom's Cabin*, first appeared in the *Era* as a serial in 1851-52. By this time the paper had moved its offices to 427 Seventh Street NW.

9 614 F Street NW

ARCHITECT'S HOUSE—Thomas U. Walter lived here while serving as architect of the Capitol. He is best remembered for overseeing construction of the Capitol dome, started in the 1850s along with the two wings. The building's continued construction during the Civil War was seen as a sign of national purpose. Walter also supervised extension of the nearby Patent Office and General Post Office buildings, and was a prime force in the establishment of the American Institute of Architects in 1857.

The Hecht Company parking garage occupied this site for much of the 20th century until razed in 1990.

10 619 F Street NW

EARLY FEMINIST—Two-time presidential candidate and suffragette Belva Ann Lockwood lived on this site for nearly 40 years. Lockwood was the presidential nominee of the National Equal Rights Party in 1884 and 1888. According to a profile by

Margaret C.B. Christman in the National Portrait Gallery's *Fifty American Faces*, Lockwood decided on a career in law after relocating to Washington from upstate New York in 1868. She gained her degree from National University Law School in Washington after being refused admission because of her sex at Georgetown University and Columbian College (now The George Washington University). Lockwood lobbied successfully for laws providing equal pay for equal work for female government employees and equal opportunities for women to practice law before any court in the United States. When her bill to permit women lawyers equal access to all courts was passed in 1879, she became the first woman admitted to practice before the United States Supreme Court. Her law offices occupied the English basement of the 20-room house, which became a local center for proponents of equal rights and, later, world peace.

Model Building. When an 1836 fire destroyed Blodget's Hotel and the government postal facilities it housed, Robert Mills constructed a monumental new building on the same site (E Street between 7th and 8th Streets NW) for the General Post Office. Congress had declared marble to be the preferred material for constructing government buildings and the marble General Post Office, photographed by John Plumbe, Jr., about 1846, was considered a model fireproof and permanent public building.

⑪ Southeast corner of 7th and F Streets NW

DESEGREGATION STRUGGLE—Between June 1951 and January 1952, picket lines were set up every Thursday night and Saturday opposing the Hecht Company department store's denial of service to black customers at its basement lunch counter; they could shop, but not be served food. Desegregation strategists targeted restaurants in department stores whose main business came from black patrons. Former picket-line members, attending the February 1991 Conference on Washington, D.C. Historical Studies at the Martin Luther King Memorial Library, recalled dressing in their finest suits and dresses, even on the hottest days of summer, to assure a dignified presence. One picket-line sign asserted that "Negroes are Fighting and Dying in Korea, But Hecht's says 'We Won't Serve Colored Here'." On Christmas Eve, the protesters sang carols with alternative lyrics to drive home their

Map on page 106

Inventor's Temple. The monumental original wing of the Patent Office (now the National Portrait Gallery) facing F Street, shown in this ca 1846 photograph by John Plumbe, Jr., contrasted dramatically with the residential scale of downtown Washington. Exhibits here included inventions, the Declaration of Independence, and other government collections. Greenhouses behind the building were relocated to the Mall in the early 1850s, near where the U.S. Botanic Garden is today, as the Patent Office was extended around the block.

protest message to last-minute shoppers. After a six-month protest, the lunch counter was opened to all.

In 1986, the Hecht Company's downtown store relocated to the northwest corner of 12th and G Streets NW.

12 E Street between 7th and 8th Streets NW

FROM HOTEL TO POST OFFICE—Intended by its developer Samuel Blodget to be the prize in a public lottery to raise money for public buildings, the hotel constructed here in 1793 and thereafter referred to as Blodget's Hotel was one of the city's largest buildings. In 1816 foreign observer David Baillie Warden described its elevated site as surrounded by "richly wooded hills" forming "scenery unequalled in beauty in America." The lottery failed to raise the cost of construction. The building was never a successful hotel, but it housed the city's first theater in 1800, the Patent Office and federal and city post offices for over two decades after 1810, and served as the temporary Capitol in 1814, when it was the only public building left standing by the British. Patent Superintendent William Thornton claimed to have halted the British attempt to destroy the building by asking: "Are you Englishmen or Goths and Vandals: This is the Patent Office, the depository of the ingenuity of the American Nation, in which the whole civilized world is interested. Would you destroy it?" Years later, on December 15, 1836, the building burned down accidentally, destroying 7,000 patent models.

The building currently standing was designed by Robert Mills and constructed between 1839 and 1866 to serve as the General Post Office. The first federal edifice to be built entirely in marble, it was considered by Charles Dickens when he visited the city in 1842 to be "a very compact, and very beautiful building." After the Post Office Department relocated to the Romanesque Revival structure at 12th Street and Pennsylvania Avenue in 1897, the building housed the General Land Office, the Bureau of Education, a variety of commissions, and, after World War I, the headquarters of General of the Armies John J. "Black Jack" Pershing. The Tariff Commission, now the International Trade Commission, was headquartered here from 1921 to 1989. The building was turned over to the Smithsonian Institution in 1984 for restoration and museum use, but lack of funding stalled further development. In 1996, *Washington Post* critic Benjamin Forgey urged that the building be saved, stating that "our shameful neglect of this certifiable treasure ought to end." At that time the General Services Administration proposed to lease the building for private development, presumably in a manner that would preserve its historic spaces. However, the building remained mothballed three years later.

⓭ West side of 7th Street, midway between E and F Streets NW

TELECOMMUNICATOR—The first telegraph office in the United States was opened here on April 1, 1845, by the inventor of the telegraph, Samuel F.B. Morse. The building was an ordinary two-story house with an outside stairway leading to the telegraph office on the second floor. The office operated under the direction of the Post Office Department, which occupied the building now on this site, the first-built portion of which faced E Street and extended halfway through the block, up to the point where the telegraph office was located. The post office building was extended through the entire block in the 1850s.

The telegraph was first connected between this location and Baltimore. An 1846 Washington city directory announced that "Intelligence may be transmitted at the rate of one quarter of one cent for each telegraphic character...messengers are in constant attendance at each terminus of the line for the prompt delivery of messages, etc."

Ninth & G. This ca 1910 postcard view south from 9th and G Streets shows the Patent Office Building on the left, then the headquarters of the Interior Department, of which the U.S. Patent Office was a part. Towering in the center is the Washington Loan & Trust Building, which was doubled in size in 1926 and later became a Riggs Bank branch. Along the right side are retail shops, and down the street toward Pennsylvania Avenue were the Gayety, Leader, Plaza, Imperial, Empress, Academy of Music, and Palace Theaters.

Streets for People? This 1920s photo of the intersection of 9th and F Streets next to the Patent Office shows the impending competition for the streets posed by the arrival of the automobile. The front steps of the Patent Office were removed in the 1930s to benefit motor traffic; in the 1970s the byway was converted to a pedestrian mall but has since been returned to its former status as a street.

14 Block bounded by F, G, 7th, and 9th Streets NW

FROM PATENTS TO PORTRAITS—Now home to two Smithsonian museums, the earliest part of the building here is more than 150 years old. L'Enfant's 1791 plan for the city reserved the site for a shrine to American heroes. It remained unoccupied except by squatters until construction of the Patent Office building began in 1836. The building drew more than 100,000 visitors annually as the de facto national museum before the Smithsonian Castle was completed in the 1850s. The exhibits were a showcase of the nation's resources, economic productivity, and historical achievements, including thousands of American inventions, examples of manufacturers' products, the Declaration of Independence, George Washington's uniform and military gear, and tens of thousands of natural history specimens. By the 1860s the exhibit halls continued for a quarter-mile around the top floor where, according to Boyd's *Washington City Directory:* "You may see the models of most everything that has ever been invented or grown out of the Yankee brain."

The building housed many early government offices, including the original Department of the Interior and the precursor to the Department of Agriculture. Clara Barton worked here in the 1850s as a confidential clerk to the Patent Commissioner, the first woman in federal employment to receive pay equal to that received by male clerks. During the Civil War, the building served as a temporary barracks and military hospital, where Walt Whitman read to the wounded. In 1865 Whitman worked in the building as a clerk in the Bureau of Indian Affairs. Whitman's biographer Justin Kaplan relates that in that year James Harlan, a staunch Methodist from Iowa, took office as secretary of the interior and promptly launched a cleanup campaign, instructing his staff to report employees who were disloyal, inefficient, or who "disregard...the rules of decorum & propriety prescribed by a Christian

Civilization." Harlan fired two bureau heads, 80 clerks, including Whitman, and the entire force of women copyists, who were thought to present an influence "injurious to...the 'morals' of the men." Harlan searched Whitman's desk and found the heavily edited manuscript of *Leaves of Grass* which Whitman was updating for publication in 1867. The work failed the morals test and Whitman was sacked on June 30. Whitman's allies immediately found him another post in the attorney general's office, where he served for several years and was treated with respect for his burgeoning reputation as an American writer.

President Abraham Lincoln's second inaugural ball was held here March 6, 1865, five weeks before his assassination at nearby Ford's Theatre. According to a *New York Times* report, the dancing was a great success, but the "supper was a disaster." At midnight 5,000 guests jammed space prepared for 300. "In less than an hour the table was a wreck and the array of empty dishes and the debris of the feast were positively frightful to behold."

In the 20th century, the building housed the Civil Service Commission before being converted by the Smithsonian in the 1960s to accommodate the National Collection of Fine Arts (now the National Museum of American Art) and the National Portrait Gallery. Among the portraits there is the one commissioned by President Lyndon B. Johnson, painted by artist Peter Hurd. Johnson condemned the completed work as the "ugliest thing I ever saw." It is now on permanent display.

⑮ 518 9th Street NW

TEMPERANCE DIGS—Long the site of the Holly Tree Hotel and Dining Rooms, which for many years was the city's leading first-class temperance hotel and restaurant. An 1884 trade directory ad boasted that it served the "most flavorous drip coffee," oysters

Idle Hours. This 1941 photo shows one of a number of places of adult recreation and amusement that characterized mid-20th-century 9th Street NW between F and D Streets.

Map on page 106

served in every possible style, and 15 to 25 full meals at a set rate of 25 cents. Lunches were a lot less (a sandwich, pudding, and glass of milk was a dime). The proprietor at the time was a Mr. J.D. Croissant. This site is now occupied by an office building.

⑯ 901 F Street NW

MASONS, SWEETS, AND POLLSTERS—Completed in 1868 as the Grand Lodge of the Masons, this handsome building served as the Julius Lansburgh furniture store from 1921 to the early 1970s. When renovated for offices and linked to a new building on the adjacent site on Ninth Street, the complex will house among others the Washington headquarters of the Gallup Organization on the upper floors of the existing building and retail spaces below. Significantly, the project will preserve both the exterior and major portions of the interior of this landmark building, which is listed on the National Register of Historic Places. The Masons' grand meeting hall, a 25-foot-high room occupying the second floor, will be preserved for conferences. The new building will cover the former location of Velati's Caramel shop, which had entrances at 620 Ninth Street and around the corner on G Street. A beloved candy and confectionary store, Velati's closed on the site in the mid-1970s, although the Hecht Company's Store at 12th and G Streets continues to carry sweets under the Velati's name.

⑰ 900 F Street NW

FROM BANKS TO BEDS—In 1999, following another adaptive reuse of a downtown landmark building, Courtyard by Marriott was creating a hotel in the Washington Loan & Trust Company Building, completed on this site by former government architect James G. Hill in 1891, and most recently occupied by Riggs Bank.

A 1926 addition consistent with the original facade design doubled the size of the building, making its newest use feasible. The hotel will serve as a downtown showplace for the Marriott chain, preserving the building's grand street level interior spaces. This is a prime example of the benefits of providing tax incentives for commercial projects that sensitively adapt historic properties.

⑱ H Street near 9th Street NW

ORPHANAGE—Here on "Mausoleum Square" near the present site of the Martin Luther King Memorial Library was the location from the 1830s to the 1880s of the Washington City Orphan Asylum for homeless white children. Established about 1815 and initially directed by first lady Dolley Madison, the orphanage was one of four in the city, Georgetown and Alexandria. Congress tried to help the two city institutions in 1832 by granting them public lots assessed at $10,000. Historian W.B. Bryan relates that 15 years later the asylum's trustees had only sold two of the 29 lots, and at a depressed value. President Andrew Jackson also tried to help by directing the "public sale of the Numidian lion given him by the King of Morocco" and dividing the $3350 profits between the city orphanages. The asylum relocated to S and 14th Streets NW about 1880.

Mausoleum Square, on H Street between 9th and 10th Streets NW, was the burial ground for the Burnes family and later the Van Ness family—two families of great prominence in the early history of the city.

⑲ 511 10th Street NW

FORD'S THEATRE—It was in this building, on Good Friday evening, April 14, 1865, that John Wilkes Booth shot Abraham Lincoln. Before Ford's Theatre was established here the site was occupied by the First Baptist Church. It was bought by the Ford brothers of Baltimore, who turned the building into a theater. The structure burned to the ground in 1862, proof to some that the use of a church for a theater forever cursed the site. John T. Ford built a larger theater on the spot, which opened in August 1863. Prior to his assassination, President Lincoln had seen eight plays at the theater, including one in 1863 in which John Wilkes Booth was the leading actor. Following the assassination and resulting conspiracy trial, both the public and the government opposed the building's reopening as a theater.

In 1866 the building was purchased by the government and used as the Army Medical Museum, exhibiting macabre examples of various war wounds and the remains of John Wilkes Booth's spinal column pierced by a carbine bullet.

Disaster struck the sadly deteriorated building on July 9, 1893. According to one account the government had "patched, bolstered, remodeled, braced and propped until nothing of the original was left." About 500 War Department clerks were processing Civil War pension records for the survivors of some 300,000 Army dead when the weight of stored government records and the effects of an excavation under the building caused the floors to cave in, killing 22 and wounding 108.

The tragedy had a long-lasting effect on federal employment. In the days following the collapse, anti-government feeling grew to a fevered pitch. An indignation rally staged by friends and relatives of the dead and injured turned into a mob and came close to violence as they denounced "government murderers." Newspapers, meanwhile, blamed congressional demagogues for the deaths of the government clerks, charging that the lives of lower-level employees had been imperiled by administrators trying to prove their frugality to congressmen demanding reduced government spending. On the day following the collapse, the *Washington Post*

Assassination Site. Ford's Theatre as it appeared in about 1910 next to the National Cycle Repair Company.

Map on page 106

Shopping Center. F Street between 15th and 7th Streets NW was for many years the heart of the city's retail district. This is how it looked in the 1920s. The Sun Building is partially visible at the far left.

said: "For years the clerks and other Federal employees have been huddled in innumerable death-traps to lose their health by slow degree or die outright in sudden accidents, in order that a few selfish impostors might flaunt themselves before a crowd of gulls."

In the 1960s the building was restored as a theater by the National Park Service, aided by a series of photographs taken by Mathew Brady for the government just after the shooting. As far as possible, the newly opened theater looked as it did on the night of the assassination. Performances resumed with its reopening.

20 516 10th Street NW, opposite Ford's Theatre

THE PETERSEN HOUSE—President Lincoln was taken here after being shot because it was feared that moralists would disapprove of him dying in a godless theater on Good Friday. He died here early in the morning of April 15, 1865, despite the efforts of five physicians, and it was on this spot that, according to Lincoln's personal secretary, that Secretary of War Edwin Stanton uttered the words that marked Lincoln's death: "Now he belongs to the ages."

William Petersen, who owned the house, was a Swedish-born tailor whose lodgings were popular with Union soldiers during the Civil War. The Oldroyd family bought the house in the 1880s and ran a Lincoln Museum there for many years. The building is now owned and administered by the National Park Service.

21 The block bounded by 10th, 11th, F, and G Streets NW

THE LAST WOODIES—Partners Samuel Walter Woodward and Alvin Mason Lothrop launched their Washington retail enterprise, the Boston Dry Goods House, in the market space on Pennsylvania Avenue. Six years later, they relocated to this site in anticipation that the commercial center of the city would move north from Pennsylvania Avenue. They were right. Woodward & Lothrop expanded on the block and beyond, serving for a century as an anchor of the downtown commercial community.

The building covers its share of history, as expansion brought the loss of several venerable institutions, including the St. Vincent's Female Orphan Asylum and St. Vincent's Academy on the southwest corner of 10th and G Streets NW. According to Woodies' institutional history, *From Founders to Grandsons*, John B. McLeod's Central Academy was located there prior to the orphanage from 1816 to 1835. On the F Street side stood one of the first—if not the first—churches in Washington: St. Andrew's, a Presbyterian church organized in 1794.

The store was a major force in the commercial development of the city and its suburbs: "Without Woodies," humorist Art Buchwald once wrote, "Washington would be just another small town surrounded by Bloomingdales...." Buchwald's prediction is now being tested, as Woodies closed in 1995. The Washington Opera purchased the building for 18 million dollars but decided the cost of renovating for a downtown opera house was prohibitive and sold it in 1999 to developer Douglas Jemal for 28.2 million dollars. Jemal plans a mixed retail and residential establishment.

㉒ North side of G Street between 10th and 11th Streets NW

WOODIES NORTH—As Woodies thrived across G Street, this location became its logical expansion site and in 1946 it purchased the Palais Royal Department Store at 11th and G, another Washington retail institution that had been located on several different downtown sites following its establishment in 1877. Woodies used and expanded the building as an annex. When permission was granted to tear it down in 1985, it was lamented as the city's oldest department store and an example of the Chicago school style of commercial architecture. The site is now occupied by the Washington Center office building.

Christmas Shopping. F Street looking east from 13th Street is decorated for holiday season shoppers in this 1950s photograph.

Map on page 106

STREET LORE

PHANTOMS. Those working with old maps and histories of the city often encounter street names that no longer exist. The names date back to before 1893, when streets outside the original boundaries of Georgetown and the City of Washington were named by developers who paid no attention to names given by other developers. There was, in fact, much duplication, with two Baltimore streets, three Joliets, two Philadelphias, and three Lowells. Over time many of these names were discarded.

 Northwest corner of 12th and F Streets NW

ICE CREAM PIONEER—The original site of Fussell's Ice Cream Parlors. The name on the door was that of Jacob Fussell, who began the American ice cream industry in Baltimore in 1851. The Fussell company's Washington outpost opened in 1856, across the street from the Great Falls Ice Company (at the southwest corner of 12th and F Streets NW), making this intersection something of a summer mecca in the days before air-conditioning. Fussell had a store in New York City as well.

As a moderately successful milk dealer, Jacob Fussell was constantly oversupplied with cream, but found that he could dispose of it in the form of ice cream at 25 cents a quart. Before this, ice cream was either made at home or prepared on order by a caterer.

The father of the American ice cream industry was a man of fierce conviction. He was an ardent abolitionist who once barely escaped a pro-slavery lynch mob in Baltimore. A close friend of Abraham Lincoln, he was a delegate to the Republican convention that nominated Lincoln. In Baltimore Fussell built a housing project, Fussell Court, for newly freed slaves.

The ice cream parlor later moved to 1427 New York Avenue NW, where on hot days it would sell between 300 and 600 gallons of ice cream.

24 1209 F Street NW

STRAWBERRY DREAMS—Former site of Reeves Bakery and Restaurant, which for decades had been known for its strawberry pie, blueberry doughnuts, chicken salad sandwiches, and other old-fashioned favorites. Television personality Willard Scott recalled from his childhood, "For 40 cents you could kill yourself in there."

It first opened in 1886 and rose from its own ashes after a 1984 fire that gutted it. The pre-fire Reeves featured a lunch counter described as being "as long as Ohio."

In the *Washington Post* restaurant critic Phyllis Richman observed that Reeves was popular among First Ladies: Lady Bird Johnson brought daughter Lynda by for coffee milkshakes, Bess Truman often had lunch there, and Pat Nixon often took one of Reeves' strawberry pies home with her. Richman also reported that Helen Hayes recalled going to Reeves as a young girl for lemonade or chocolate sodas.

Reeves closed on September 29, 1989, and reopened nearby in 1992 at 1306 G Street. The old building was razed to make way for a new office building at 1201 F Street.

㉕ 1215 F Street NW

HISTORIC FIRE—Former site of the Dulin and Martin china store, which burned in January 1928. It was one of the most spectacular fires in the history of the city, fought by the entire fire-fighting force of the District along with 29 Maryland and Virginia companies, including 10 from Baltimore. High winds blew sparks and burning debris for blocks, raising fears that the entire business district would go up in flames as had happened in Baltimore and Chicago. More than a thousand firemen kept those fears from being realized, and although several sustained injuries, there were no deaths. The most dramatic moment came with the rescue of three firemen hanging from a fourth-floor ledge.

㉖ Northeast corner of 13th and F Streets NW

UNCLE SAM'S BANK—The nation's private central bank, chartered by Congress in 1791 and headquartered in Philadelphia, opened a branch on this site in 1801, after the federal government relocated to Washington. Its purpose was to collect, disburse, and

Soldiers' Hangout. Downtown 9th Street provided many attractions for the troops during World War II.

Map on page 106

The Gayety. Famous theater for burlesque and vaudeville, on the east side of 9th Street near E Street NW, as it looked in April 1937 when photographed by John Vachon of the Farm Security Administration. The Gayety observed the segregated practices of the day and relegated black patrons to the balcony. Morrison Hansborough, a longtime Washingtonian, remembers that as a teenager in the 1930s, he would sit in a balcony seat from where he saw such legendary burlesque queens as Ann Corio and Georgia Southern and heard what he describes as some fine bands. In 1949, the Gayety closed its doors, replaced the following year by the Sam S. Shubert Theater, which presented legitimate stage productions there until 1960. Jimmy Lake, Jr., son of the owner, believes that snazzy dresser in the photograph is Billy Hagen. He writes, "Billy was the baggy-pants, putty-nosed comic who would growl 'Cheese and Crackers' whenever he wanted to beef up a punch-line. So much for profanity in those more innocent days."

manage public funds for the government. However, its initial 20-year charter prevented any new banks from being chartered in its jurisdiction, so the new City of Washington had no local bank until after 1811. In the meantime, Georgetown and Alexandria banks, already established, served the day-to-day banking needs of the locals.

27 1325 F Street NW

MOVIE SCENE—In the basement of a building on this site in 1893, Washington inventor Charles Francis Jenkins, with the assistance of Thomas Armat, constructed an early movie projector that was successfully demonstrated to the public three years later in New York City. The site was later that of Harris and Ewing, the city's leading photographic gallery for most of the 20th century.

28 1317 F Street NW

OLDEST SKYSCRAPER?—The claim has been made that the Sun building may be the nation's earliest surviving "skyscraper." Here is how the *Washington Post* handled this assertion in 1987 when the structure was 100 years old: "The oldest standing skyscraper in America—maybe the first—an exquisite nine-story example of Romanesque Revival architecture, is celebrating its 100th anniversary this year. Although New York and Chicago are normally associated with skyscrapers, the oldest example is in neither city but rather in Washington...." Now restored to its original beauty, it was designed by Alfred B. Mullett for the Washington bureau of the Baltimore *Sun*. Mullett also designed the Old Executive Office Building (the State, War and Navy Building), next to the White House. A tower, later removed, further accented the original building's verticality.

㉙ 1321 F Street NW

SCHOOLCRAFT HOME—Enthologist Henry R. Schoolcraft lived in a house on this site. He began studies of Ojibwa Indians after marrying an Ojibwa woman while on government assignment in what is now Minnesota. These and other studies provided a scientific introduction for Americans to the characteristics of diverse Indian tribes, culminating in his six-volume *Historical and Statistical Information Respecting...the Indian Tribes in the U.S. in the 1850s.*

Earlier, William Thornton, original architect of the Capitol, lived here. The site is now occupied by the International Office Building at 1319 F Street.

㉚ 1333-1335 F Street NW

PRESIDENTIAL BULLPEN—James Madison lived in a three-story brick home on this site until becoming president in 1809. Later, John Quincy Adams lived here while secretary of state from 1821 to 1825. He also left when elected president, which probably makes this site something of a presidential record-setter for the city.

㉛ 1336-1338 F Street NW

MAN OF TREACHERY—The National Press Building now covers the site of the residence of Aaron Burr. Burr narrowly lost to Thomas Jefferson in the 1800 presidential election and thus became vice president as the Constitution then specified. In 1804, while vice president, he challenged Alexander Hamilton to a duel in New Jersey and killed him. Burr served out his vice-presidential term, although indicted for murder in New York and New Jersey. While still in office, he plotted to form an army and seize Western territory along the Mississippi. Thwarted, he was tried for treason, acquitted on a technicality, and left for Europe. He returned to New York in 1812 and resumed his law practice.

㉜ 14th and F Streets NW

NATIONAL PRESS BUILDING—The journalistic landmark sits on the site of the Ebbitt House, a hotel which for decades was part of Newspaper Row. William McKinley, President from 1897 to 1901, resided in the Ebbitt House as a member of the House of Representatives from Ohio. The cornerstone of the present 14-story building was laid by President Coolidge on April 8, 1926. Hugh Morrow in his history of the National Press Club, *Dateline Washington*, termed it a "125,000-ton monument to the fantastic finances of the 1920s."

Occupied in 1927 on the eve of the Great Depression, the building became bankrupt within a few years. Officers of the club lobbied directly with President-elect Franklin D. Roosevelt and Congress in 1932 for an amendment to the bankruptcy law. The result of their work was Section 77-B of the statute, which allowed for corporate reorganization. The Press Club filed within 15 minutes of the bill finally being signed into law in 1934.

By 1949 the Press Building had bounced back and could boast of a vast array of news offices as well as shops and the Fox Theatre. In 1982 a massive reconstruction was begun, which is now complete. A popular part of the new complex is the ground-level mall with shops and restaurants. But to some, it came at an aesthetic price. Architectural historian James M. Goode says the "elegant lines" of the original 1927 limestone facade were destroyed in the remodeling.

The renovated National Press Club is housed on the top two floors of the building. Over time, it has welcomed such world-famous speakers as Churchill, Ghandi, deGaulle, Khrushchev, Lindbergh, and Carnegie. Sixteen consecutive presidents have been card-carrying members. When he retired from CBS, commentator Eric Sevareid said of the club, "It's the

Map on page 106

Dancing. Jimmy Lake's 9th Street nightclub billed itself as the Spot of the Town, as seen in this 1939 photo.

Westminster Hall, it's Delphi, it's Mecca, the Wailing Wall [for] everybody in this country having anything to do with the news business; the only hallowed place I know of that's absolutely bursting with irreverence."

33 609 14th Street NW

CONFEDERATE-TO-BE—Jefferson Davis resided in a house once on this site during the years he lived in the city as a member of Congress, prior to the Civil War.

34 West side of 14th Street, between F and G Streets NW

MARK TWAIN—Samuel L. Clemens lived here while working on Capitol Hill and writing *Innocents Abroad*. In the 1930s this became the site of Garfinkel's department store, a Washington institution that went out of business in 1990. Newly renovated, the old Garfinkel's building has been renamed Hamilton Square and converted to contain offices on the upper floors and major retail outlets on the lower levels. This building's renovation, along with that proposed for the former Woodward & Lothrop department store location three blocks away, signal the revitalization of the city's once thriving but long dormant downtown commercial sector.

35 Northeast corner of 14th and G Streets NW

CHURCHES—Site of Foundry Methodist Church, erected as a thanks offering by Henry Foxall shortly after his foundry in Georgetown escaped destruction by the British in August 1814. Serving as a center for Methodism in Washington, successive churches on this site welcomed many notable worshippers, from James Madison in Foxall's day to President Rutherford B. Hayes (1877-81). According to James M. Goode's *Capital Losses*, street-car noise and other urban pressures, together with the continuing migration of parishioners to residential areas on the edge of the city, caused the congregation to relocate to a newly constructed church at 16th and P Streets NW in 1904. An office building was then erected on this site and now contains the popular Red Sage restaurant.

36 **725 14th Street NW**

PUBLIC ACCOMMODATION—Thompson's Restaurant, once located on the ground floor of the Colorado Building, was the target of a United States Supreme Court decision in June 1953 that ended discrimination against African Americans in public accommodations in Washington. Civil rights activist Mary Church Terrell and others maintained that long-neglected laws passed in 1872 and 1873 mandated that such businesses provide equal access for all "well behaved, respectable" persons. The Supreme Court agreed, and the 90-year-old Terrell and her colleagues were finally served three years after their first attempt in 1950. At that time, according to *The Guide to Black Washington*, "the only places in Washington where blacks could be seated to eat were the cafeterias at federal office buildings, the 17th and K Street YWCA, Union Station, National Airport, the Methodist Building Cafeteria, the Hains Point Tea House, and the American Veterans Committee Club on New Hampshire Avenue." This case and others in the early 1950s broke down long-established barriers and customs maintaining segregation in virtually every area of local life—recreation, food service, entertainment, schools, and housing.

The few exceptions to the segregated norm included the D.C. Public Library and the public transportation system. According to one account, the transportation systems allowed equal access because of a charter granted by Congress during the Civil War to a local railroad company stipulating that its services be nondiscriminatory. Successive transportation companies retained the original charter stipulation; transportation services were desegregated while segregation persisted in virtually all other sectors of local life.

Map on page 106

THOMAS CIRCLE, SHOWING ST. LUKE'S CHURCH, WASHINGTON, D. C.

© C.C.BUCKINGHAM

Thomas Circle Then. Not only was the circle much larger in this ca 1928 postcard but virtually all the buildings have been razed with the exception of the two churches in the middle of the picture. In fact, a third church, the National City Christian Church, was added to this vista in 1930. It covers the spot to the left of the circle, where a large tree blocks the view of a three-story building.

The Franklin Square Area

① 714 K Street NW

CANDY STORE—Former site of the Davis Confectionary and Ice Cream Saloon, established in 1881 by Josephine Davis, a pioneering black businesswoman. Directories of the time identified her this way: "Mrs. Davis was born and educated in Philadelphia, and is granddaughter of Bishop Allen, the first colored bishop ordained in the United States." Part of her success was due to the facts he had brought with her from Philadelphia a franchise to sell Whitman's chocolates. The site is now covered by an office building.

② 925 11th Street NW

DIES AND STAMPS—For over 70 years, the Baumgarten Company operated on this site, providing engraving and printing services and making dies and stamps for Washingtonians. Established before the Civil War, the company relocated to this site in the 1920s. According to the current proprietor James Baturin, quoted in a *Washington Post* article when the firm relocated to 17th and G Streets in March 1996, the company had "filled orders for every president since Lincoln."

③ 1219 I Street NW

LITTLE LORD FAUNTLEROY—Former home of Frances Hodgson Burnett, who wrote *Little Lord Fauntleroy* here as a serial for *St. Nicholas* magazine in 1886. Journalist Frank Carpenter described her attic work area as a "large room hung with

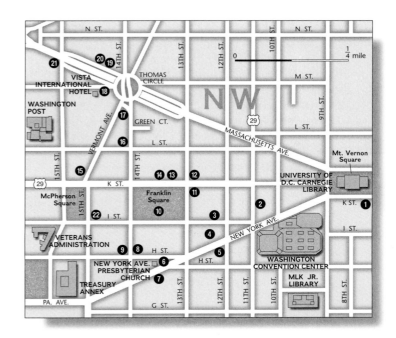

J STREET. There is no J Street in the city, which has given rise to the urban legend that this was planned as an insult to Chief Justice John Jay. Not so, according to the Historical Society of Washington, D.C., which long ago ran this one down. J was omitted because the letters I and J looked almost identical when written in the script of the 19th century. There is, in fact, a Jay Street named for John Jay in the northeast quadrant of the city.

There are no X, Y, or Z Streets either, and the two B Streets, which once ran on the south and north sides of the Mall, long ago became Independence and Constitution Avenues respectively.

I STREET. The name of this street is often spelled out as Eye so that it will not be confused with 1st Street.

paintings. A tiger skin lies in the middle of the floor, and warm red curtains tone down the glaring light of the Washington sun. A desk, half a dozen easy chairs, and a sofa make up the furnishings. Amid these surroundings Mrs. Burnett has written most of her recent works."

Anne H. Oman reported on the residence in an October 17, 1980, article in the *Washington Post*, "In 1936, 50 years after the publication of *Fauntleroy,* movie magnate David O. Selznick placed a plaque on the house to honor the author of this 'deathless classic.' The plaque was removed in the last few weeks, probably by the ghost of Burnett herself. For the house where the quintessential good boy was created now serves as a pornographic book and movie outlet, conveniently across the street from the Trailways bus station." Oman pointed out that Burnett, whose novels were mostly set in English gardens at tea time, was born in England but wrote most of her books here. She was married to a local physician. In 1882, Burnett entertained Oscar Wilde, who undoubtedly would have appreciated the irony of what the future held for the site.

④ 1207 New York Avenue NW

TOY STORE—The former site of A. Stuntz's Fancy Store, where Abraham Lincoln took his sons Tad and Willie to buy toys. Willie died of typhoid fever in 1862. After Lincoln was assassinated, workers inventorying and packing family belongings from the White House found a room of unused toys that had been bought for Willie.

Stuntz's remained for many years one of the most famous toy stores anywhere and boasted a wide clientele. In *Toys in America,* Inez and Marshall McClintock wrote, "With such a following over a period of so many years, some people wondered why Stuntz's never made a fortune. The question was once answered by General Sherman's daughter, who said, 'You can buy more for a penny at Stuntz's than anywhere on earth." The store was razed in 1913.

5 812 12th Street NW

LOGAN HOUSE—George S. Boutwell, Senator from Massachusetts and later Secretary of the Treasury (1869-73), and later Gen. John A. Logan, Commander of the Army of the Tennessee during the Civil War and afterward Senator from Illinois, resided in a house on this spot. In 1868 Logan succeeded in setting aside Memorial Day as a time to honor the Civil War dead. The same year, according to George Rothwell Brown's account, he mounted a campaign to "select St. Louis as the new Capital, and to transport there all the existing public buildings in Washington" in one of many efforts to relocate the nation's capital to a more central part of the country. In spite of this affront to the city, Logan is memorialized by his statue in Logan Circle, renamed from Iowa Circle in 1930.

6 1313 New York Avenue NW

HISTORIC CHURCH—The original New York Avenue Presbyterian Church, established in 1803, was attended by Presidents John Quincy Adams, Andrew Jackson, William Henry Harrison, Millard Fillmore, James Buchanan, Abraham Lincoln, and Andrew Johnson. The present church building was erected in 1951, its cornerstone laid by President Harry S. Truman.

7 Incorporating 1312-1320 New York Avenue NW

FROM ANCIENTS TO AUTOMOBILES—Boston businessman Franklin Webster Smith created a 34-acre exhibit here in 1898 called "Halls of the Ancients," an early theme park intended to celebrate ancient civilizations and to promote Smith's fantastic scheme to build the "National Galleries of History and Art." The galleries would have occupied a 40-acre site ranging along Virginia Avenue between 17th and 23rd Streets NW. Dozens of buildings

Louise Home. Created by W.W. Corcoran in 1871 and named for his wife and daughter as "testimonial to their devoted concern for the poor and unfortunate," the Louise Home was located at 15th Street and Massachusetts Avenue NW.

Map on page 129

ROAD CONDITIONS. One of the recurring themes in the diaries kept in and the letters written from Washington in the early 19th century was the miserable condition of the roads. "The entrance or avenues, as they are pompously called, which lead to the American seat of gov't, are the worst roads I passed in the country....Deep ruts, rocks and stumps of trees every minute impede yr. progress and threaten yr. limbs with dislocation," wrote Charles W. Janson in 1806. On a visit to the city in 1840, the Chevalier de Bacourt wrote, "This is how it is in Washington...streets not paved, swept or lighted." Some 150 years later roads are still a familiar source of complaints as motorists demand that the city move faster in repairing potholes.

would have copied the architecture of ancient civilizations and contained related exhibits, culminating with an "American Acropolis" on the hill where the former Naval Observatory now overlooks the Kennedy Center. Smith failed to secure funding for the larger project, but for several years the Halls of the Ancients on New York Avenue presented a microcosm of what he had in mind. Smith was less interested in displays of "dead things" than in explanations of how they were used and their effect on people. His approach was to provide the visitor total immersion "into the midst of the domestic, social, and religious life of the people...their surroundings, in other words, before they became mummies." He thought big. Egypt was represented by an entrance hall with 70-foot-high columns after the monuments at Karnak and a cast of the Rosetta stone. Other exhibits included a 10,000-square-foot reproduction of a Roman house, with 15,000 square feet of surface decoration copied from ancient sites. In 1926 the building was razed to make way for the Capital Garage.

The Capital Garage, a beautifully decorated classic Gothic—replete with gargoyles—1,200-car multi-level facility was the epitome of the blessings that the automotive age could bestow on a city. At the time it was determined to be the largest privately owned building in the city. In 1927, when you could park here for five dollars a week, *The Book of Washington* gave "this splendid institution" major billing as one of the city's attractions and called it a "distinct contribution to the beauties of Washington."

During World War II it was preempted by the government to store war records and became a garage again after the war. For a while the government stored Adolph Hitler's specially built Mercedes here, and luminaries ranging from Shirley Temple to Jacqueline Kennedy parked here. It remained in use until November 1973 and was razed a short time thereafter.

8 **14th and H Streets NW**

PIONEERING INSTITUTION—According to historian Constance McLaughlin Green, free black Henry Smothers started a school for black children at this intersection about 1822. It was continued by John Prout, who charged 12 1/2 cents per month tuition.

9 **Northwest corner of 14th and H Streets NW**

CAVE-INS—This was the site of two mammoth construction cave-ins that began on November 19, 1990. Miraculously, no one was killed. The five-stories-deep hole took up a large portion of the block, extending from the east side of the Southern Building on H Street NW to the south side of the United Press International building on 14th Street NW. The cave-ins extended to within a half-block of the McPherson Square Metro station entrance at the southwest corner of 14th and I Streets NW. The site was being prepared for the 12-story City Center office building when the cave-ins occurred.

10 **Franklin Square, bounded by 13th, 14th, I, and K Streets NW**

WHITE HOUSE WATERING HOLE—This plot was purchased by the government in 1829 because it contained excellent springs whose waters were piped to the White House and Executive Offices as early as 1832; the springs were still the source of water at the outbreak of the Spanish-American War in 1898. Speculation was widespread that the President could be poisoned if Spanish sympathizers tainted the open springs, and they were closed off.

During the Civil War, the 12th New York Volunteers, commanded by Gen. Daniel Butterfield, camped here while in the city on the way to the front lines. Remnants of the 27th New York Volunteers encamped here after fleeing the First Battle of Bull Run.

School. The Franklin School at 13th and K Streets NW, a time when it was still a major source of civic pride as an experimental institution. It looks much the same today, although the two bell towers seen in this picture were long ago removed.

Map on page 129

CITY LORE

A FEW FIRST AND A COUPLE OF ONLYS. Washington is the first American planned city—it did not spring up around a fort or natural harbor. The first zinc was produced here in 1835, the first television broadcast was made here in 1925, and the first news dispatch sent by telegraph came from Washington in 1844. Georgetown University was Washington's first college and is also the oldest Catholic institution of higher learning in the nation. Gallaudet University is the first and only college for the deaf and hearing-impaired in the country. Dunbar High School was the first African-American high school in America. From the Mexican War to Desert Storm, victorious armies have marched through the city, but only one hostile army has paraded here— the British in 1814.

⑪ Southeast corner of 13th and K Streets NW

EXPERIMENTAL SCHOOL—Completion of the Franklin School by architect Adolph Cluss in 1869 signaled a new city commitment to educational reform. Building the modern 14-room school required every cent in the school construction budget for four years. But as a pace-setting urban school building, it achieved international recognition for functionality and design. The building was used as an elementary school until 1925 and as D.C. school administrative offices from 1928 to 1968. The building was restored in the early 1990s.

Experimenting with his invention called the photo-phone, Alexander Graham Bell transmitted sound on a light beam between the school and his laboratory on L Street in 1876. The invention was never a commercial success.

⑫ 1013 13th Street NW

LAST TABLOID—Site of the *Washington Daily News*, whose building was clobbered with a 4,000-pound wrecking ball in December 1972, a short time after the Scripps-Howard newspaper chain terminated its publication. During the demolition, which included the church building next door (also owned by the paper), Scripps-Howard tried to sell the late Ernie Pyle's desk for $5,000, but in the confusion it went for $35. The destruction of the building recalled A.J. Liebling's line that the wrecking ball was the "supreme force in American journalism." Now an office building covers the site.

⑬ 1321 K Street NW

ANTITRUST MAN—John Sherman, younger brother of Gen. William Tecumseh Sherman, lived in a house formerly on this site. Once he arrived in Washington in 1855 as a congressman from Ohio, he never went home. Instead, he served in the House, the

Senate, as President Rutherford B. Hayes's secretary of the treasury, and then three more Senate terms before becoming President William McKinley's secretary of state in 1897. Ill health forced him to retire, and he died in the house in 1900. Today he is best remembered as author of the Sherman Antitrust Act (1890). The One Franklin Square office building covers this and the next site.

⑭ 1323 K Street NW

STANTON'S PLACE—Edwin M. Stanton, President Abraham Lincoln's secretary of war, lived and died in a house on this site in 1869. President Andrew Johnson retained Stanton as secretary of war after Lincoln's assassination, but the two men clashed over Johnson's moderate attitude toward Reconstruction of the South. When Johnson fired Stanton in 1868, Stanton refused to leave his office at the War Department for several weeks as the Congress began impeachment proceedings against Johnson. When the impeachment attempt failed, Stanton finally moved out.

⑮ 1022 Vermont Avenue NW

PLACE FOR ALL TREES—James Wilson, Secretary of Agriculture from 1897 to 1913, lived in the house that once stood on this site. Wilson, who was born in Scotland but grew up in Iowa, increased the scope and importance of the Department of Agriculture during his years of service to Presidents McKinley, Roosevelt, and Taft. In 1899 he first proposed the creation of a National Arboretum as a "place for all trees that will grow in Washington, D.C." Congress did not approve the idea until 1927.

STREET LORE

15TH STREET NW. For most of this century the stretch of 15th Street extending from the Washington Hotel to K Street was known as "Little Wall Street" for the number of banks and brokerage houses (to say nothing of the Treasury Department) located here. From 1881 to 1962 Washington had its own stock exchange, located in the Woodward Building on 15th Street between New York Avenue and H Street. As the exchange lost its appeal—in 1906 a seat on the exchange was $10,000, but the price dropped to $25 in the World War II era—and a number of financial institutions relocated to K Street, Connecticut Avenue, and other locations downtown, the term Little Wall Street dropped from use.

CITY LORE

GREATER WASHINGTON. Washington D.C., which started with a broad canvas of open space, was from its early days called the "City of Magnificent Distances." But for a long time that was about all that one could brag about. Charles Dickens, upon seeing all that was still unfinished, added "...and the City of Magnificent Intentions." Dickens, like other visitors used to the great capitals of Europe, was shocked by the place. Many would have agreed with his 1842 remark that Washington consists of spacious avenues "that begin in nothing and lead nowhere."

It took a while to fill those streets and create a greater metropolis. One hundred years later, the city was the nerve center of a nation fighting a World War, and it's population grew to 750,000 by the end of the war.

At the turn of the 21st century, the nation's capital has realized much of its designer's plan, and Dickens's Magnificent Intentions have to a large degree been realized. For all the federal office buildings, monuments, and museums, it is also a city of neighborhoods populated by regular citizens from

continued on next page

16 **1407 L Street NW**

WALT WHITMAN AGAIN—The great American poet rented a room in a building on this site in 1862 from William Douglas O'Connor for $7 per month. During this period Whitman spent many hours in nearby military hospitals visiting Civil War wounded (see Whitman House, p. 32).

17 **South side of Thomas Circle, between 14th Street and Vermont Avenue NW**

FIRST APARTMENT BUILDING—Site of the elegant Portland Flats apartment building, erected in 1879 and said to be the first apartment building in Washington. Among others, J. Sterling Morton of New York, originator of Arbor Day and secretary of agriculture in Grover Cleveland's second administration (1893-97), resided here. The building was razed in 1962.

18 **1400 M Street NW**

HIS HONOR—It was in room 727, when this was the Vista International Hotel, is that then-Mayor Marion Barry was videotaped and arrested by the FBI for smoking crack cocaine on January 18, 1990. At the time of the arrest the room rented for $153 a night as a single and at $173 for double occupancy.

19 **1407 Massachusetts Avenue NW**

CATHEDRAL PLANNER—Right Rev. Henry Y. Satterlee, the first Protestant Episcopal bishop of Washington (1896-1908), lived and died in a house formerly on the site now occupied by the National City Christian Church. He planned and began work on the Washington National Cathedral.

20 **1435-1441 Massachusetts Avenue NW**

OLD GERMAN EMBASSY—The German Embassy was located here from 1893 to World War II. Three million dollars in bills were discovered when the United States took control after the war began. The German staff was confined at a resort hotel in White Sulphur Springs, West Virginia. The elegant buildings on this elevated site were demolished in the late 1950s. It is now a parking lot along a ramp above Massachusetts Avenue. The handsome iron fence is a reminder of the earlier grandeur of the site.

21 **Southwest corner of 15th Street and Massachusetts Avenue NW**

FADED GENTILITY—Founded by William W. Corcoran as a home for impoverished Southern gentlewomen, the Louise Home stood here from 1871 to 1947, when the building was razed and the residents relocated to the Codman House at Decatur Place and 22nd Street NW. It closed in 1976, but the residents and Corcoran's endowment were taken over by the Lisner Home at 5425 Western Avenue NW, which now operates under the name Lisner Louise Dickson Hurt Home.

22 **15th and I Streets NW**

POSH HOTELS—Once site of the Bellvue Hotel and before that La Normandie, home to Adlai E. Stevenson, Vice President to Grover Cleveland from 1893 to 1897 and grandfather of the Adlai E. Stevenson, who ran unsuccessfully for president in 1952 and 1956.

Map on page 129

CITY LORE

continued from previous page

Anacostia to Chevy Chase to Brookland to Foggy Bottom, from MacArthur Boulevard to Martin Luther King, Jr., Avenue. Its neighbors, such as Fairfax and Montgomery Counties, in Virginia and Maryland respectively, have grown dramatically in the last 20 years. Locals would name places as distant as Middleburg, Virginia, and Annapolis as part of greater Washington, along with neighborhoods as close as Kalorama and Adams-Morgan.

Multi-modal. This rather
remarkable image, showing
the intersection of Pennsylvania
and New York Avenues at 15th
Street NW, displays five modes
of transportation (streetcar,
horse-drawn carriage, automobile, bicycle, and foot).

The White House Neighborhood

❶ 1600 Pennsylvania Avenue NW

THE WHITE HOUSE—Home to presidential families and a few others. For instance, John Eastman points out in *Who Lived Where* that Meriwether Lewis, as secretary to Thomas Jefferson, lived at the White House from 1801 to 1803 while planning the Lewis and Clark Expedition.

The first President to live here was John Adams, who moved in on November 2, 1800, before the building was completed. First Lady Abigail Adams found that the building had no privy or water and wrote, "I will use the unfinished barnlike room on the east side of the house for a laundry." This comment gave rise to the oft-told tale that she hung her family's wash in the East Room.

The mansion has seen customs that seem odd to us today. Presidents once kept the noon hour free six days a week for Americans who wished to stop by and shake the President's hand. Herbert Hoover finally put an end to the practice because, as he pointed out in his memoirs, the "average of 30 to 40 persons per day at Theodore Roosevelt's receptions had increased to between 300 and 400 per day under Coolidge. And I soon found myself wasting a whole hour every day shaking hands with 1,000 to 1,200 people."

The White House has became symbolic of the presidency itself and one often hears of "White House reaction" or the "White House says." As a symbol it has its ups and downs. During Prohibition it symbolized the nation's inability to deal with illegal booze. A well-known reporter, Edward F. Folliard of the *Washington Post*, ducked

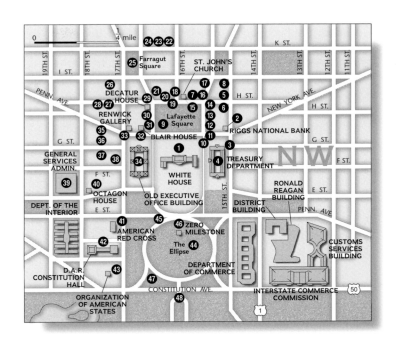

THE WHITE HOUSE. When first occupied in 1800, the official name of 1600 Pennsylvania Avenue NW was the President's House. Later, it was called the Executive Mansion. In 1901, Teddy Roosevelt changed the official name to the White House for the simple reason that this had become its popular name. In recent years the building has required a new coat of white paint every four years, but according to an item in *USA Today* in late 1990, a new and hardier paint was about to be used that would cut back the need to repaint to once every 5 to 12 years.

out one day to buy a pint of gin from his favorite bootlegger. The supplier had just run out, so the two jumped into the bootlegger's car and drove to the White House, where the bootlegger got out of the car and retrieved a large burlap bag from the hedge. He took out a half-dozen gin bottles and returned the rest. The stunned reporter was told that this was a safe hiding place because nobody would expect anyone to be so audacious. Later, after the bootlegger found a new venue, Folliard told the story in print and the short article became national news as it moved over the Associated Press wire. The public questioned how local police could enforce a ban that was ineffective even on the grounds of the White House.

An interesting discovery was made here in 1975 when Indian artifacts were found during excavations for the White House outdoor swimming pool. They represented evidence of Native American presence here dating back some 10,000 to 20,000 years according to archaeologists Robert L. Humphrey and Mary Elizabeth Chambers.

❷ Northwest corner of 15th Street and Pennsylvania Avenue NW

SECOND BANK OF THE UNITED STATES—A federally chartered but privately managed bank that held federal funds, the Second Bank became the target of a showdown between President Andrew Jackson and bank president Nicholas Biddle. Jackson made the bank's power and financial control a campaign issue in 1832, and after his reelection he removed federal deposits and relocated them to selected "pet" banks in the states.

William W. Corcoran, famous banker and patron of the arts, worked here for eight years before entering the business himself. In 1845 the firm of Corcoran and Riggs purchased what was left of the Second Bank building, vaults, and some assets.

③ Southwest corner of 15th Street and Pennsylvania Avenue opposite G Street NW (current north end of the Treasury Building)

OLD STATE—The State Department occupied a building on this site from January 1820 until October 1866. The Webster-Ashburton Treaty with Britain was signed here in 1842, fixing the boundaries between Maine and Canada.

④ 15th Street at New York and Pennsylvania Avenues NW

TREASURY DEPARTMENT—The first section of the Treasury to be built was that containing the Ionic colonnade along 15th Street NW, designed and erected between 1836 and 1842 by architect Robert Mills. Mills oversaw the most extensive federal building program in the city prior to the Federal Triangle project of the 1920s and 1930s, delivering the first sections of three permanent fireproof buildings (the Treasury, Patent Office, and General Post Office) that set a standard for federal offices to follow. Politically motivated controversy dogged Mills, and he narrowly avoided being forced to tear down the first section of the Treasury in 1838 when Congress objected to its location. After a six-month wrangle, Congress voted to proceed. The building was extended around the block by other architects in the 1850s and 1860s.

The first inaugural ball of President Ulysses S. Grant (1869) was held in the north section of this building.

In 1882, Frank Carpenter reported that this building "...has the biggest spittoon on record. An oblong wooden box, as big as a bed, it is filled with sawdust. It lies at the foot of the four-floor spiral staircase, and the Treasury employees delight in squirting their juice over the marble banisters down the stairwell. Such target practice, they think, is a good game."

The President's House. This John Plumbe, Jr., daguerreotype of 1846 shows the building in reverse (a characteristic of daguerreotypes when a reversing prism was not employed).

Map on page 139

STREET LORE

EAST EXECUTIVE AVENUE. A phantom street that lives on in the old road maps in the glove compartments of cars and as a pedestrian walkway closed to vehicles. The long-established block-long street that ran between the White House and the Treasury Department no longer exists, a victim of concern for White House security. In March 1983, it was closed to vehicular traffic with the placement of two immense flower pots in the roadway. Pedestrians were banned in 1984, and in 1986 plans were announced to convert, in the words of the *Washington Post*'s Sarah Booth Conroy, "a serviceable city street into a well-guarded extension of the White House grounds; a tree-lined promenade that will double as an arrival court for White House visitors." It once again opened as a pedestrian avenue. In May 1995, Pennsylvania Avenue NW in front of the White House along with portions of other avenues adjoining the White House grounds were closed. These dramatic moves were prompted by a fear of terrorism and the fact that security had been seriously breached. On September 12, 1994, a stolen Cessna aircraft crashed on the grounds of the Executive Mansion and skidded into a corner of the building. On October 29, 1994, at least 29 shots from a semiautomatic rifle were fired at the White House.

5 Northwest corner of 15th and H Streets NW

HOME TO HOTEL—Site of the residence of Gen. George B. McClellan when he was restored to the command of the Army of the Potomac by Lincoln in 1862.

Later this was the site of the original Shoreham Hotel, where Representative Thomas B. "Czar" Reed lived while speaker of the House in the last decade of the 19th century. The Shoreham, built by former Vice President Levi P. Morton and named for his native town in Vermont, advertised itself as "absolutely fireproof."

6 Southwest corner of 15th and H Streets NW

WORMLEY'S HOTEL—Site of Wormley's Hotel in the 1870s. It was owned and operated by James T. Wormley, a prominent black caterer, restaurateur, and land owner who had operated a hotel since 1858 on I Street between 15th and 16th Streets NW. Wormley obtained this luxury hotel from Rep. Samuel Hooper of Massachusetts, who had built it in 1871. Wormley's was an elegant hotel frequented by a distinguished clientele including members of Congress and diplomats. Many important gatherings were held in its private dining rooms, including one noted in James H. Whyte's book on Reconstruction in Washington, *The Uncivil War*: "It was, ironically, at this Negro-owned hotel that the agreement [was made in 1877] by which the Democratic leaders consented to the election of Rutherford B. Hayes as President provided that Federal troops were withdrawn from the South."

Wormley died in October 1881, and all of the hotels in the city flew their flags at half-staff for several days. Wormley's Hotel was later reopened as the Colonial and then, in 1906, razed to make way for the Union Trust Company.

This structure was joined to a smaller building that contained John Welcker's restaurant, which opened during the Civil War and soon established itself as one of the best restaurants in the nation. The Belgian-born Welcker proudly displayed a letter from Charles Dickens, who had been a guest of the restaurant in 1868, to the effect that this was the finest restaurant in the world. With hearty breakfasts at $5 to $8 and dinners from $10 to $12, his prices were only slightly less than the fabled Delmonico's of New York.

7 1525 H Street NW

ASHBURTON HOUSE—The parish house that now adjoins St. John's Church was originally a private residence and later the official residence of British envoy Lord Ashburton. In 1842 Ashburton and Daniel Webster used the residence to negotiate the treaty establishing the borders between the United States and Canada. As the site of the British legation, it was also where E.R. Bulwer-Lytton, a diplomat working as the pseudonymous poet Owen Meredith, is said to have written the long, poetic romance *Lucile* in 1860.

8 1500 I Street NW

HOUSE OF MIRTH—Site of the residence of wealthy businessman and publisher of the *Washington Post* John R. McLean, after whom the Virginia suburb of McLean was named in 1906. The house was used for many gala parties and was described by one newspaper as a "home so dedicated to entertainment that it consisted mostly of anterooms wrapped around a gigantic ballroom."

Before demolished in 1939 to make way for the Export-Import Bank building (at 811 Vermont Avenue NW), it served for a short while as the headquarters of the New Deal Works Progress Administration (WPA), which had an enormous impact on the arts and public works.

Man of War. The Honorable William H. Taft in his office in the War Department when the Executive Office Building was known as the State, War and Navy Building. This somber image of the usually jolly man was captured by a photographer from the H.C. White Co. of Bennington, Vermont, in 1908.

Map on page 139

Poseur. This F Street merchant chose to pose his horse and wagon with the Treasury Department and the Corcoran Building (right) in the background.

9 Lafayette Square, opposite the White House

WHERE ANDREW JACKSON DOMINATES—The dominant feature of this park is the statue of Gen. Andrew Jackson in the center. It was the first equestrian statue erected in America. A congressional resolution of 1848 provided that the statue include metal from brass guns captured by Andrew Jackson during the War of 1812 at the Battle of Pensacola, Florida, as well as the four guns at the base that were captured by Jackson at the Battle of New Orleans.

Eleven paces northwest of the Jackson monument is the Bernard Baruch Bench of Inspiration. It was on this bench that the famous financier and philanthropist would take a break from running the War Industries Board during World War I and dispensing advice to Presidents from Woodrow Wilson through John F. Kennedy. The bench was dedicated to Baruch in 1960 on the statesman's 90th birthday. Baruch, who had become a millionaire before he was 30, had another "park bench office" in New York in Central Park. "In this hectic Age of Distraction," Baruch once said, "all of us need to pause now and then in what we are doing to examine where the rush of the world and of our own activities is taking us. Even an hour or two spent in such detached contemplation on a park bench will prove rewarding. The importance of such periodic stocktaking was one of the most valuable lessons I learned from my early experiences."

The park is marked by memorials to those of foreign birth who assisted the American Colonies in the Revolutionary War. At the southeast corner is a memorial to the Marquis de Lafayette, major-general in Washington's army. On the pedestal are Rochambeau and Duportail of the Army, and de Grasse and d'Estaing of the Navy. There are also monuments to Steuben, the Prussian drillmaster of Valley Forge, and Kosciuszko, Polish soldier and statesman.

The statue of Lafayette is holding clothes and pistol near a bare-breasted Columbia who appears to be offering him a sword.

Countless wags have wondered whether Columbia should be saying, "Give me back my clothes and I'll give you your sword."

The name Lafayette Square does not come from the statue as many people assume—the statue of Jackson stood alone in Lafayette Square for many years after its dedication in 1853—but from the day in 1824 when the gallant Frenchman visited Washington and people overflowed the park to get a glimpse of him. Earlier the park had served as an open-air market, military encampment and a site from which to witness the burning of the White House in 1814. The populist Andrew Jackson dispensed punch and whiskey from tubs on the square and troops guarding the White House during the Civil War camped here. President Grant set up Lafayette Square as a small zoo, including his pet deer and prairie dogs, which stunk, drew complaints, and were removed.

The park, which covers seven acres, was purchased in 1791 for $469. In 1964 the estimated value of the property was 12.5 million dollars. Today it would defy valuation.

⑩ Near the northeast corner of Madison Place and Pennsylvania Avenue NW

ASSASSINATION SPOT—Today this is the site of the Treasury Annex, built in 1919. In front of a house here in 1859, enraged New York Congressman Daniel E. Sickles (later a Union Army general wounded at the Battle of Gettysburg) shot Philip Barton Key, son of the author of "The Star-Spangled Banner." According to George Rothwell Brown, the shooting took place the day after Sickles's wife confessed to having an affair with Key. Unaware that Sickles now knew, Key on that day gave his usual signal to Mrs. Sickles from Lafayette Park, a wave of his hanky. But it brought out the congressman instead of his wife. Sickles confronted and shot Key, who died a short time later up the street in the Washington Club.

The trial was a national sensation when Mrs. Sickles's written confession, with all its racy details, was made public. Sickles was acquitted after a 20-day trial on the grounds of temporary insanity, the first successful use of that defense in the United States.

⑪ Northeast corner of Pennsylvania Avenue and Madison Place NW

CIVIL WAR HEADQUARTERS—The site of the headquarters of the Department of Washington during 1863. The department was the military entity of the city, responsible for its defense; the department reached a troop strength of 31,000 by 1864.

⑫ Formerly 17 Madison Place NW, now 717 Madison Place NW

DEATH-DEFYING HOME AND THEATER—Now the United States Court of Claims Building, formerly on this site was the house built by Commodore John Rogers in 1831. Prior to the Civil War, after Rogers had moved, the building was a boarding house and a club for congressmen known as the Washington Club. Secretary of State William H. Seward lived here during the Civil War and narrowly avoided being assassinated in the house the night of April 14, 1865. Conspirator Lewis Payne attacked Seward in his bedroom the night of Lincoln's shooting and tried to slit his throat. Seward had suffered a broken jaw and arm in a serious carriage accident, and the bandages and a steel apparatus supporting his jaw saved him. He survived and two years later negotiated the purchase of Alaska from Russia for 7.2 million dollars (called at the time "Seward's Folly").

James G. Blaine, Republican Speaker of the House, Senator, and presidential candidate, lived here while he served as President Benjamin Harrison's secretary of state from 1889 to 1892. The house was demolished in 1895 to make way for the Lafayette Square Opera house, later called the Belasco Theater. *Rider's Washington*

Old and New. Robert Mills's monumental Treasury Department (constructed in 1836-65) hovers over the old State Department, representative of the first generation of federal office buildings erected prior to 1820. Shortly after this photograph was taken, the older building was demolished to make way for the north wing of the Treasury.

reported in 1924 that a plaque on the building said it was "of steel skeleton construction, stone terra cotta, mackite, and brick, to prove that an opera house can be made safe at all times from fire and panic." The theater, built in 1895, lasted until 1964. During World War II it was the famous Stage Door Canteen, visited by more than two million military personnel, and during the Korean War it was the USO Lafayette Square Club.

Helen Hayes once told reporters her stage debut was as a five-year-old singer at the Belasco.

⑬ 21 Madison Place NW

TAYLOE HOUSE—This three-story yellow house marked by a plaque was built by Benjamin Ogle Tayloe, and later was the home of Senator Don Cameron of Pennsylvania. During the McKinley administration, when occupied by Senator Mark Hanna, it was called the "Little White House." It has been said that Hanna created big-money presidential elections as McKinley's campaign manager in 1896 when he outspent rival candidate William Jennings Bryan by 25 to 1. The Congressional Union for Woman Suffrage set up its headquarters here on January 1, 1916.

⑭ Southeast corner of Madison Place and H Street NW

CUTTS-MADISON HOUSE—Dolley Madison lived here after her husband died in 1836, until her own death in 1849. The former First Lady acquired the house from her brother-in-law Richard Cutts to settle a debt owed the estate of President Madison. Later it was the home of Charles Wilkes, who led the United States expedition to the South Pacific (1838-42) that charted the Pacific and identified Antarctica. The expedition also returned with dozens of shiploads of scientific collections that helped form the basis of an unofficial national museum in the Patent Office building in the

1840s before being transferred to the Smithsonian Institution. The house was also headquarters of Gen. George B. McClellan during the Civil War. In 1878 the Cosmos Club was organized here. The club relocated to 2121 Massachusetts Avenue NW (the former Townsend mansion) in August 1952.

15 Northeast corner of 16th and H Streets NW, adjacent to Lafayette Park and a neighbor of the White House

PRESIDENTS' CHURCH—Madison, Monroe, John Quincy Adams, Jackson, Van Buren, Harrison, Tyler, Fillmore, Buchanan, and Arthur were among the early chief executives who attended services at St. John's Church. It was erected in 1816 from the architectural design of Benjamin Henry Latrobe, who was also its first organist.

It came to be known familiarly as the "Presidents' Church," and its attraction for presidents continued into the modern era. Just prior to announcing a pardon for former President Richard M. Nixon, President Gerald Ford attended a private service at St. John's. More recently, on the morning of January 20, 1989, President-elect Bush, Vice President-elect Quayle, and some 500 guests attended a special pre-inaugural service here.

16 Northwest corner of Vermont Avenue and H Street NW

ABOLITIONIST—Senator Charles Sumner, the first American statesman of note to advocate the freeing of the slaves, and William L. Marcy, secretary of state in the administration of Franklin Pierce, lived in a house on this site.

17 Southwest corner of Vermont Avenue and I Street NW

ARLINGTON HOTEL—The Arlington Hotel was constructed here in 1869 by William W. Corcoran, who joined the Charles

Pickets. Suffragists picketing at the White House fence, ca 1916.

Map on page 139

Popular Corner. One of the most-photographed corners in the city, 15th and Pennsylvania at the Treasury Department, is depicted here about 1920, during the period just before automobiles claimed the streets.

Sumner house to the west and the Reverdy Johnson (Zachary Taylor's attorney general) house to the north to form a large luxury hotel. Financier J.P. Morgan maintained an elegant suite in the hotel, and Andrew Carnegie gave a dinner here in 1890 costing $10,000. It stood until 1912, when it was demolished to make way for the Department of Veterans Affairs, then known as the Veterans Bureau.

⓲ Northwest corner of 16th and H Streets NW, 1 Lafayette Square

HAY-ADAMS HOTEL—Attached homes on this spot belonging to longtime friends John Hay, poet and biographer of Lincoln who lived here while secretary of state (1898-1905), and Henry Adams, historian and man of letters, were destroyed in 1927 to make room for the hotel. The Hay residence fronted H Street NW (no. 1603) while the Adams residence was on 16th Street NW.

⓳ 1607 H Street NW

SLIDELL HOUSE—John Slidell, Senator from Louisiana; Gideon Welles, Lincoln's Secretary of the Navy; and Daniel Lamont, Grover Cleveland's Secretary of War, successively resided in a house on this site. On November 8, 1861, Slidell and James Mason (a Washington native born on Mason's—now Roosevelt—Island), acting as diplomats for the Confederacy, were taken from the British ship *Trent* by a Union warship commanded by Slidell's former neighbor Charles Wilkes. Slidell and Mason were on their way to Europe to plead for diplomatic recognition of the Confederacy. The seizure and imprisonment of these men set off an international diplomatic incident, for the War of 1812 had begun when Americans objected to the British impressment of American sailors. British tempers eased when the Confederate prisoners were released.

The site is now covered by the Hay-Adams Hotel.

20 1623 H Street NW

BUSY GUY—George Bancroft, Secretary of the Navy (1845-49) and historian, lived in a house once standing at this address. As secretary, he established the U.S. Naval Academy. A lover of floriculture, Bancroft originated the popular American Beauty rose in his garden here. Known as the "father of American history," Bancroft also completed in the house his 10-volume *History of the United States* which was a bestseller in its day. The house was demolished in 1922, and now the site is occupied by the United States Chamber of Commerce.

21 Northeast corner of Connecticut Avenue and H Street NW

ORATORY DORMITORY—The United States Chamber of Commerce since 1925 has occupied the site at 1611 H Street NW of the mansion of William W. Corcoran, banker and philanthropist. Previously it was Daniel Webster's residence when he was secretary of state (1841-43), and his desk is housed in the Chamber of Commerce building. Senator, noted orator, and wit Chauncey M. Depew lived here also. Around the turn of the century, Depew may have been the nation's most popular after-dinner speaker. In 1888 he was a prominent candidate for the Republican presidential nomination, and in 1899 he was elected U.S. senator from New York.

The Chamber of Commerce, the Treasury Annex, and the Veterans Bureau were the first parts of a 1902 plan that would have seen the demolition of all the buildings around Lafayette Park to form a new core of government and quasi-governmental buildings. It was dropped after World War I because the government had grown so much in the interim. A larger site was found for the construction of the Federal Triangle, which began in 1928.

An even earlier scheme of 1838 called for placing "all the departments of Government" in buildings to "be constructed on

Arlington Hotel. Widely described as the most opulent hotel in the city after the Civil War, it is shown here before it was enlarged in 1889. The building was razed in 1912 to make way for the building, which now houses the Veterans Administration.

Map on page 139

STREET LORE

16TH STREET NW. From March 4, 1913, to July 24, 1914, this street was, by act of Congress, known as Avenue of the Presidents. The renaming, which never caught on and was dropped because people persisted in calling it 16th Street, was the idea of Mary Foote Henderson, who also lobbied for the creation of Meridian Hill Park (unofficially called Malcolm X Park).

A small stretch of 16th Street NW, near the then-embassy of the Soviet Union at 1125 16th Street NW, was renamed Andrei Sakharov Plaza in the mid-1980s to protest Soviet treatment of the Nobel Prize–winning physicist and dissident. As of this writing, the signs are in place and official city maps list it as Andrei Sakharov Plaza.

Lafayette Square" itself. It was at this time that architect Thomas U. Walter proposed tearing down the Treasury Department building under construction along 15th Street because of its alleged instability and interference with the view of the President's House.

22 1601 K Street NW

HERO'S HOUSE—Adm. George Dewey, hero of the Spanish-American War, lived and died in a house on this site. The house stood until about 1940. This site and the next are now covered by the Solar Building at 1000 16th Street NW.

23 1603 K Street NW

TAFT HOUSE—William H. Taft lived in a house once standing on this site while secretary of war, and here he received the news of his nomination to the presidency.

24 1625 K Street NW

THE LITTLE GREEN HOUSE ON K STREET—The house once standing on this site featured in the multiple scandals of the Harding administration. The house was rented for several months beginning in May 1921 by Howard Mannington, an Ohio influence peddler; and two associates, M.P. Kraffmiller, a railroad car builder, and Fred A. Caskey, a lawyer. Francis Russell's biography of Harding, *The Shadow of Blooming Grove, Warren Harding in His Times;* describes the house as a clearinghouse for favor-seekers and sleazy deal makers, and the site of poker games among Harding's cronies from his home state—the Ohio Gang—and their friends. Due to the involvement of the corrupt head of the Prohibition Bureau, liquor deliveries were made to the house accompanied by armed tax agents.

At about the same time, a house at 1509 H Street NW, the "Little House on H Street," was occupied by Harding intimates Attorney General Harry Daugherty and Jess Smith. According to Russell, this house served the same role for patronage and deal-making as the K Street house. Daugherty estimated he had 50 to 500 visitors daily. Millionaire Ned McLean provided the house rent free with servants, Armour & Company donated food, and Bill Orr, former pol turned bootlegger, provided liquor. Jess Smith committed suicide in 1923 when his misdeeds were exposed; Daugherty was tried twice but saved by hung juries.

㉕ Farragut Square

ENCAMPMENT—On this site Union Army artillery batteries were encamped during March 1861. It was one of the 17 public encampments called for in Pierre Charles L'Enfant's original plan for the city. According to the National Park Service history of the square, General Washington himself approved the plan.

㉖ 1736 I Street NW

PRE-PRESIDENTIAL—Site of the last Washington residence of Jefferson Davis, who spent many years in Washington before becoming President of the Confederacy. He lived here while serving as a senator from Mississippi from 1857 until January 1861. When his state seceded from the Union, Davis immediately returned home to Vicksburg, Mississippi, where he was elected President of the Confederacy in February 1861.

㉗ 1710 H Street NW

THE PRINCE SLEPT HERE—On October 5, 1860, the Prince of Wales (the future King Edward VII) was a guest in a house formerly on this site occupied by Lord Lyons, minister from Great

NAME LORE

FEW COPIES. One has to look long and hard to find an American city or town laid out quite like Washington. As George R. Stewart notes in *Names on the Land*, there were three basic patterns for laying out and naming city streets in early America. One was the "no pattern" city (the Boston model), the second called for numbers in one direction and names in the other (the Philadelphia model), and the final one called for a city of four sections with lettered and numbered streets moving out from the center of the city. This was the Washington model, which also featured broad diagonal avenues.

The haphazard Boston model was copied in New England, and the Philadelphia model was popular all over the country, but the Washington model gained few converts. Richmond, Indiana, copied it, and its influence is felt to some degree in Indianapolis. Other than that, Stewart was able to find only a few examples in Illinois and Iowa. As Stewart put it in his 1945 work, "The Americans simply did not like it."

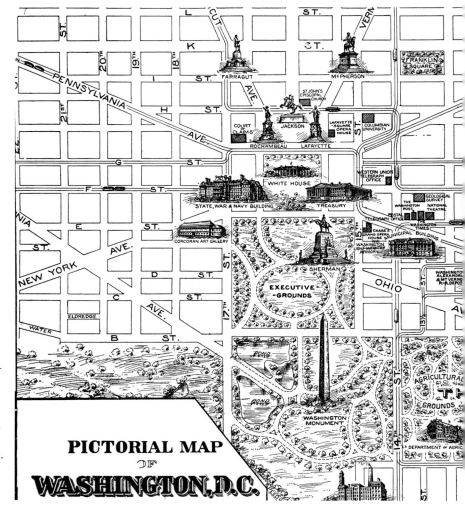

Changes Ahead. This 1907 tourist map shows Washington before the dramatic changes of the 20th century. The Mall is wooded, with wandering walks and drives, and is without most of the monuments and museums that dominate it today. The B Streets north and south of the Mall have not yet become Constitution and Independence Avenues. In years to come, the huge Federal Triangle complex will be built between the Mall and Pennsylvania Avenue, and Indiana Avenue will disappear under government buildings and highways. Louisiana Avenue will be renamed Indiana Avenue and a new Louisiana Avenue created near Union Station. Missouri and Maine Avenues will be relocated to the Upper Northwest and Southwest respectively.

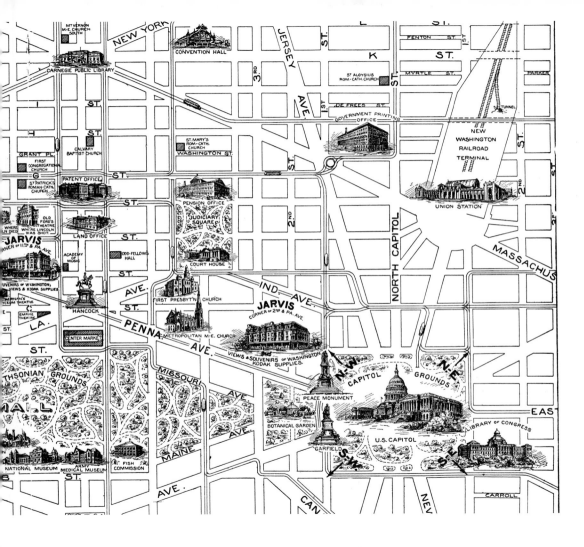

The White House Neighborhood 153

Signal Corps. These two buildings, which once stood on the north side of G Street between 17th and 18th Streets NW, housed the headquarters of the U.S. Signal Service for many years. The house to the right was the home of Jefferson Davis when he served as President Pierce's secretary of war before he became President of the Confederacy. The Davis structure was razed in 1902.

Britain. This was also the site of a house in which Adm. Porter resided and where the District of Columbia Society of the Sons of the American Revolution was organized on April 19, 1890.

28 1718 H Street NW

THE FAMILY—An exclusive men's club was located on this site between approximately 1907 and 1954, consisting of 40 members calling themselves "The Family." The building was purchased in 1954 by the organization for Diplomatic and Consular Officers Retired (DACOR) and continued as a social club. DACOR has since moved to 18th and G Streets NW.

29 748 Jackson Place, the southwest corner of Jackson Place and H Street NW

DECATUR HOUSE—Commodore Stephen Decatur built this house in 1818-19 from a design by Benjamin Henry Latrobe, and died here on March 22, 1820, from his wounds after his "gentleman's duel" with Commodore James Barron. Over the years it was occupied by Henry Clay (while secretary of state), Martin Van Buren, Edward Livingston (who served in Congress as a representative from New York and then as representative and senator from Louisiana, and as secretary of state from 1831 to 1833), George M. Dallas (vice president from 1845 to 1849), Judah P. Benjamin (Louisiana senator who served as secretary of war and secretary of state of the Confederacy), and Gen. E.F. Beale. (Beale experimented with the idea of using camels in the military and led a camel corps from Texas to California in 1857). Threatened with demolition on three occasions in this century, Decatur House is now owned by the National Trust for Historic Preservation, which obtained it in 1956 and converted it to a historic house museum and bookstore.

30 736 Jackson Place NW

TEMPORARY WHITE HOUSE—Once the home of James G. Blaine, in 1902 it became the residence of President Theodore Roosevelt for six months while the West Wing was added to the White House. As journalist George Rothwell Brown noted later, "Up to this time the President's offices were on the second floor of the White House, and the privacy of the presidents and their families was constantly invaded by all sorts of callers, including hordes of office seekers."

31 722 Jackson Place NW (formerly No. 14)

EWELL HOUSE—This site was long known as the Ewell House, for its first occupant, Dr. Thomas Ewell, who lived here in 1820-24. It is one of those locations that underscore the phenomenally rich history of Lafayette Square and the city.

Where to start? Vice President Schuyler Colfax was the 13th occupant of the private residence that stood on this spot from 1820 to 1930. Colfax was elected with Ulysses S. Grant in 1868, but failed to be renominated because of his implication in the Credit Mobilier scandal. The third occupant was New Jersey Senator Samuel Southard, whose report in 1835 led to federal rescue of the city from bankruptcy and began regular federal financial support to the District. The fifth occupant (1831-41) was New Hampshire Senator Levi Woodbury, who served as secretary of the treasury for Presidents Jackson and Van Buren. Daniel Sickles, New York congressman and general, lived here in 1858-64 during which time (1859) he killed Philip Barton Key, son of Francis Scott Key, who was having an affair with Mrs. Sickles (see Assassination Spot, p. 145).

Later residents included Elihu Root, secretary of war in Teddy Roosevelt's Cabinet (1903-05), and publisher William Randolph Hearst while he served as a member of the 58th and 59th Congresses.

Ewell House was razed in 1930 and replaced by an eight-story building for the Brookings Institution that was dedicated in 1931 and remained until July 1960. During those years the Brookings Institution had a remarkable impact on the nation and the world, including its role as the primary architect of the Marshall Plan, which rebuilt Europe after World War II.

Brookings was no stranger to the square, as it and the two groups that had merged to form the institution (the Institute for Government Research and the Institute of Economics) were formerly located at 744 Jackson Place.

The modern Brookings building was razed in 1963 when the Kennedy administration decided to restore the historic character of the square. City planning historian Frederick Gutheim called the redevelopment of the square in the 1960s "a turning point in the adaptive use of older buildings and more sympathetic recognition of urban continuity."

32 1651 Pennsylvania Avenue NW

BLAIR HOUSE—Now used as the President's guest house, this was the home of Francis Preston Blair, who left it to his son, Montgomery Blair, postmaster general from 1861 to 1864. Francis Preston Blair was a Jacksonian Democrat who published the *Congressional Globe,* a privately-published forerunner of the *Congressional Record.* In *Inside Blair House,* Mary Edith Wilroy and Lucie Prinz discuss the sale to Francis Preston Blair: "On December 6, 1836, Blair bought the house for $6,500. He was delighted to find that there was even room for some livestock. He kept a horse and a cow, which was so productive that Blair was able to leave a pail of milk for his President on the White House steps every morning."

Facade. For his 1937 inauguration, President Franklin D. Roosevelt reviewed the parade from this reviewing stand built to resemble the Hermitage, the home of President Andrew Jackson in Tennessee.

Other notables residing here included historian George Bancroft when he served as President Polk's secretary of the navy in the 1840s and Thomas Corwin, President Fillmore's secretary of the treasury in the 1850s.

It was here that the command of the Union Armies at the outbreak of the Civil War was offered to Gen. Robert E. Lee by Colonel Montgomery Blair in the name of Abraham Lincoln.

In 1942 the administration of Franklin D. Roosevelt bought the original Blair portion of the mansion for $175,000. An oft-heard story of the impulse for buying the house was that the idea came from First Lady Eleanor Roosevelt. Wilroy and Prinz recount the incident that might have caused her to decide that the days of the White House functioning as a hotel were over:

"It is reliably reported that Mrs. Roosevelt, up early one morning striding through the White House living quarters on her way out on one of her many trips, encountered a corpulent figure, dressed in a nightgown, pacing the hall. In one hand he held a cigar, in the other a snifter of what might have been brandy. It was six-thirty.

'Winston, where are you going at this time of the morning?' she is said to have inquired. 'To see Franklin,' he answered. 'Oh no, you're not. You've kept him up half the night as it is,' Eleanor Roosevelt replied firmly. 'Now please just go back to your room and let him rest.'"

President Truman lived at Blair house with his wife Bess and daughter Margaret from 1948 until 1951, while the White House underwent its most extensive remodeling since it was rebuilt after the British burned it in 1814. In 1950, during this period of reconstruction, two Puerto Rican nationalists tried unsuccessfully to shoot their way through the front door of Blair House in an attempt to assassinate Truman.

Today heads of state and other dignitaries occupy Blair House on official visits to the city.

33 **Northeast corner of 17th Street and Pennsylvania Avenue NW**

RENWICK GALLERY—Created in 1859 by James Renwick, Jr., for banker-millionaire William W. Corcoran, it was the city's first art gallery. It was modeled after the new Louvre in Paris, though Renwick put his distinctive imprint on the structure when he created the French Second Empire design and then had it built in red brick and brownstone.

The Civil War intervened while the building was being completed, and it spent the years 1861 through 1869 as a government supply depot. The Army used it for its clothing department during the war. Corcoran had little to say in the matter because his sympathy for the South led him to go abroad in 1862. He remained in Europe until the close of the war. Corcoran rented his nearby house at the northeast corner of H Street and Connecticut Avenue NW to the French minister in order to prevent the United States from seizing it while he was abroad.

The building became an art gallery after the war, but was sold to the government after the Corcoran collection was moved to its present New York Avenue location in 1897. It was turned into the U.S. Court of Claims in 1899. Under government ownership it deteriorated so much that by 1956 the court began pushing for its demolition and replacement with a new building. In *Historic Buildings of Washington, D.C.,* Diane Maddex reports on how it was saved: "President Kennedy's interest in preserving the historic character and scale of Lafayette Square...was instrumental in sparing the gallery that for most of its existence had served as everything but a gallery." It was transferred to the Smithsonian Institution by President Lyndon B. Johnson. The Smithsonian restored it to showcase American design and crafts.

34 **The southeast corner of 17th Street and Pennsylvania Avenue NW**

OLD EXECUTIVE OFFICE BUILDING—Originally the State, War and Navy Building, it was constructed between 1872 and 1888 in the style of the French Second Empire. When it opened it was the largest office building in the world—"and most magnificent," according to one guidebook. However, the architectural style was one that almost instantly went out of fashion, and for many years the building was ridiculed as an overly ornate confection.

The architect, Alfred B. Mullett, committed suicide in 1890 after years of wrangling with the government over his fee for the structure.

The construction of the building nonetheless had an important effect on the city. In 1870, when the $500,000 needed to start construction was authorized by Congress, St. Louis and other cities were making serious bids to have the center of government relocated. The appropriation of the money for this immense (then and now) structure settled the issue.

During the administration of President William Howard Taft (1908-12), his pet cow Pauline grazed behind this building.

The building was renamed the Executive Office Building in 1949. In more recent times, Fawn Hall shredded documents in Room 392 for her boss, Col. Oliver North, an action revealed during investigation of the Iran-contra scandal in the Reagan presidency.

35 **1732 Pennsylvania Avenue NW**

SCOTT HOUSE—Site of the house in which Gen. Winfield Scott, hero of the Mexican War, resided. He was the Whig candidate for president in 1852 but was defeated by Franklin Pierce. He is honored with a statue in Scott Circle at Massachusetts Avenue and 16th Street NW.

Going Home. The caisson carrying the casket of Franklin D. Roosevelt as it passes the Treasury Building.

36 North side of G Street NW between 17th and 18th Streets

JEFF DAVIS AGAIN—Jefferson Davis lived on a site toward the middle of the block while secretary of war between 1853 and 1857 during the Franklin Pierce administration.

The War Department's Signal Office was located on this and an adjacent site during the late 19th century. A variety of antennae, gauges, and other sensing and measuring devices on the roof testified to the increasing importance of nationwide communication of security and weather information as improvements were made in telegraphy and electricity. *Keim's* 1884 guidebook noted that the office was connected with "different stations in all parts of the country, through the lines of the general telegraphic companies."

37 1732 G Street NW

DOWNTOWN ATHLETIC ACTIVITIES—Former site of a downtown YMCA that was previously the Columbia Athletic Club, a group whose playing fields were once located on Roosevelt Island. The CAC abandoned its fields on the island in 1892 when ferry service ended. This site is now 1776 G Street NW.

38 600 block of 17th Street NW

HEADQUARTERS—In 1861 Gen. Winfield Scott, Union commander, established his headquarters in a building once on this site. Gen. Ulysses S. Grant had his headquarters here in 1865 while in command of all Union Armies.

39 Southwest corner of 18th and F Streets NW

TEAPOT DOME—Now offices for the General Services Administration, this 1917 building originally housed the Interior Department. In a fifth-floor dining room here in 1922, the illegal deal that created the Teapot Dome scandal was consummated.

President Harding's secretary of the interior, Albert B. Fall, secretly leased federal oil reserves to private companies, accepting more than $400,000 in cash and gifts in exchange. Fall was later fined $100,000 and sentenced to a year in jail for his crime.

The name of the scandal came from a Wyoming rock formation over one of the oil reserves. Francis Russell says in his Harding biography, *The Shadow of Blooming Grove, Warren Harding in His Times,* that Teapot Dome became a "stone symbol of government corruption."

The paneled dining room was destroyed by a fire on August 30, 1991.

40 1799 New York Avenue NW, in front of the headquarters of the American Institute of Architects

OCTAGON HOUSE—Now owned by the American Institute of Architects Foundation and preserved as a historic home, this is called by some the city's most interesting house. President James Madison and first lady Dolley Madison lived here after the burning of the White House by the British in 1814. Madison ratified the Treaty of Ghent here which ended the War of 1812. The signing took place on February 17, 1815, in the front circular room on the second floor. Sarah Booth Conroy of the *Washington Post* has deemed it "Washington's second most famous haunted house (the most famous is, of course, the White House)." The house was built by Col. John Tayloe III, whose ghost has been known to ring bells here. His daughter, who died in a fall, has seemed to appear in "wavering candlelight." The ghost of a murdered slave girl screams in the night from time to time.

Although the house has only six sides, these sides have eight angles—hence the name Octagon.

Old Navy. This photograph from about 1875 shows the Navy Department building on 17th Street, one of four similar government office buildings flanking the President's Mansion by the 1820s (War and Navy on the west, State and Treasury on the east). While the Treasury Department was replaced between 1836 and 1865, it was not until 1888 that the State, War and Navy Building (today's Old Executive Office Building) was completed on this site to accommodate the growing needs of those offices.

Map on page 139

Pearl Harbor Night. The White House ablaze with light as President Franklin D. Roosevelt confers with Cabinet officials and leaders of Congress on the bleak night of December 7, 1941.

41 17th Street NW, on the west side between D and E Streets

RED CROSS—Home of the American Red Cross Society, erected, beginning in 1913, "in memory of the heroic women of the Civil War." Three buildings—the Headquarters, West Building, and D.C. Chapter—comprise the white-marble complex on the block that was once a rough slum known as "O'Brien's Court."

42 The block bounded by 17th, 18th, C, and D Streets NW

D.A.R. BUILDINGS—A complex of three connected buildings including Constitution Hall and the headquarters of the Daughters of the American Revolution. The plenary sessions of the 1921 Conference on the Limitation of Armaments were held in the Genealogical Library.

Congress exempted Constitution Hall from taxes in the 1920s with the provision that it be made available for cultural events. It was the city's cultural center for some 20 years until in 1939 it denied Marian Anderson, the black singer, the opportunity to sing here because of her race. The D.A.R. later changed its stand. Anderson sang here in 1943 in a gala for United China Relief and again in 1953, but the role of the auditorium as a cultural center would never be the same. Officially the hall maintained a "white artists only" policy until 1952, and Anderson's 1943 appearance was an exception.

43 17th Street between Constitution Avenue and C Street NW

MOST EXPENSIVE HOUSE IN THE U.S.—The former site of the residence of Gen. John Van Ness, who married the daughter of David Burnes, original proprietor of the grounds now occupied by the White House, Treasury Building, Old Executive Office Building, and much of downtown Washington.

When Burnes sold his lands to the nation in 1792, as President Washington assembled the parcels needed to build the city, he retained the use of his home. Upon his death in 1799, it passed to his daughter, along with his new-found wealth from land sales. She married Congressman John Van Ness of New York in 1802, and the Van Nesses engaged Benjamin Henry Latrobe to design an elegant mansion, which, upon completion in 1816, was said to be the most costly private residence ever built in the United States. It was also said to have been the first house in America with hot and cold running water in each room. The family retained the Burnes cottage on the grounds, where it was venerated as the oldest house in the city until torn down in 1894.

After the Civil War, according to James M. Goode's *Capital Losses*, the property was used as a "German beergarden, florist's nursery, headquarters of the street cleaners, and, finally for the Columbia Athletic Club before being sold to the Federal Government in 1907."

Andrew Carnegie then contributed $900,000 toward the erection of the present building, which cost a total of 1.1 million dollars to build. The old Van Ness mansion, its barns, and stables were torn down and the cornerstone for the new building laid on May 11, 1908. The carriage house designed by Latrobe remains. The monumental marble building opened in 1910 as an architectural symbol of the coexistence of the nations of the Western Hemisphere and as headquarters of the Pan-American Union (founded in 1890) and its successor, the Organization of American States.

44 Land immediately south of the White House fence on the present-day Ellipse

WHITE LOT—During the Civil War this was known as the White Lot, because of a white fence at the south end of the White House lawn that separated the White House grounds from a pasture.

Old Herdic. Horse-drawn rear-entry omnibus of the Herdic Phaeton Company. These vehicles were a familiar 19th-century sight as shown in this 1891 photograph of the station by the White House and Lafayette Square. The Boundary Road destination referred to today's Florida Avenue, which formerly divided the City of Washington from the County of Washington, within the District of Columbia.

Map on page 139

Building Washington. This photograph shows the east wing of the Treasury Department under construction on December 1, 1857. To the right is the old State Department, dating from 1818, soon to be displaced by the north wing of the Treasury. To the rear are elegant homes surrounding Lafayette Square, then a prime residential area.

Cattle grazed there while waiting to be slaughtered for Army beef at a temporary slaughtering area on the grounds of the unfinished Washington Monument.

In addition, there were camps on the White Lot. As reported by Richard M. Lee in *Mr. Lincoln's City,* "Two small temporary camps were built on the White Lot—Rush and Reynolds Barracks. They were used when the need arose as hospitals, barracks for soldiers on duty in the city, or as bivouacs for troops passing through. Pennsylvania regiments on their way to and from Virginia customarily camped here."

45 **South of the White House grounds, on the northwest area of the Ellipse**

BUTT-MILLET MEMORIAL—Memorial fountain erected in memory of Maj. Archibald W. Butt and Francis D. Millet, who lost their lives on the *Titanic.* Butt was a military adviser to Presidents Roosevelt and Taft, and Millet was a popular artist. The fountain was designed by Daniel Chester French, who also created the statue of Abraham Lincoln at the Lincoln Memorial. It was erected in 1913.

Another memorial to the victims of the *Titanic* is located next to Fort McNair.

46 **The northern border of the Ellipse, just south of Executive Avenue and E Street NW**

ZERO MILESTONE—The point from which all distances to Washington, D.C., are officially measured. It is a 4-foot-high pink granite marker that was dedicated on July 4, 1923, as a gift from the Lee Highway Association.

47 **17th Street and Constitution Avenue NW, at the southwest corner of the Ellipse**

SECOND DIVISION MEMORIAL—A monument dedicated in 1936 to the famed World War I Army division. The focal point of the memorial is a huge bronze hand holding a flaming bronze sword aloft. In 1962 a new wing was added to the monument. Just as an 8-inch-thick slab of granite was being put into place, workmen heard the sound of rustling newspapers and discovered two sleeping, disheveled men inside. This near-entombment created quite a fuss at the time.

48 **Constitution Avenue NW, south of the White House**

SWIMMING HOLE—Where President John Quincy Adams took morning dips in the Potomac, which reached this point in the 1820s (one must recall that the present Constitution Avenue was a canal that widened into the Potomac at 17th Street NW). Constance McLaughlin Green reports that an eager woman reporter, Anne Royall, "supposedly stood over his clothes on the bank until he granted her an interview."

IMPORTANT WASHINGTON TIPS

POLITICAL TIP. "Washington is the town of the politically triumphant. Better to be dead than out of office, if you belong to a political set."
—Helen Nicolay from *Our Capitol on the Potomac,* 1924

GENERAL TIP. "Washington is not a nice place to live in. The rents are high, the food is bad, the dust is disgusting, the mud is deep, and the morals are deplorable."
—Horace Greeley, *New York Tribune,* July 13, 1865

TIP FOR PUNDITS. "Washington City is the poorest place in the United States from which to judge the temper of the nation. Its citizens have a different outlook on life than those of the individual states, and the atmosphere is artificial and enervating."
—Columnist Frank Carpenter, *Carp's Washington,* 1882

Connecticut Avenue Bridge and Lions,
Washington, D. C.

Leonine Approach. This vintage postcard carries the following description: "Connecticut Avenue Bridge and Lions. Showing the massive lions at approach to Connecticut Avenue Bridge, leading to the 'Zoo,' 'Rock Creek Park,' and Washington's most fashionable suburbs." The lions were removed in 1994 and put into storage. In early 1999, under the direction of Mayor Anthony A. Williams, restoration began with plans to have them back in place by the end of the year 2000.

The Dupont Circle and Adams-Morgan Area

① 1701 K Street

SHEPHERD'S ROW—This was once the site of three stone-faced homes contained in one building, constructed by Alexander R. "Boss" Shepherd in 1872 and known as Shepherd's Row. Shepherd lived in the corner house, and Charles W. Fairbanks resided here while Vice President between 1905 and 1909. One of the houses on this site served as the Imperial Russian Embassy and from 1914 to 1951 as the Washington Club. The structure was designed by Adolph Cluss, D.C.'s most famous Victorian architect. It was demolished on August 31, 1951, and is now the site of an office building.

② 1127 Connecticut Avenue NW

THE MAYFLOWER HOTEL— A guidebook once described it as "big, busy convention hotel with a big history...." Completed in time for Calvin Coolidge's inaugural ball in 1925, it was built on the site of an ancient cypress swamp discovered during the excavation. "The Kingfish" himself, Huey Long, lived here while in the Senate from 1932 to 1934. In 1933, President-elect Franklin D. Roosevelt and his family stayed in Rooms 776 and 781 while waiting to move into the White House. It is also where Harry Truman declared that he would win in 1948. Gene Autry once rode his horse Champion into the banquet room, and J. Edgar Hoover dined here almost every day for 20 years before his death in 1972. Trivia expert Fred Worth has noted that in 1942 a member of a Nazi sabotage team that had landed in the U.S. on a German submarine surrendered to FBI agents in Room 351.

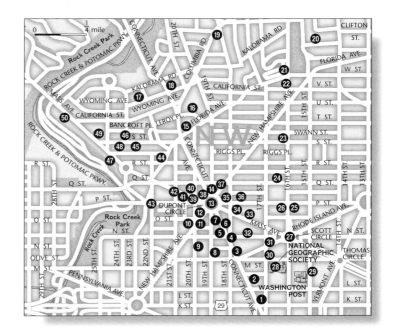

The Old British Legation. This was a landmark at Connecticut Avenue and N Street NW from 1872 to 1931. It was described as the city's finest example of mid-Victorian architecture.

③ 1223 Connecticut Avenue NW

SPEAKEASY—This was the site of the Mayflower Club, reputed to be the swankiest speakeasy in the city during Prohibition. It offered gambling as well as illegal booze, and catered to what was then called high society. The club featured a 30-foot bar and was decorated in a Halloween motif. The art focused on famous people playing jazz, so one could find likenesses of George Bernard Shaw tooting the clarinet and Ghandi playing the piano. In 1999 the building was occupied by a restaurant.

In February 1932 the police mapped all the illegal speakeasies in the city that had been raided in 1931. There were 1,155 that had been raided and another 516 locations where illegal buys had taken place.

④ Connecticut Avenue and N Street NW

STATUE OF JOHN WITHERSPOON—Patriot and a signer of the Declaration of Independence, Witherspoon unified and led the Presbyterian Church in America.

The statue by William Couper was originally placed in front of the Church of the Covenant, renamed the National Presbyterian Church in 1947. The church was located at this site from 1877 to 1966. Since then the church has attempted to have the statue moved to its new site at 4101 Nebraska Avenue NW, but the city has refused.

⑤ 1300 Connecticut Avenue NW

FORMER SITE OF THE BRITISH LEGATION—Great Britain's decision to locate its diplomatic offices here in 1872 helped establish the area as an exclusive residential neighborhood. The most notable resident of the legation (which became an embassy in 1893) was British diplomat and jurist James Bryce, author of *The American Commonwealth,* a classic work on American government. After the British moved in 1931 to their current Massachusetts Avenue location, the site was used for the present headquarters building of the International Association of Machinists. At one time the ground floor housed the Washington bureau of the Associated Press.

❻ 1331 Connecticut Avenue NW

BELL HOME—This site was the last residence of Alexander Graham Bell, the inventor of the telephone and a very public figure in the city for most of his adult life. The Bells began building the three-story brick and stone house in the summer of 1891. It featured an annex that the inventor used for weekly Wednesday night gatherings of "notable men."

❼ 1350 Connecticut Avenue NW

DUPONT CIRCLE BUILDING—From the 1940s to the 1980s, this building was the city's mecca for activist public interest organizations, grant-funded non-profits, and small entrepreneurs. "The only office building in this city with a soul," claimed one ten-year resident in a 1986 *Washington Post* article. Over the years it housed such groups as the Environmental Law Institute, Zero Population Growth, the graphic arts studio/office of former Takoma Park mayor and political activist Sammie Abbott, and the poetry magazine *Black Box*, which specialized in producing cassette tapes of poets reading their own work, including Washington poet E. Ethelbert Miller. Established as an elite 700-unit apartment building in the 1930s, during World War II it was taken over for government offices, including the Office of Civil Defense, directed by Eleanor Roosevelt. When converted to a commercial office building after the war, offices still sported the attributes of the earlier apartments—bathrooms, fireplaces, outmoded plumbing, and heating.

Harvey's North. The once-famous restaurant depicted in the 1930s after moving from Pennsylvania Avenue to 1107 Connecticut Avenue near the Mayflower Hotel. At this point in its history its motto was: "No visit to Washington is complete without a visit to Harvey's." Gone from the scene today, Harvey's in its two prime locations served the likes of Mark Twain, Ulysses S. Grant, and Walt Whitman.

DUPONT CIRCLE. This circle was on the outskirts of the original City of Washington in a section called "The Slashes." This location became a prime target of wealthy real estate investors as massive public works projects of the 1870s, including the paving of Connecticut Avenue, began to transform a backward community into a fashionable capital city. Western mining fortunes in the names of Stewart, Clark, and Hearst poured into the "Pacific Circle" area in the last quarter of the century as streetcars helped the city expand northward. In 1882 the circle was renamed after Union Adm. Francis S. du Pont. Although his ironclad ships were defeated at Charleston, South Carolina, in 1863, he was nevertheless immortalized here in Washington's best known circle, now a mini-park managed by the National Park Service. Today the former mansions of the rich serve as clubs, association headquarters, professional offices, and embassies, or have been replaced by hotels, banks, and office buildings. But a strong residential flavor prevails despite the intrusions of commerce and entertainment.

Among its postwar tenants was the 1948 presidential campaign office of Thomas F. Dewey. In 1986 the building was sold, renovated, and converted from a center for no-frills, low-budget organizations to an upscale office building.

8 1215 19th Street NW

ROOSEVELT MANSION—Theodore Roosevelt lived in this house from 1889 to 1895, while Civil Service commissioner. In 1987, after the home (now known as the Roosevelt mansion) had been turned into an office building, it was sold to an international conglomerate for a record four million dollars, or $288 a square foot. At the time the price was deemed to be the highest ever paid for finished office space in the Washington area.

9 1229 20th Street NW

ORIGINAL BREWERY—Here was the original site of Christian Heurich's Lager Beer Brewery and Tavern, started in leased quarters after Heurich's arrival in the District from Baltimore in 1872. In the late 1870s, he tore down the first structure and erected a new four-story brewery on this spot. It was destroyed in an 1892 fire. He rebuilt an even larger brewery near the site of the present Kennedy Center.

10 1308 20th Street NW

PRESIDENT'S LADY—The widowed Edith Bolling Galt—whose deceased husband had been the proprietor of a jewelry store still operating today as Galt and Brothers Jewelers at 607 15th Street NW—lived in a house on this site before she married President Woodrow Wilson on December 18, 1915. She was his second wife. The house was demolished in 1960 to make way for an apartment building.

11 1307 New Hampshire Avenue NW

CHRISTIAN HEURICH MANSION—The home of The Historical Society of Washington, D.C. (formerly the Columbia Historical Society). The society moved into the building on August 25, 1956. Christian Heurich, the beer baron, who died at age 102 (on March 3, 1945), decorated many of the walls with mottoes appropriate to his calling. One reads: "There is room in the smallest chamber for the biggest hangover."

12 1400 New Hampshire Avenue NW

HEARST HOUSE—George Hearst, creator of the Hearst fortune and father of newspaper magnate William Randolph Hearst, lived a lavish life here with his wife, Phoebe, in the 1890s. George successively discovered and owned the nation's largest gold mine, in South Dakota, and the world's richest copper lode, in Anaconda, Montana. George was a bit crude for Washington society, but Phoebe contributed mightily, founding the national Parent-Teacher Association, financing the National Cathedral School for Girls, and supporting many educational and charitable endeavors. Later the building served as the Italian Embassy, a World War II officer's club, and, according to the Chronicler of the Columbia Historical Society, a "Russian Bible House" in 1951.

13 Underneath Dupont Circle

WASHINGTON UNDERGROUND—Two tunnels under Dupont Circle were opened in 1949 to relieve congestion on the city's busiest trolley line and abandoned in 1962 when trolley service ended. Thereafter dozens of plans were offered for the use of the tunnels, including a health spa, shopping mall, and final resting place for

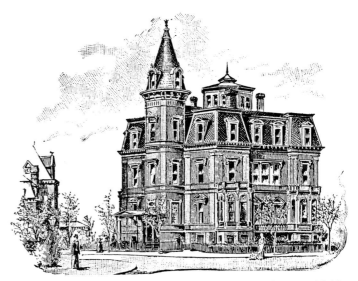

Castle of Yore. Built in 1873 by Nevada Senator William Stewart with his mining riches, it was known as Stewart's Castle. The gigantic town house, located on the northwest corner of Connecticut Avenue and Dupont Circle, was demolished in 1901.

Map on page 165

the ashes of the dead. Finally in the early 1990s the area was reopened as a food court, which failed, and the area is presently closed.

⑭ 1519 Connecticut Avenue NW

TELEVISION HISTORY—Site of the first licensed television station in America, established in 1928 with the assigned call letters W3XK. It was the brainchild of inventor Charles Francis Jenkins, who experimented with the medium here until 1932. Jenkins was only able to transmit images of dark silhouettes.

⑮ Northeast corner of Florida and Connecticut Avenues NW

DEAN ESTATE—This block, lying just beyond the original boundary of Washington, was cleared in the early 1950s for a 26-million-dollar development by Morris Cafritz. The chronicler of the Columbia Historical Society reported that the project required clearing the grounds of a home known successively as Oak Lawn, Temple Heights, and the Dean estate, after Edward C. Dean, president of the Potomac Terra Cotta Company. The property extended to the crest of the hill along Columbia Road and included the venerable Treaty Oak, legendary site of an early treaty between Indians and colonists. Wood from the tree was offered to historical societies. The Universal Building now on the site was part of the complex.

An earlier, but unbuilt, project proposed for this site, according to an article by *Washington Post* writer William F. Powers (July 4, 1992), was Frank Lloyd Wright's visionary scheme in 1940 for a 2500-plus-unit apartment and hotel complex comprising 14 linked towers of various heights and including a "1,000-seat cinema-theater; a banquet hall; retail shops; a cocktail lounge with a 400-foot-long crystal bar; an art gallery; [and] nine bowling alleys." Called Crystal Heights, the project was never approved—because of bureaucratic opposition, height restrictions, and possibly, Powers suggested, because the project was too conceptually and financially ambitious for a conservative city on the brink of World War II. Thus the city lost the opportunity for a building by Wright.

⑯ 1919 Connecticut Avenue NW

WASHINGTON HILTON—The "gull-winged" hotel opened in 1965 as the 60th hotel in the Hilton chain and was dubbed the unofficial palace of Washington by Conrad Hilton. It featured such innovations as extra-long beds, five underground levels, and a three-court tennis club. On March 30, 1981, at the T Street lower-level entry to the hotel, John Hinckley shot President Ronald Reagan, his press secretary James Brady, and FBI agent Raymond Martin. A protective portico has since been constructed at the entrance.

⑰ 2215 Wyoming Avenue NW

SYRIAN EMBASSY—Last residence of former President and Chief Justice William Howard Taft, who died here in 1930. He bought this home in 1921 when he became chief justice. The building is now the Syrian Embassy.

⑱ 2101 Connecticut Avenue NW

2101—This elegant apartment house built in 1908—with gargoyles—has been known for decades simply as 2101. To build it, three great mansions were torn down, including the G.W. Woodward house. From the start, it was meant to be the best on the market, with each apartment as large as a good-size house (minimum: three bedrooms, three baths, maid's room with bath, and a heated sun porch).

⑲ Southeast corner of 18th Street and Columbia Road NW

KNICKERBOCKER DISASTER—On January 28, 1922, the show-case Knickerbocker Theater on this spot collapsed under the weight of a 26-inch snow that had begun falling more than a day earlier. Some 300 neighborhood residents had trudged through the knee-deep snow to see the comedy hit "Get Rich Quick Wallingford." As the title and credits were being shown on the screen, a small crack ran across the ceiling that could be heard by patrons in the balcony. Bits of plaster fell and then there was a loud sickening hiss as the roof and its load of snow folded in on the balcony. The balcony broke loose and slid down into the orchestra. After a 32-hour rescue operation, 98 people were found dead and 136 injured. Eventually the architect and the owner both committed suicide. It was later rebuilt as the Ambassador Theater.

⑳ Area bounded by Florida Avenue, Columbia Road, and 14th and 15th Streets NW

OLDE CAMPUS—This 46-acre tract was purchased for about $7,000 by local Baptists in 1820 to establish Columbian College, precursor of The George Washington University. It was a non-denominational institution to prepare gospel ministers and offer a general college education. Its medical faculty operated the City Hospital, located downtown in the 1840s. Historian Constance McLaughlin Green wrote that the Marquis de Lafayette, on a celebrated national tour (1824-25) commemorating his Revolutionary War service in the American cause, attended the first commencement along with President Monroe and the Cabinet.

Fred A. Emery, president of the Society of Natives, District of Columbia, told the Columbia Historical Society in 1930 that he could remember when many streets in the neighborhood were named after college officials. Chapin Street was College Street.

INSIDE THE BELTWAY

SYMBOLIC STREETS. Some streets do special tasks, both in symbol and reality. New York has its Wall Street and Madison Avenue, Los Angeles its Rodeo Drive and Hollywood Boulevard. In Washington, Massachusetts Avenue is known as Embassy Row because of its embassies (Britain, Brazil, Ireland, India, Australia and more). K Street has become synonymous with lawyers and lobbyists, while Pennsylvania Avenue is known far and wide as the Avenue of the Presidents. If you're headed for Maine Avenue, you are probably thinking about seafood and P Street and Seventh Street are addresses for art galleries.

Outside the city is I-495 which is more commonly known as the Beltway. Besides being a major force in local transportation, it has become symbolic of thinking inside the boundary it describes. "Inside the Beltway" has become a popular metaphor for the parochialism and political intensity of official Washington. On the other hand, "Outside the Beltway" refers to the rest of the nation—the Real World.

Belmont, Harvard, and Girard Streets were Staughton, Bacon, and Binney, respectively, after former presidents. The chronicler of the Columbia Historical Society reported in 1960 that some of the original stone wall remained near Clifton Street and University Place. The college moved downtown in 1882.

㉑ Formerly on the northwest corner of Florida Avenue and 16th Street NW

HENDERSON CASTLE—Missouri Senator John Brooks Henderson, best known as drafter of the 13th Amendment to the Constitution, which abolished slavery, built an enormous residence here in 1888-92 when the area was still semi-rural. Mrs. Henderson had a proprietary attitude toward the neighborhood, developing several of the mansions along 16th Street, lobbying Congress to purchase and create Meridian Hill Park across the street, and working to make 16th Street the city's Embassy Row. Among the mansions is the Polish Embassy at 2640 16th Street NW.

Mrs. Henderson's social functions were legendary, if somewhat quirky. An article by *Evening Star* writer John Sherwood in November 1975 pointed out that she was a vegetarian who eschewed liquor, tobacco, coffee, and tea, and was author of a lengthy tome entitled *The Aristocracy of Health.* One famous night in 1906 she held a party for colleagues in the prohibition movement and dumped the contents of her exclusive wine cellar into the 16th Street gutters. When her renaming of 16th Street as "Avenue of the Presidents" failed to catch on, she devoted her energies to beautifying it by planting trees. After World War I, she dedicated them to D.C. troops killed in battle, with veterans' names on bronze plaques.

The senator died in 1923, Mrs. Henderson in 1931. According to Sherwood, the house ironically became an after-hours bottle club in the 1930s. Neighbors Eugene and Agnes Meyer, owners of the *Washington Post,* tired of the partying and finally bought the place. It was demolished in 1949 and the land later sold and developed into an extensive complex of town houses in 1976, the Beekman Place condominiums.

㉒ 2100 16th Street NW

HUGHES HOUSE—Justice Charles E. Hughes lived here when nominated for the presidency in 1916. He lost to Woodrow Wilson but served Presidents Harding and Coolidge as secretary of state (1921-25) and returned to the Supreme Court as Chief Justice (1930-41).

㉓ 1814 16th Street NW

MAIN STREET ADDRESS—Writer Sinclair Lewis lived in a small house on this site from 1919 to 1920 while struggling to complete *Main Street,* one of his most famous novels. According to biographer Mark Schorer, Lewis rented an office room at nearby 1127 17th Street NW, produced over 200,000 words in nine months, and delivered the manuscript hoping to sell 10,000 copies. Within a year 180,000 had sold, eventually to be millions.

㉔ 1615 Q Street NW

CAIRO HOTEL—Architect and developer Thomas Franklin Schneider, fresh from experiencing Chicago's World's Fair in 1893, provided Washington with a steel-framed skyscraper still reigning as one of its tallest structures—after the Washington Monument, the dome of the Capitol, and the Washington National Cathedral. By far the tallest private building in the city when constructed in 1894, the Cairo's 12-story, 146-foot height far exceeded the reach of local firefighting equipment. Now converted into condominiums, the Cairo started as a luxury apartment building and later served as a hotel. As noted in James M. Goode's *Best Addresses,* initial appointments and amenities included an ornate lobby, a ballroom, a drug store, a bowling alley, a billiard parlor, and a tropical garden on the roof, where refreshments were served to Washingtonians enjoying the spectacular view. The Cairo's most striking architectural feature, its grand entryway, echoed the acclaimed arched entrance to Louis Sullivan's Transportation Building at the Chicago Fair.

Concern for safety and neighborhood aesthetics led to regulations limiting the height of residential buildings to 90 feet and commercial buildings to 110 feet, except along selected wider avenues, such as Pennsylvania, where buildings to 130 feet were allowed. These guidelines were incorporated into Congress's Height of Buildings Act in 1910, still in effect.

㉕ 1530 P Street NW

CARNEGIE INSTITUTION—Since 1910 this has been the headquarters of the Carnegie Institution of Washington, founded in 1902 by Andrew Carnegie for the encouragement of investigation, research and discovery, and the application of knowledge to the improvement of mankind.

㉖ 1620 P Street NW

ASTRONOMER—Simon Newcomb (1835-1909), long called America's greatest astronomer, lived and died in a house once on this site.

Cairo Hotel. This luxury hotel at Q and 16th Streets NW billed itself as away from the noise and bustle yet conveniently located. When completed in 1894, it was the tallest private building in the city.

Map on page 165

STREET LORE

BATAAN AND CORREGIDOR STREETS. The two short streets adjoining Scott Circle to the east and west were named in 1961 to commemorate two World War II battles, at the request of Philippines Ambassador Carlos P. Romulo. Prior to that, they were nameless, which had been something of an irritation to the few people whose houses faced them. Complaints, including one from Mrs. Gifford Pinchot, widow of the governor of Pennsylvania and pioneering conservationist, whose home faced one of the unnamed streets generated press reports on the dilemma (for example, the *Washington Post's* "2 Nameless Streets Flank Scott Statue" of February 6, 1953). Mrs. Pinchot was given a temporary Rhode Island Avenue address by the District because the side of her house faced on that avenue.

㉗ Scott Circle at Massachusetts Avenue and 16th Street NW

SEX CHANGE—The statue by H.K. Brown of Gen. Winfield Scott is of note because the horse that Scott is riding underwent a sex change when it was about to be cast. Scott's living relatives decided that it was more appropriate to have him riding a stallion than a mare (even though he did ride a mare into battle).

㉘ South side of M Street NW between 16th and 17th Streets

THE GEOGRAPHIC—On this site is the headquarters complex of the National Geographic Society, organized in 1888 for the diffusion of geographic knowledge. For many years, it has been the world's largest non-profit scientific and educational association. Explorer's Hall, the museum portion of the newer headquarters building at 17th and M Streets NW, houses a freestanding globe of the world, said to be the world's largest. This new building, designed by Edward Durrell Stone, was formally dedicated in 1974 and created something of a sensation when the society paid for it—eight million dollars—in cash. The ten-story headquarters features such amenities as a pear-tree-shaded courtyard and three levels of underground parking. The older colonnaded building on 16th Street NW was built in 1913 and houses the society's boardroom. It was a long-established piece of Washington Cold War lore that the Central Intelligence Agency posted agents on the top floor of this building to observe the comings and goings across 16th Street at No. 1125.

㉙ 1125 16th Street NW

PULLMAN MANSION—This mansion was built in 1910 by Mrs. George M. Pullman, who never actually lived there. It spent much of its life as the Russian Embassy, first under Czarist Russia and then under the U.S.S.R., after the United States granted it diplomatic recognition in 1934.

30 Northeast corner of 17th and M Streets NW

SUMNER SCHOOL—The Sumner School, completed in August 1872 to replace the older M Street School for black children, torn down in 1871. The Sumner School was named for Massachusetts abolitionist Charles Sumner and was a key institution for black education during the decades of segregated schools. For many years it housed the office of the superintendent of "Colored Public Schools for the District of Columbia and Georgetown." Today it is a showcase restoration used by the District government for exhibits, conferences and receptions.

31 Northeast corner of 17th Street and Rhode Island Avenue NW

SHERIDAN HOUSE—Famed Civil War Gen. Philip H. Sheridan resided in a house once on this site. Sheridan is honored with a monument at Sheridan Circle on Massachusetts Avenue and 23rd Street NW, which was sculpted by Gutzon Borglum in 1908. Borglum would later—between 1927 and 1941—create the monumental sculptures of Mount Rushmore.

32 1739 N Street NW

TABARD INN—Small hotel and restaurant composed of three former town houses. In one of them, in 1863, Edward Everett Hale wrote his "Man Without a Country," which for decades was one of the nation's most popular and commonly recited stories. It is the tale of a fictional U.S. Naval officer named Philip Nolan who was involved with Aaron Burr's treason. As he goes into exile, Nolan expresses the desire never to hear or read the name of the United States again, a wish that is fulfilled for 55 years.

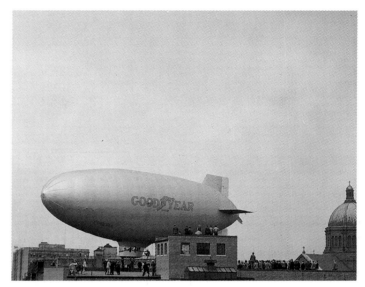

Roof Event. The Goodyear blimp touches down atop an automobile dealership that once stood at 17th and M Streets NW. The picture appears to have been taken from the roof or an upper floor of the Sumner School and looks over the property that is now home to the National Geographic Society.

Map on page 165

TALE OF TWO STATES

MASSACHUSETTS AVENUE. This is the longest street in the city and the only one to run through three quadrants (Southeast, Northeast, and Northwest). Sixteenth Street NW is the second longest. The section of Massachusetts Avenue NW near Dupont Circle is also known as Embassy Row, as a quarter of the embassies in the city are located here, many in the mansions of the American rich of an earlier era.

CALIFORNIA STREET. Almost all states have avenues named for them, but not California, nor Ohio, which gives its name to a drive along the Mall.

33 1735-1775 Massachusetts Avenue NW

THINK TANK—To erect the Brookings Institution building on this site, eight elegant houses were torn down in 1958, including the former home of World War I nationalist and League of Nations opponent Senator Henry Cabot Lodge of Massachusetts.

34 1785 Massachusetts Avenue NW

MCCORMICK APARTMENT BUILDING—One of the six sumptuous apartments in this building was that of financier and Secretary of the Treasury Andrew W. Mellon, who was also an avid art collector. Art dealer Lord Joseph Duveen rented the floor below in 1936, filled it with 21 million dollars worth of paintings, gave Mellon the key, left town, and wound up selling him the lot. Mellon gave his paintings to the nation and established the National Gallery of Art. The building is now the headquarters for the National Trust for Historic Preservation.

35 1801 P Street NW

IRAQI EMBASSY—Closed since the Persian Gulf war in early 1991, this building was once the home of Mabel Boardman, who helped organize and direct the American Red Cross in the early 20th century. Like its neighbors, the house was an entertainment center in its day. According to an article by *Washington Post* writer Sarah Booth Conroy on February 10, 1991, Boardman saved the nearby Herbert Wadsworth mansion in 1932, relocating to it the Sulgrave Club she formed earlier at 1801 Massachusetts Avenue NW. Boardman bequeathed the house to the Washington National Cathedral in 1946. The cathedral in turn sold it to the Hungarian Reformed Federation of America in 1950. The house was purchased by the Iraqi government in 1962 for $394,000.

36 **1722 Church Street NW**

CHURCH RUINS—The site of St. Thomas Episcopal Church, which burned down in 1970; the parish garden remains a community meeting place. Franklin D. Roosevelt worshiped at the church for years.

37 **1500 New Hampshire Avenue NW**

LEITER HOUSE—The former Dupont Plaza Hotel occupies the site of an elegant mansion built in 1891 by Chicago department store and real estate tycoon Levi P. Leiter. Leiter's son Joseph took over in 1913, and continued to make the residence a center for lavish entertainment. Joseph reportedly prepared for Prohibition by stashing away $300,000 worth of the choicest liquors and wines.

38 **1913 Massachusetts Avenue NW, northwest side of Dupont Circle between Connecticut and Massachusetts Avenues NW**

ONCE A CASTLE—Now occupied by a branch of Riggs Bank, from 1873 until 1901 this was the site of Stewart's Castle, an immense mansion built by Nevada Senator William Stewart. Stewart made a fortune in his 20s in the California gold fields, then repeated the feat with the Comstock silver lode in Nevada. Building and maintaining the mansion—with proper staff—taxed even Stewart's wealth. For many years he leased the residence to the Chinese legation, before selling it to William A. Clark, another wealthy western senator. Clark tore down the Victorian castle in 1901, intending to rebuild in a then-fashionable classical mode, but decided to move to New York City instead. Riggs Bank built its branch here in 1924.

The Dry Years, Washington Style. This 1922 photograph shows a 500-gallon still filled with confiscated liquor. The exact location of this scene has been obscured by time, but similar raids were common throughout the city during Prohibition.

Map on page 165

LOVERS' LANE. Washington is one of the few cities to have one of these—officially, that is. This one runs between Massachusetts Avenue and R Street NW inside Rock Creek Park. Long closed to vehicular traffic and resembling a gravelly country lane more than a city street, it is missing on most modern street maps. The northern entrance to Lovers' Lane is just west of the Massachusetts Avenue bridge over Rock Creek Park.

The lane got its official name in 1900, long after it had gotten its reputation as a popular trysting place.

39 2000 Massachusetts Avenue NW

BLAINE MANSION—Originally this building was a mansion owned by Maine Senator James G. Blaine, post-Civil War Republican party leader, Speaker of the House, Secretary of State, and presidential candidate in 1884. George Westinghouse rented it in 1898 and bought it in 1901. The inventor of air brakes installed an elevator in this, his last home. In the 1920s it became the site of the Japanese legation. Today it accommodates various professional offices.

40 2009 Massachusetts Avenue NW

THE LONGWORTHS—Home of Nicholas Longworth, Speaker of the House of Representatives from 1925 to 1931. He will always be remembered as the man who married Theodore Roosevelt's sharp-tongued daughter Alice. She lived in this house as a widow for nearly 50 years, a society-page icon and quotable to the end. She died here on February 20, 1980.

41 2012 Massachusetts Avenue NW

SPENCER MANSION—The mansion built on this site was one of many erected by wealthy Americans attracted to Washington in the late 19th century. It is now called the National Headquarters Building, containing the National Federation of Business and Professional Women's Clubs and the Business and Professional Women's Foundation and Research Center.

42 2020 Massachusetts Avenue NW

WALSH-MCLEAN MANSION—This imposing structure was built by mining baron and Senator Thomas F. Walsh for three million dollars in 1903, and sold in November 1951 to the

Indonesian government for about $350,000. It is in use today as the Indonesian Embassy. Walsh's only child Evalyn married Ned McLean, the only son of fabulously wealthy businessman and *Washington Post* owner John McLean, thus uniting the two family fortunes and setting in motion over two decades of frenzied spending and ostentatious living by the couple, including the purchase of the Hope Diamond. Longtime Washingtonian Francis A. Young informed the authors of an interesting anecdote. Walsh is said to have saved the first gold nugget from the Chief Ouray Mine that launched his fortune, enclosed it in crystal, and set it into the floor of the entrance area of the building to celebrate his wealth. The artifact is no longer there, according to the Indonesian Embassy.

43 22nd and P Streets NW

CLASSICAL GAS—The gas station on this site was designed in 1937 with arched windows and classical columns to reflect the appearance of the nearby Church of the Pilgrims. Earlier the Washington Hunt Club had occupied the location, just above Rock Creek. In 1973 Gulf Oil officials agreed with a Commission of Fine Arts request to restore the building rather than tear it down. Commission official Charles H. Atherton expressed the relief of preservationists to an industry trade magazine: "So much of our life today is being homogenized. Here we have a little building that has a unique sense of place—a unique character of its own...it is refreshing to see something like this." The site became a Mobil station in the early 1990s.

44 2131 R Street NW

YOUNG FRANKLIN—Home of Franklin D. Roosevelt and his family from 1918 to 1920, two of the years he served as an assistant secretary of the Navy. The 17-room, 6 1/2 bath house is now

---

STREAM LORE

SLASH RUN. One of the most notorious of the lost creeks and runs of the District was Slash Run, which ran from about 16th Street and Columbia Road NW through the Kalorama section and passed within a block of Dupont Circle until the 1870s, when it was buried in conduits and sewer pipes. John Claggett Proctor points out in *Proctor's Washington* (1949) that the city's open streams were used to furnish water for and then remove the offal of the many slaughterhouses. He adds, "Slash run was at an early day one such stream, and in the course of time there was a number of slaughterhouses built on it." Rain would routinely cause Slash Run to overflow.

---

the residence of the ambassador of Mali. Earlier the Roosevelts lived for several years in a house that once stood at 1733 N Street NW.

TOURIST TIP

INDECENT EXPOSURE. Seen in the *National Intelligencer* of May 17, 1851: "Indecent Exposure. A number of lads were seen a few days ago bathing and running about the bank of the Washington Canal, in a state of nudity, directly in front of the dwellings on Missouri avenue...it is hoped that the city police will arrest all such offenders, as their bathing in the Washington Canal and in the Tiber creek, near dwelling-houses and the railroad station, is not only an offence against public decency, but in violation of a city ordinance."

45 2300 S Street NW

HOOVERVILLE—Residence of Herbert Hoover while he was secretary of commerce under Presidents Warren G. Harding and Calvin Coolidge, and until his inauguration as President.

46 2301 S Street NW

KALORAMA—Here on the heights above the new federal city was located the estate of Joel Barlow, Revolutionary War-era poet, liberal political writer, and confidant of Thomas Jefferson and James Madison. The latter would travel from the President's Mansion to visit Barlow "in the country," according to journalist George Rothwell Brown's account. A backer of steamboat inventor Robert Fulton, Barlow is said to have let Fulton test his "submarine torpedo" in a pond on the estate, although some reports suggest that the test was performed in Rock Creek in the valley below. The residence, "Kalorama," a Greek name meaning "beautiful view," was demolished in 1889 when S Street was extended between Florida and Massachusetts Avenues to make way for the development of the neighborhood that now bears the name.

47 2306 Massachusetts Avenue NW

HAVEN FOR THE ARTS—Here on Sheridan Circle overlooking Rock Creek Park, widowed artist and socialite Alice Pike Barney dedicated herself to bringing high culture to early 20th-century Washington. Fortified by inheritances from her father and husband, both self-made millionaires, she engaged Waddy Wood, architect for many elegant homes in the nearby Kalorama neighborhood, to design this extraordinary town and studio house, completed in 1903. Barney, a student of James McNeill Whistler, made the house a gallery for her paintings and a center for cultural and political elites of the day. Author G.K. Chesterton, ballerina Anna Pavlova, actress Sarah Bernhardt, and Presidents Theodore Roosevelt and William Taft were among the notables entertained there.

According to an article by Benjamin Forgey in the *Washington Post* (March 18, 1995), Barney also championed the founding of the Sylvan Theater at the Washington Monument, the launching of the Corcoran Gallery's Biennial and the establishment of a "truly national art gallery," eventually created in the form of the Smithsonian's National Museum of American Art, which now curates the Alice Pike Barney art collection. Many of Barney's fundraising events benefited the Barney Neighborhood House in Southwest Washington. Francis A. Young reminded the authors that when he lived in that area in the 1950s and attended it after school, it was one of the most highly regarded social agencies in the city. Barney's Studio House was bequeathed to the Smithsonian Institution in 1960, when it served for a decade as the headquarters location for the American Association of Museums. In the mid-1990s the Smithsonian began to seek an appropriate buyer for the historic but costly-to-maintain property.

48 2340 S Street NW

WOODROW WILSON HOUSE—Residence of Woodrow Wilson upon his retirement as president until the time of his death, after which Mrs. Wilson continued to live here for some years. Wilson made a speech from the balcony of this house on Armistice Day 1923, three months before his death. The property is now open to the public, operated as a historic house by the National Trust for Historic Preservation.

49 2419 Massachusetts Avenue NW

RINEHART RESIDENCE—Once the home of writer and playwright Mary Roberts Rinehart, best known for her humorous stories and detective novels. Her books *The Circular Staircase* (1908) and *The Man in Lower Ten* (1909) are considered classics of the detective genre.

50 2520 Massachusetts Avenue NW

JAPANESE EMBASSY—At the beginning of World War II, it was on this lawn that the staff of the embassy burned code books, secret letters, and other documents after the bombing of Pearl Harbor. Until a transfer of diplomats could be arranged, the ambassador and one envoy were confined to their rooms at the Washington Hotel and the rest of the staff remained at the embassy.

Wartime Concert. Watergate concerts performed twice weekly from a barge anchored just above Memorial Bridge were popular summer evening attractions from 1935 to the 1960s. Up to 12,000 listeners would gather on the steps and terraces flanking the parkway and, as seen in this World War II photo, in canoes on the Potomac. It has been suggested that the sailor standing in this picture may have just finished singing the national anthem. Even in wartime those in canoes were excused from standing up in the notoriously tippy vessels.

Foggy Bottom

❶ Northwest corner of 19th and G Streets NW

CONFEDERATE NAVIGATOR—On this site was the home of geographer Matthew F. Maury. Among his accomplishments, he wrote the first textbook of modern oceanology, *Physical Geography of the Sea,* and prepared a chart of the ocean bottom to prove that a transatlantic cable was practicable. In 1861 he resigned from the U.S. Navy to enter the Confederate Navy. Maury Hall at the U.S. Naval Academy in Annapolis is named after him. He was considered the greatest oceanographer of his day.

❷ Southwest corner of 19th and I Streets NW

BAPTISTS—According to a plaque on the site today, the First Colored Baptist Church of the City of Washington took over this location in 1833 from the city's first Baptist congregation. The Nineteenth Street Baptist Church worshiped here from 1871 to 1975.

❸ 2099 Pennsylvania Avenue NW

ONCE THE FRANKLIN HOTEL—An office building with a newly assigned Pennsylvania Avenue address is planned for the I Street site of the former Franklin Hotel where Lafayette stayed in 1824 during his triumphal 16-month U.S. tour commemorating the American Revolution. William O'Neale erected a building here in the 1790s and expanded over the next two decades into a hotel, boarding house, and tavern business spreading over three buildings. Another prominent hotel owner, John Gadsby, took over the

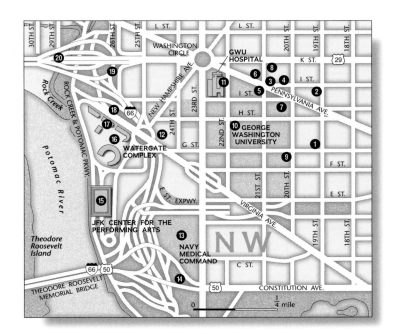

NEIGHBORHOOD LORE

FOGGY BOTTOM. Originally a nickname for the section of the city known as Hamburgh, the term presumably alluded to smoke and fumes from a gas plant, a brewery, and a glass factory once located here. Others insist the name was an allusion to the fog that comes in off the Potomac. A valuable insight into the name was contained in a comment by columnist Jeremiah O'Leary in the *Washington Star* (September 17, 1967), which ran with a historical overview photo of the area taken from the Washington Monument: "I never really understood how Foggy Bottom got its name until I saw the 1885 photo depicting the section as the waterlogged, barren area it once was." O'Leary noted the visible presence of the gas works "which gave Foggy Bottom some of its flavor until recent years." The gas works dominated the neighborhood from 1857 until 1948, when the Washington Gas Light Company converted to the use of natural gas.

site in the mid 1820s and converted the buildings into row houses. Before the conversion the hotel accommodated Andrew Jackson and other politicians, including Jackson confidant Senator John Eaton of Tennessee, who married the innkeeper's spirited daughter, Mrs. Margaret (Peggy O'Neale) Timberlake, after news of her Navy husband's suicide at sea. When Eaton became Jackson's secretary of war, Washington society, led by the wife of Vice President John C. Calhoun, snubbed the couple, resulting in tensions that led to Eaton's resignation. Jackson himself was sympathetic to Peggy because of slanderous charges earlier made against his late wife.

The site was occupied by the Park Lane Apartments (then 2025 I Street) in 1929, and in 1980 the building was converted into an office building (now demolished), which accommodated a diverse array of causes and practitioners attracted by the ambience and reasonable rents. A *Washington City Paper* article by Alan Green (November 6, 1992) listed as sometime tenants various physicians, the American Bar Association, Lyndon Larouche for President, League of Women Voters, the Sons of the American Revolution, the National Society of Descendants of Lords of the Maryland Manors, an acupuncturist, a jazz society, various writers and artists, and an aromatherapist, along with perhaps the most notable of the group, Michael Moore, maker of the film *Roger & Me*, which he sold to Warner Bros. for three million dollars. Green noted that Moore relocated to California in June 1991.

❹ 2017 I Street NW

MONROE HOUSE—James Monroe lived in a house on this spot when elected president. In 1817 Monroe became the first president since the federal government was located in Washington to take his oath of office away from the Capitol, which had been burned by the British in 1814. On the morning of March 4, he joined fellow Virginian and neighbor James Madison for the ride to the inaugural ceremonies at the temporary Brick Capitol on Capitol Hill. Monroe resided here for the first six months of his administration while the restoration of the Executive Mansion, which had also been burned, was completed.

Meteorologist Cleveland Abbe, who headed the U.S. Weather Bureau in the 1890s, lived here from 1877 to 1916. He pioneered daily weather forecasts and lobbied for international standard time agreements. The Washington Arts Club located here in 1916 and continues at this site today. A prominent figure living here was Frances Benjamin Johnston, a famous photographer assigned by President McKinley to document the Spanish-American War and commissioned to document Washington, D.C., schools for an exhibition that appeared at the Paris Exposition in 1900. The Arts Club was her last Washington residence.

5 **2106 Pennsylvania Avenue NW**

MAYOR'S HOUSE—Dr. William B. Magruder, mayor of Washington from 1856 to 1857, lived and died in a house that stood on this site. Magruder was forced to call out the Marines to put down the election riots of 1857. Six individuals were killed in the ensuing action.

6 **2107 Pennsylvania Avenue NW**

SENATOR SAM—Gen. Samuel Houston, governor of Tennessee, United States senator, and twice president of the Republic of Texas (1836-1838 and 1841-1844), resided in a house on this site. Part of a complex of row houses referred to as the Six Buildings, the house also served as the first Navy office of the United States in 1800. In the 1930s, No. 2107 became the address of an A&P grocery store, but by 1973, according to the *Polk's Directory*, there no

Ballplayers. Christian Heurich's Brewery produced both beer and basketball players, shown in this 1935 photo.

Map on page 183

SWAMPY CITY. Many have portrayed the city as a swamp. For example: "Washington lies securely in an area which the guidebooks call an amphitheatre and what you and I call a swamp," said Alistair Cooke in *One Man's America* (1952). It all began with a line attributed to Thomas Jefferson, when he referred to the area as "that Indian swamp in the wilderness."

longer was a 2107 Pennsylvania Avenue NW. There was the legendary Circle Theater at 2103, a repertory movie house, and a bar known as Tammany Hall at 2109. All buildings on the block, save the offices of the Federal Mediation and Conciliation Service, were razed by 1990, and the space formerly occupied by the Six Buildings is now an office building housing offices of the World Bank and the International Finance Corporation.

7 Space bounded by H, I, 20th, and 21st Streets at Pennsylvania Avenue NW

MARKET SPACE—President Jefferson declared this site the Western Market in 1802. It was first located on the north side of Pennsylvania Avenue on the wedge formed with I Street. According to a government report in 1856, the market was relocated that year to 21st and K streets and the triangular space remaining was enclosed with "a handsome iron railing." It was razed in the 1960s.

8 Southeast corner of 21st and K Streets NW

WESTERN MARKET—The market was located on this site from the 1850s to the 1960s. The chronicler of the Columbia Historical Society reported in April 1961 that the decision to close the 32-booth market caused anguish to "Georgetown matrons" and long-time vendors alike, including poultry dealer Preston Burrows, *charcutier francais* George Jacob, Robert Pitle of Hudson Brother's fresh groceries, and Paul L. Muir, "who has the corner on the best imported and domestic cheeses." Joint tenant Safeway Stores was also displaced to make way for an office building.

⑨ 2000 G Street NW

LOST AT SEA—Army Maj. Archibald W. Butt, personal aide to presidents Theodore Roosevelt and William Howard Taft, resided in a house on this site. Major Butt lost his life on the *Titanic* in 1912. The Washington College of Law was located here in the 1920s. It had been founded in 1896 by Ellen Spencer Mussey and Emma M. Gillett, lawyers who wished to provide opportunities for legal education for women at a time when local universities, except Howard, refused to admit women. According to the 1927 *Book of Washington,* graduates of the three-year program received a bachelor of laws degree; additional work led to a master of laws or master of patent law.

⑩ Area roughly bounded by Pennsylvania Avenue, 20th, F, and 23rd Streets NW

CAMPUS OF THE GEORGE WASHINGTON UNIVERSITY, incorporating the Cloyd Heck Marvin Center, Lisner Auditorium and Smith Center—In 1795 President George Washington urged that a national university be established in the nation's capital, and to that end donated 50 shares of stock in the Potomac Company then constructing a canal system along the Potomac River. The commissioners of the District reserved for the university an elevated 19-acre site bounded by 23rd, 25th, C, and E Streets NW (now the site of the Naval Medical Command, near the Department of State). Washington's canal project failed, his stock lost value, and the university remained a vision, never to be established at the designated site.

In 1821, Baptists founded Columbian College at what is today the area bounded by Florida Avenue, Columbia Road, and 14th and 15th Streets NW. The college was seen at the time as a response to Washington's wish and developed as a non-denominational institution over the 19th century into what became The George Washington University in 1904. By that time the institution had established schools for medicine (1824), law (1865), and journalism (1869), among others, and expanded to various downtown locations. The university began to acquire land and facilities in the Foggy Bottom area in 1882 and has never stopped.

Lisner Auditorium was added in 1946 and became an important downtown cultural center. Washingtonian Donald Lief reminded the authors that when Ingrid Bergman inaugurated the Lisner in 1946 with a two-week engagement in "Joan of Lorraine," the audience was integrated, and that although Catholic University's theater was already integrated, "this event really broke the color line in DC entertainment." The manager of the National Theatre had said that a "policy of mixed audiences would be suicidal."

GWU is the largest university in the city, and its rapid expansion over the last several decades has caused some people in the neighborhood to dub it "The Thing That Ate Foggy Bottom." In 1999, the campus contained 74 buildings spread over 18 city blocks, and served over 19,000 students.

⑪ 901 23rd Street NW (the block bounded by 22nd, 23rd, and I Streets NW, Pennsylvania Avenue, and Washington Circle at its southeast corner)

THE GEORGE WASHINGTON UNIVERSITY HOSPITAL— It was here that President Ronald Reagan was brought for emergency surgery after being shot by John Hinckley on March 30, 1981. Each year the hospital admits over 17,000 patients and responds to approximately 250,000 emergency and walk-in requests.

⑫ The 5-sided block bounded by Virginia Avenue, New Hampshire Avenue, and 24th, G, and H Streets NW

TANKS—Until 1954 this was the site of two enormous gas storage tanks owned by the Washington Gas Light Company. With the removal of these tanks and the relocation of the State Department to 23rd and D Streets NW, Foggy Bottom was able to establish itself as a neighborhood with high real estate values.

⑬ West side of 23rd Street between C and E Streets NW

NAVY MEDICAL COMMAND—This area, originally bounded on the west by 24th Street, comprised a 19-acre square first suggested for a national university. Today the headquarters of the Naval Medical Command, this complex includes a domed building, visible from the Kennedy Center and surrounding highways, which was the original naval observatory of the United States. Completed in 1844, it was viewed as America's "Lighthouse in the Sky" by John Quincy Adams, convinced it would make American astronomers internationally competitive. Passers-by would set their watches at noontime when a large black ball dropped from a pole on top of the dome to mark the hour. By the 1870s the observatory housed the world's most powerful telescope, and its grounds had become a popular picnic area. With the construction of the new Naval Observatory north of Georgetown (Massachusetts Avenue at 34th Street) in the 1890s, the grounds were turned over to the Naval Medical Hospital and related institutions.

In front of the observatory (Building 2), above the E Street Expressway at 23rd Street, is a statue dedicated in 1904 of Declaration of Independence signer Benjamin Rush, who founded Dickinson College and co-founded the University of Pennsylvania Medical School and the first American antislavery society. Rush was a strong advocate of the education of women, temperance, and various humanitarian concerns. He is also regarded as the father of American psychiatry. In 1961 Secretary of the Interior Stewart Udall attempted to have the statue moved on loan to Dickinson College in Carlisle, Pennsylvania, but the move was thwarted. As the *Washington Star* put it on November 22, 1961, "Ever since his service in the House...the second-youngest member of President Kennedy's cabinet has made no secret of his belief that Washington has too many statues."

⑭ South of the Naval Medical Center, off 23rd Street NW, to the left of the ramp to Theodore Roosevelt Bridge (I-66)

BRADDOCK'S ROCK—Here can still be seen portions of Braddock's Rock, an enormous rock formation that extended into the Potomac River as a natural quay before extensive landfill operations in the early 20th century pushed back the river's edge. According to writer George Rothwell Brown, "Gen. Braddock never landed there, and never saw it. Still, it is a good, reliable Washington myth." It's true that the doomed British officer, assisted by the young Virginia Col. George Washington, passed through the area in 1755 before being routed by the French and Indians at Fort Duquesne (Pittsburgh). But there's no evidence that he stepped on the rock that bears his name.

⑮ Formerly 25th, 26th, D, and Water Streets NW

KENNEDY CENTER—On this site in 1892 German immigrant Christian Heurich constructed a fireproof brewery that stayed in operation until 1956. During its heyday it produced 100,000 barrels of Senate Beer per year. Historian Margaret N. Burri has recounted that Heurich rode out the Prohibition era, from 1919 to 1933, by running an ice-making plant, then resumed his beer business. Heurich was 90 by then and continued to manage the beer company until he was 102. It was a fortresslike building taking up the whole block, large enough to boast a gymnasium used as a site for early professional basketball.

The production of beer stopped in 1951. In 1955 the Arena Stage Company moved in, and for the next six years the theater that occupied the gym was known as the "Old Vat." The theater moved to new modern quarters at Sixth and M Streets SW in September 1961 and, in honor of its previous location, added its informal "Old Vat Room" to the new facility in 1976.

The prominent plant was razed in the early 1960s to make way for the John F. Kennedy Center for the Performing Arts, a memorial to the slain President that opened on the site in 1971. Historian James M. Goode reminds us that the first site chosen for the Kennedy Center was Seventh Street and Constitution Avenue NW, but this idea was blocked by the Smithsonian, which planned to use it for the future National Air and Space Museum.

16 Virginia Avenue NW and Rock Creek Parkway

WATERGATE COMPLEX— Developed in the 1960s on the former site of the "Old Gas House," part of the works of the Washington Gas Light Company. High-density real estate and highway construction in the l960s completely changed the character of this formerly residential and light industrial area at the junction of Rock Creek and the Potomac once known as Hell's Bottom.

Seldom recalled after history gave the name Watergate a political meaning was that the complex was designed and built as an independent urban community—albeit an expensive one—with its own shops and services.

Near the Watergate complex was once a skating rink, as well as a riding stable that former Washingtonian Pat Hollyfield remembers as the starting point in the late 1920s and early 1930s for a horseback circuit that would lead around the Lincoln Memorial and back.

Comfy Inn. Colonial decor was the norm at the Watergate Inn overlooking the Potomac in Foggy Bottom from 1940 until it was razed to make way for the Kennedy Center in 1966.

NAME LORE

WATERGATE. This name is a direct allusion to the water gate at the edge of the Potomac River, due west of the Lincoln Memorial and flanking the Arlington Memorial Bridge. For many years a barge containing a band shell anchored here for the summer just offshore, to form a free outdoor concert hall. An arc of stairs 206 feet wide was constructed on the riverbank to provide seats. During World War II, a common photographic image of Washington was that of servicemen and their dates in canoes around the band barge. The water gate is still there, but noise from low-flying planes approaching nearby National Airport brought the riverside concerts to an end.

⑰ 2600 Virginia Avenue NW

WATERGATE OFFICE BUILDING—Once the site of the offices of the Democratic National Committee, in which five men in business suits were arrested for illegal entry in the early morning hours of June 17, 1972. There is a small engraved plaque on the sixth floor pinpointing the spot where the Watergate scandal began. The name of this building was used to describe not only the break-in but also the widening circle of events surrounding it.

⑱ 2601 Virginia Avenue NW

ROOM WITH A VIEW—On June 17, 1972, from the balcony of Room 723 of the Howard Johnson Motor Hotel, a cohort spotted police approaching the burglars in the Democratic Party offices at the Watergate.

⑲ 2618-2620 K Street NW

THE PETER MANSIONS—Mr. and Mrs. Thomas Peter resided in houses located here. Mrs. Peter (Martha Parke Custis) was the granddaughter of Martha Washington. General Washington was a guest here and spent his last night in the city—August 5, 1799—at this home.

According to Grace Ecker's *A Portrait of Old George Town* (1951), the Peters used her inheritance from George Washington to build their mansion, Tudor Place, after acquiring the property in 1805. It became one of the most elegant homes in Georgetown and an expression of the Peters' prominence and good fortune (see Tudor Place, p. 217).

Both houses were later the residences of the British ministers Anthony Merry, Francis James Jackson, and David M. Erskine. The last lived here from 1805 to 1809 and was considered a friend of America in the years prior to the War of 1812.

Tom Moore, the poet, visited Mr. and Mrs. Merry in 1804 and penned satirical verses about the early capital city:

...this Embryo Capital, where fancy sees,
Squares in morasses, obelisks in trees,
Which second-sighted seers, even now adorn!
With shrines unbuilt and heroes yet unborn!

㉟ 29th and K Streets NW

PATRIOTIC BRIDGE—Prior to 1800 there was a bridge that crossed Rock Creek at this point. It was said to contain large rocks from each of the 13 original Colonies and a keystone with this motto: "May the Union last as long as this bridge."

D.C.'s Brew. German immigrant Christian Heurich's brewery operated for about 20 years at 1223-1235 20th Street NW, between M and N Streets, until relocating to expanded quarters with double the capacity in Foggy Bottom in 1892. The early brewery depicted here produced up to 50,000 barrels a year.

Map on page 183

Iron Bridge. Shown here about 1880, this iron truss bridge carried M Street across Rock Creek when the stream was still navigable past the bridge.

Georgetown

① Northeast corner of 30th and M Streets NW

UNION TAVERN—Built here in 1796, Union Tavern played host to President John Adams in 1800, when he visited to inspect progress on the nation's new capital before relocating the government from its temporary site in Philadelphia. Adams was roundly welcomed with 17 toasts at the nearby City Tavern, but lodged at the Union. Other guests during that early era included the French minister Talleyrand (who tried to get Napoleon not to sell the Louisiana Purchase to the United States), inventor Robert Fulton, Napoleon's youngest brother Jerome Bonaparte, author Washington Irving, Francis Scott Key, and visitors to the new capital who preferred staying in Georgetown rather than in the largely unbuilt, Washington. George Washington, to the contrary, recorded in his diary on February 8, 1798, that he "dined at the Union Tavern" but he decided to sleep at Thomas Law's, on Capitol Hill.

The Union was a favorite stopping place for congressmen in the early 1820s. Rebuilt in 1836 after a fire, it was a temporary hospital during the Civil War, attended by author Louisa May Alcott among others.

The building survived into the 20th century, only to be replaced in the 1930s by a gas station prior to the construction of the present bank building in 1983.

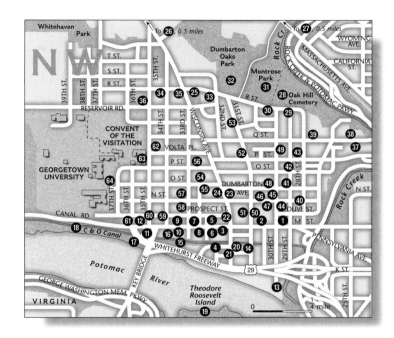

Bucolic Fill-Up. Photographer John Vachon captured this D.C. filling-station-with-painting in 1937 while documenting the fabric of American life, a Depression-era project sponsored by the Farm Security Administration. This station, one of a number of Ott's service stations in the city, was located on the northwest corner of 36th and M Streets NW.

2 3051 M Street NW

OLD STONE HOUSE—Built in 1765 by cabinetmaker Christopher Layman, the Old Stone House is considered the District's oldest surviving structure and only building dating from the pre-Revolutionary era. The late Robert W. Lyle of the Georgetown Branch Library's Peabody Room told the authors that the oft-told story that Pierre Charles L'Enfant and President George Washington met here during the planning and layout of the District of Columbia in 1791 has been disproven. But the building is known to have served a variety of artisans during the 19th century as a combination shop and residence. A used-car dealer occupied the site in the 1950s before the building was purchased for preservation by the National Park Service.

3 3208-3210 M Street NW

VARIED PAST—The earliest parts of this renovated building date from its incarnation as a branch of the Bank of Columbia, operating from 1796 to 1806. Later occupants included the Bureau of Indian Affairs, the Georgetown City Hall, a hotel, and finally the firehouse for Engine Company No. 5 until the 1940s. Declaring it a "rubbish dump" and pigeon shelter, proponents of the National Firefighting Museum and Fire Prevention Center tried to have the city-owned building turned over for a museum in 1972. Instead in 1981 it was sold at auction to become a fast-food franchise and in 1999 is the site of an upscale women's clothing store.

4 Behind the 3200 block of M Street NW down to the Potomac River

CHANGING WATERFRONT—Capitol Traction Company's powerhouse, with its looming twin smokestacks, was the "ultimate symbol of the area's change from seaport to industrial neighborhood," according to historian Kathryn Schneider Smith.

The Georgetown waterfront was peppered with warehouses when the town served as a center for shipping Maryland tobacco. Wharves and a ferry landing lined the Potomac's shore below. Occasional traveling circuses set up here as well, before 3222 M Street NW (now the Georgetown Park shopping mall) became the Georgetown terminus of the horse-drawn streetcars of the Washington and Georgetown Railroad Company in 1862. Later, car barns and works of the successor Capital Traction Company would spread south through Grace Street and along the waterfront. With electrification of the streetcars in the 1890s, industrial power plants replaced warehouses and the B&O Railroad spur was run down the center of K Street in 1910 to deliver coal. Nearly a century later, after streetcar operations ceased around 1962, commercial and residential buildings have replaced industry and a "multi-use" recreational path now occupies the railroad right-of-way to Maryland.

❺ 3219 M Street NW

THORNTON HOUSE—Formerly this site was the residence of Dr. William Thornton, who was trained as a doctor but is better known as the architect of the United States Capitol, Octagon House, and Tudor Place, as well as superintendent of patents from 1802 to his death in 1828. While Thornton's address has been given as 3221 or 3223 M Street, the late Robert W. Lyle of the Georgetown Branch Library's Peabody Room told the authors the spot was definitely 3219.

❻ 3236-40 M Street NW

THE NEW GEORGETOWN—Clyde's restaurant and bar, says restaurant critic Phyllis Richman, "practically invented modern-day Georgetown." A special happy hour menu entitled "Afternoon Delights" inspired songwriter Bill Danoff of the Starland Vocal Band to write a hit song of the same name. The group's gold record still hangs in Clyde's bar.

Industrial Zone. An image of the Georgetown waterfront, taken about 1925. Shown here are the twin-stacked Capital Traction streetcar power-house at the foot of Wisconsin Avenue (center), and the rigs and ramps of the Columbia Concrete and Dredging Company. Key Bridge can be seen in the background. Some of these facilities were razed for the Whitehurst Freeway, completed in 1949. Others persisted until the conversion of the area into office and residential buildings in the last two decades. In his 1932 work, *Rambling Through Washington*, Theodore Dodge Gatchel cautions visitors, "Now just a word of caution to the visitor, who perhaps may expect too much in old Georgetown. There are many lovely homes, quaint churches and a fine college, but there are also factories, shops, garages, tenements, cheap lodging, housing, unsightly stores, vacant lots and disgraceful alleys."

Map on page 193

NAME LORE

WASHINGTON, D.C. The city got its name in 1791 as the new commissioners, Thomas Johnson, Daniel Carroll, and David Stuart, wrote to L'Enfant, "We have agreed that the federal district shall be called 'The Territory of Columbia' and the federal city, 'The City of Washington.'" As George R. Stewart notes in *Names on the Land*, "...the Commissioners had no authority to name the city, but no one questioned their choice, and it was established."

The city was named while its namesake was still very much alive, and evidence suggests that George Washington modestly referred to it as the Federal City.

❼ 3278 M Street NW

SADDLERY—The W.H. Stombock Saddle Shop operated here from 1895 to the 1960s. Started during the days of horse-drawn transportation, the store changed with the times to repair the leather upholstery of automobiles in the 20th century and perform numerous specialty projects. Stombock provided the harness used by crippled President Franklin Roosevelt to pull himself to a standing position during his first inaugural. Dominican Republic dictator Rafael J. Trujillo, who shopped here for his grandson, was reputed to be a heavy spender.

❽ South side of M Street opposite Potomac Street NW

MARKET HOUSE—This location was designated as a market site when Georgetown was formed in 1751, and a frame market-house was constructed here in 1796. At one point the building had two stories with meeting rooms above for use by town officials, in keeping with European tradition. The current building was erected in 1865 and used as a market until the 1930s, after which for a time it was an auto parts store before being leased by the city for renewed use as a market. In 1999 it was Dean & Deluca Georgetown.

❾ North side of M Street, at Bank Street between 33rd and 34th Streets NW

FIRST LOCAL—Site of the Bank of Columbia, established in 1793, the first bank within the limits of the District of Columbia.

❿ 3350 M Street NW

FORREST-MARBURY HOUSE—Dating from about 1788, it was here that Georgetown mayor Uriah Forrest gathered local landowners on March 29, 1791, so that President George Washington could persuade them to sell land for establishment of the nation's capital. The transaction was completed the next day at Suter's Tavern (see Elusive Tavern, p. 202).

William Marbury acquired the house on December 6, 1800. Marbury's suit to retain a local judgeship awarded him by outgoing President John Adams established the doctrine of judicial review in an 1803 Supreme Court decision.

After the house left the family in 1895, a succession of stores and clubs occupied the site. In 1987 it was purchased by a real estate partnership in a condition described by one of its developers as "trashed... about to fall." Now renovated, the building is the Ukranian Embassy.

⑪ M Street NW entrance to Key Bridge

KEY MANSION—Francis Scott Key, author of "The Star-Spangled Banner," resided in a house on a site just to the west of today's Key Bridge from 1805 to 1830. A prominent Washington lawyer, Key was asked to journey to Baltimore in 1814 to plead for the release of an American civilian held there on a British ship. Negotiations were successful, but Key and his friend were prevented from leaving the harbor when the British launched their attack on Fort McHenry. The fort's commander defiantly flew the large garrison flag (now preserved in the Smithsonian) as the British bombardment continued through the night of September 12, 1814. One account says that Key's colleague lost his glasses during his capture and repeatedly asked if Key could still see the flag as the night wore on, thus inspiring the words "O say can you see... that our Flag was still there." Completed after the fort's successful defense, Key's words were quickly circulated and set to music, although not officially adopted as the national anthem until 1931. James M. Goode relates that early in the 20th century this home

Car Barn. Built in 1895 as a station for connecting street car lines, the building at 3600 M Street is today used for offices.

Coal Business. The coal storage terminals operated by Wm. King & Son are an example of the diverse commercial uses of the Georgetown waterfront at the turn of the 20th century.

was the Key Museum, during World War I an American flag factory, and later the target of various abortive preservation efforts. The house finally succumbed to the Whitehurst Freeway ramp in 1949, after President Harry Truman pocket-vetoed a bill to relocate it to the east side of Key Bridge.

The Francis Scott Key Foundation has established and donated to the United States a small park honoring Key about a hundred yards east of the former site of the house.

⑫ 3600 M Street NW

OLD TRANSIT BUILDING—Built as the Georgetown Union Station in 1895, this multi-story structure was a transfer and terminal point for streetcar lines from Virginia and trolley lines from suburban Maryland and downtown Washington. Relocation of secret material from the Pentagon into this building in 1959 required electronic sensors to be installed in the walls. The owner of the 1788 landmark Prospect House at 3508 Prospect Street NW complained of cracks in its walls from the nearby construction. After trolleys were phased out in the 1960s, the building was occupied by O. Roy Chalk's Capital Transit Company, which operated the city's bus lines until local transit was taken over by Metro. The building, now known as the Car Barn, was renovated for offices, with the addition of upper stories and a roof terrace for social events.

⑬ K Street at 30th Street NW

UPSCALE COMPLEX—Washington Harbour, an upscale condominium/retail/office development, opened in 1986. It succeeded the Libby and Wheatly lumberyards. In the early 1900s, cement, barge, and dredging operations occupied the site.

⑭ 1054 31st Street NW

IBM PRIMITIVE—IBM's ancestor company operated here from 1892 to 1911 in the form of inventor Herman Hollerith's Tabulating Machine Company. As a new engineering graduate from Columbia University working at the Census Bureau in 1880, Hollerith became intrigued with speeding up the tabulation of the national census. On a trip to the West in 1884, he observed railroad conductors using punched tickets to identify passengers as a means of thwarting train robbers. According to his daughter's account, when the conductor punched Hollerith's characteristics, "light hair, dark eyes, large nose, medium height," onto his ticket, Hollerith decided "tabulating cards should be punch-photographs of each person in the census." He developed a prototype battery-operated tabulating machine and demonstrated it in 1887 by punching and rapidly tabulating cards with data from Baltimore's death records. The count was achieved by recording electrical currents passing through similarly aligned holes. After further improvements and the invention of a keyboard punch machine, he won the competition for counting the 1890 national census. His approach tabulated the 62.5-million count in only six weeks, months faster than a lower total had been tallied by hand in 1880. More government and business applications followed. Hollerith sold out in 1911 to the company that became the International Business Machines Corporation in 1924.

⑮ 3300 K Street NW

SMELLY PLANT—Coal yards on this site were replaced by the Hopfenmaier animal rendering plant in 1902, ushering in olfactory anguish for over two generations of Georgetowners. In the 1950s the sweet-smelling Washington Flour Company nearby asserted its innocence with an "It's not us" billboard above the

Great Ice Storm. A February 1881 flood caused breaking ice on the Potomac to pack the waterfront, damaging ships at Georgetown and jamming against Long Bridge at 14th Street, diverting floodwaters into downtown Washington.

Map on page 193

WATER STREET. In existence before the American Revolution, this is the oldest street inside the limits of the District of Columbia.

WISCONSIN AVENUE. Why does this street have a dogleg in a city of linear streets? Because it was a road known as the Frederick Pike before it was Wisconsin Avenue...and before Washington was a city.

Whitehurst Freeway. Commercial and residential development of the waterfront eventually replaced the malodorous enterprise; it closed in the summer of 1971.

16 **Southeast corner of 34th Street NW and the C&O Canal**

FOXALL SITE—Site of a home built in 1802 by arms manufacturer Henry Foxall. Here he attended to his shipping, real estate, and banking interests, spread Methodism, and played violin duets with his friend President Thomas Jefferson. After serving as mayor of Georgetown from 1821 to 1823, Foxall died suddenly while on a visit to his native England. By the 1880s the once-elegant house sat amid the coal operations and warehouses of an increasingly industrialized waterfront. It was razed about 1925. In 1987 urban archaeologists on the site uncovered numerous artifacts, the foundations of the original house, and the wall of a turning basin for canal barges. Archaeologists described the dig as a "hot one," both because of the famous subject and the willingness of the developer, National Mid-Atlantic Developers, to finance the work.

17 **3600 K Street NW**

DEMPSEY'S BOATHOUSE—For 58 years, this legendary boathouse operated just north of Key Bridge. It burned down and was replaced by the National Park Service Boating Center (now known as the Thompson Boat Center) at the mouth of Rock Creek in the 1960s. The Columbia Historical Society's chronicler's report for 1960 said that in earlier times "no man could take his lady canoeing unless she was fully dressed, high buttoned shoes and all," and men could canoe only in full-length bathing suits "with tops." Celebrities frequenting the place included 1940s radio star Arthur Godfrey (who met his wife there), songstress Kate Smith, and Gen. George C. Marshall.

18 **Between the C&O Canal and the Potomac River, about 1/2 mile north of Key Bridge and just south of Foundry Brook**

FOUNDRY SITE—Here was the site of Henry Foxall's Columbian Foundry. Foxall relocated from Philadelphia along with the federal government in 1800 and established a munitions business here that supplied the nation's cannon and shot for the War of 1812. The foundry was a prime target for British troops, but after destroying most of the capital's public buildings, the British retired to Baltimore rather than attack Georgetown. Foxall sold the foundry in 1815 to John Mason. There were two large buildings and several appendages, capable of turning out an estimated 300 cannon and 30,000 shot per year. Mason and other owners continued to operate a foundry here for some 50 years, with dwindling success. Late in the century, the site was a distillery, before being largely encompassed within a "huge frame structure used some years ago as an ice-house by the Independent Ice Company," according to a 1907 account. *Rider's Washington* in 1907 reported that a marble slab containing the Ten Commandments had been affixed to the still-standing foundation walls. This act may have had a point. Foxall was once a minister, and his philanthropies included construction of the Foundry Methodist Church downtown, another in the Navy Yard, and a third, for blacks, in Georgetown.

19 **Theodore Roosevelt Island, Potomac River**

OUT ON THE ISLAND—According to *Washington, City & Capital* (1937), this island has been called My Lord's, Barbados, and Analostan Island, but for most of the 19th century it was called Mason's Island, after the family that owned it from 1717 to about 1834. Banker and businessman John Mason built a summer estate there in the 1790s, propagated Merion sheep imported from Spain,

Remember the *Maine*. The flag-draped remains of many of those killed when the U.S.S. *Maine* exploded in Havana harbor carried along M Street in Georgetown on their way to Arlington National Cemetery. This event took place on March 23, 1912, after the ship was raised and these 65 dead were found and brought back to the United States.

Map on page 193

Forest Hall. The building at 1256-1262 Wisconsin Avenue, seen here in the 1940s, served in the 19th century as a social hall and Civil War hospital. By 1991 it had been stripped of its original Greek Revival Ionic facade. Today it is the site of a Gap clothing store.

and operated a ferry to Georgetown long before the river was spanned at that point (he built a causeway to the Virginia side in 1805).

During the Civil War the island was taken over by the Union Army. The 1st U.S. Colored Troops unit was located here, an ironic event given the role of Mason's descendant James as an author of the Fugitive Slave Act and defender of slavery in Congress prior to the Civil War. Mason's elegant home and cultivated grounds decayed over the 19th century as the island became a center for outings by Georgetowners. Popular pastimes after the Civil War were medieval jousting tournaments, where young men tilted to win the favor of the "Queen of Love and Beauty." By the 1890s the recreation-minded found a rod and gun club, baseball and lacrosse fields, a track, boxing matches, and tennis courts, mostly operated by the Columbia Athletic Club. The Washington Gas Light Company purchased the island in 1913 as the possible site for a gas plant, but it was finally acquired in 1931 by the Theodore Roosevelt Association and given to the nation. It is now known officially and popularly as Theodore Roosevelt Island and operated as a memorial and nature preserve by the National Park Service.

⬤20 East side of Wisconsin Avenue, south of M Street NW near the site of Grace Protestant Episcopal Church

ELUSIVE TAVERN—This is one of several nearby locations where Suter's Tavern is supposed to have stood. At the tavern on March 30, 1791, local landowners met George Washington for a second successive day (see Forrest Marbury House, p. 196) and agreed to convey the land needed to establish the Federal Territory. They yielded to Washington's persuasive argument of the day before, that competition among different landowners might preclude any deal altogether. The landowners agreed to convey any land Washington wanted with the understanding that they would receive $66.67

per acre for property needed for streets and public buildings, and retain half the building lots marked off from their former lands. According to Kenneth Bowling's *Creating the Federal City, 1774-1800: Potomac Fever,* Washington's deal gained the federal government "over 500 acres of public reservations for $36,099.35, as well as 10,136 lots and miles of streets at no cost to itself." If Suter's Tavern was in fact on this site, the commissioners—Thomas Johnson, David Stuart, and Daniel Carroll—would also have met here on September 9, 1791, to agree that the territory should be named the "City of Washington."

㉑ 1066 Wisconsin Avenue NW

VIGILANT FIRE COMPANY—Erected in 1844, the current building is the oldest standing firehouse in the District, although it ceased to be used for that purpose in 1883. With additions the building was used as a carpenter shop in the 1890s, and for Samuel C. Palmer's soda-bottling business in the early 1900s. A restaurant is now located here. A marker on the building is inscribed: "Bush, The Old Fire Dog Died of Poison July 15th, 1869. R.I.P."

㉒ 1238 Wisconsin Avenue NW

SITE OF THE OLD WEST WASHINGTON HOTEL—In 1932, during Prohibition, the 83-year-old hotel manager was hauled away by police when liquor was found on the premises. The poor man, who had managed the hotel for nearly 50 years, was able to claim the dubious distinction of being the oldest person arrested in the District for violating the prohibition laws. West Washington was the designation given to Georgetown in the 1880s.

STREET LORE

WHITEHURST FREEWAY. This elevated highway was completed in 1949 by the firm of Alexander and Repass, remarkable for its time because Alexander was black and Repass was white. Their friendship dated back to 1910 when both were linemen on the University of Iowa football team. They completed several successful projects (including the Tidal Basin) in Washington, despite the fact that this was a segregated city. Union rules required separate on-the-job toilet facilities for black laborers, but Archie A. Alexander refused to put up signs for "colored" and "white," agreeing only to signs that read "unskilled" and "skilled," which became its own commentary on opportunities for blacks in the construction trades. After graduating from college with an engineering degree, Alexander himself had been forced to work as a laborer.

Map on page 193

Dumbarton Theater. This archly art nouveau theater—replete with Gothic arch—at 1351 Wisconsin Avenue in Georgetown was designed to show silent films and was called the "Dummy" locally. In about 1950, the old front was taken off, and it was given a fake stone facade and renamed the Georgetown Theater. In 1999 it was a jewelry retail center.

㉓ 1335 Wisconsin Avenue NW

YURCHENKO GETAWAY—On the evening of November 2, 1985, Vitaly Yurchenko, the highest ranking KGB official ever to defect to the United States, had a memorable meal at the Au Pied de Cochon restaurant here. Yurchenko and his CIA escort had come to Georgetown to see a Russian movie. While dining at the restaurant, Yurchenko excused himself from the table, slipped out of the restaurant into the Saturday night crowd and grabbed a cab that took him to the Soviet Embassy. There he renounced his defection. The Yurchenko incident increased business at the restaurant, which immediately introduced a drink called the "Yurchenko shooter," consisting of equal parts Stolichnaya and Grand Marnier.

㉔ 1344 Wisconsin Avenue NW

DOC'S PLACE—Georgetown Pharmacy was operated here for 48 years by Doc Dalinsky, gaining a reputation as a gathering place for notables. In the early years, Doc supplied President Franklin Roosevelt with ice cream and Chesterfield cigarettes during the President's Sunday visits to his son James at 3331 O Street NW. Doc remembered Georgetown neighbor Alger Hiss as a "quiet, hell of a nice fellow," who regularly patronized his soda fountain. Later, Doc's Sundays featured the "11-year free brunch," which started, according to the *Evening Star,* when the Georgetown Inn began to supply coffee, grits, and pastries every Sunday for Dalinsky's chums, including television newsman David Brinkley, columnist Art Buchwald, and novelist Herman Wouk. Actress Lauren Bacall stopped by whenever she was in town. Success became too much for the Sunday morning institution, which ended in 1978. Dalinsky began closing on Sundays in 1979, and sold out in 1984, telling the *Washington Post* later that he'd been "married for 48 years and wanted to see what my wife looked like."

25 Southeast corner of Wisconsin Avenue and R Street NW

FROM RESERVOIR TO LIBRARY—Called Lee's Hill, after its purchase by Revolutionary War-era governor of Maryland Thomas Sim Lee, this was the location of Georgetown's million-gallon-capacity high-level reservoir beginning in 1859. It served areas in Georgetown above 100 feet in elevation. Water was pumped from the aqueduct at Rock Creek Bridge, where two four-foot-wide cast-iron pipes carried Washington's water supply across a bridge that supported Pennsylvania Avenue and connected Georgetown with the city.

The reservoir ceased to be used in 1897 when its operations were replaced by a larger reservoir at Fort Reno. In 1932, the unused structure was replaced by the Georgetown Branch Library.

26 3600 Calvert Street NW

INDUSTRIAL HOME—Located at what is today the site of the Guy Mason Recreation Center was a 19th-century social institution variously called the Poor House, Poor Farm, or Industrial Home. The cornerstone of the Poor House was laid in 1831 by the Georgetown Masonic Lodge. It was intended as a place for indigent boys to learn a trade.

27 Massachusetts Avenue at Observatory Place NW

THE OBSERVATORY—The Navy acquired this land in 1881 and relocated the Naval Observatory here in 1893 from its Foggy Bottom site at 23rd and E Streets NW. Earlier this was the site of Cornelius Barber's Italianate villa, set on picturesque landscaped grounds with ornate gardens and trees, a new fashion for Washington. According to architectural historian Daniel Reiff, the estate integrated "features of the landscape garden with those of a

Georgetown Reservoir. Scene about 1860 at what is now the southeast corner of Wisconsin Avenue and R Street NW. This elevated site was selected in 1859 for the reservoir supplying water to the upper areas of Georgetown. The man in the empty basin on the right with the cane is Montgomery C. Meigs, the army engineer in charge of constructing the D.C. aqueduct system of which the reservoir was a part. Meigs made sure to have himself photographed with his various projects. He also designed the Pension Building (now the National Building Museum) and first suggested the idea of Arlington National Cemetery to Abraham Lincoln.

Map on page 193

CUSTOMS

ON MANNERS AND CUSTOMS. American expatriate David Baillie Warden wrote in 1816 of peculiar customs witnessed in the District:

"Both sexes, whether on horseback or on foot, wear an umbrella in all seasons..."

"At dinner, and at tea parties, the ladies sit together, and seldom mix with the gentlemen, whose conversation naturally turns upon political subjects."

"In almost all houses, toddy is offered to guests a few minutes before dinner."

"Any particular attention to a lady is readily construed into an intention of marriage."

usable farm," and was probably influenced, or even planned, by horticulturist and landscape designer Andrew Jackson Downing while he was developing extensive landscaping plans for the Mall between 1850 and 1852. The house was removed in the 1890s.

The observatory is responsible for making astronomical computations for the United States Navy. It was with the 26-inch telescope of this observatory that Asaph Hall made his discovery of the moons of Mars.

The large house currently on the grounds of the observatory was for many years the residence of the chief of naval operations. During the Ford administration, the house was designated as the official residence of the vice president. The first to move in were Vice President and Mrs. Walter Mondale, who unpacked shortly after the 1977 inauguration. All vice-presidential families since then have used it.

28 R Street NW, opposite 29th and 30th Streets on the heights

OAK HILL CEMETERY—Situated on four natural plateaus, this cemetery was founded in 1848 and features a Gothic Revival chapel designed by James Renwick, Jr., just after he designed the original Smithsonian Castle. Here lie the mortal remains of John Howard Payne (author of "Home, Sweet Home"), banker and civic leader William W. Corcoran (who founded the cemetery and the Corcoran Art Gallery), Edwin M. Stanton (Lincoln's secretary of war), and Union Gen. Jesse Lee Reno, who fell at the battle of South Mountain, Maryland, on September 14, 1862. Fort Reno, a Civil War fort just north of Georgetown, was named in his honor, as was Reno Road NW. Others interred here who were once household names include James G. Blaine, Spencer F. Baird, Lorenzo Dow, Bishop William Pinkney, Joseph Henry, George Brown Goode, Jr., and Arthur P. Gorman. Visitors are urged to bring a biographical dictionary with them.

The Van Ness Mausoleum is modeled after the Temple of Vesta in Rome; it was moved here from the Van Ness family cemetery once located on M Street between Ninth and Tenth Streets NW. The gate house is a miniature Italian villa in brick.

29 2920 R Street NW

DIVERSE CAST OF CHARACTERS—George Washington's great-nephew Corbin Washington married into this property when he united with Eleanor Beall, daughter of original owner Thomas Beall. In 1859 their son was among those held hostage in John Brown's raid on Harpers Ferry. He was freed by United States Army Col. Robert E. Lee, who two years later would command the Confederate forces in the Civil War. Twentieth-century owners have included Gen. William "Wild Bill" Donovan, head of the Office of Strategic Services (precursor of the Central Intelligence Agency) during World War II, and, since 1946, Katharine Graham, publisher of the *Washington Post*.

30 South side of R Street, between 30th Street and Avon Place NW

PETER'S GROVE—This land was also derived from Thomas Beall's original holdings. David Peter built a residence called "Peter's Grove" here about 1808. Several prominent occupants followed, including the British and French ministers, before the house burned in 1860. The land was purchased in 1867 by Henry D. Cooke, brother of financier Jay Cooke. Henry was president of the First National Bank of Washington and soon to become governor of the short-lived Territory of the District of Columbia, formed in 1871.

Cooke subdivided the property west of 30th Street between Q and R into 24 large lots, and named the section Cooke's Park. He met with financial misfortune and was only able to develop four

Market House. The still-standing Georgetown Market shown about 1925.

Map on page 193

Poplar Alley. Georgetown's population was about 25 percent black into the 20th century. Many blacks lived in eastern Georgetown near Mount Zion United Methodist Church at 1334 29th Street. Poplar Alley, shown here in 1942, ran parallel to and between O and P Streets, between 28th and 29th Streets.

large double houses along the north side of Q Street. Cooke and Alexander R. "Boss" Shepherd forever altered the face of the city with a massive public works program but spent the District dry, doubling authorized expenditures with over 20 million dollars in obligations in three years. Cooke resigned in 1873 after his bank failed. The territorial government was replaced in 1874 by a three-person commission.

31 North side of R Street opposite Avon Place NW

MONTROSE PARK—During Georgetown's heyday as a port town, Richard Parrott operated a ropewalk at his home here, which he called Elderslie. (The ropewalk was a long narrow building in which ropes were manufactured by combining and twisting fibers.) The home was renamed Montrose by later owners. The grounds were a favorite area for picnics and rallies. George Washington's Revolutionary War-era tent was erected here to protect the funeral service held for his wartime friend James Maccubbin Lingan, who was killed by a mob in Baltimore for expressing opposition to the War of 1812. Periodically during the 19th and early 20th centuries, the house was vacant, the last period ending in 1910 when "Miss Loulie" Rittenhouse, who had been raised six blocks away in Dumbarton House, campaigned successfully to have Congress purchase the Montrose estate and present it to the District for a public park. The house was then razed, and a monument at the entrance to the park marks Rittenhouse's efforts.

32 3101 R Street NW (entrance at 1703 32nd Street NW)

DUMBARTON OAKS—The estate, bordering Rock Creek Park, is known locally for its splendid gardens, internationally for its pre-Columbian art museum and Byzantine research center, and historically for its role as a World War II meeting site. The land was named by its first owner after a Scottish landmark. In 1801 owner William H. Dorsey, Thomas Jefferson's appointee as judge of the Orphan's Court, built the mansion. South Carolinian John C. Calhoun lived here as speaker of the House when he and his brother owned the home, and the two supposedly entertained Lafayette here in 1824. During the mid 19th century the house sported a then-fashionable mansard roof, since removed; while owned by Edward M. Linthicum it became a District showplace.

After renovating and landscaping the 27-acre estate in the 1920s and 1930s, owners Robert Woods Bliss and his wife, Mildred Barnes Bliss, beneficiaries of the Castoria patent medicine fortune, donated the estate to Harvard University in 1941. Composer Igor Stravinsky, a friend of the Blisses, often premiered his works here and composed his noted "Dumbarton Oaks Concerto" for their 30th anniversary.

Shortly after America's entrance into World War II, parts of the mansion were made available to the federal government, including the National Defense Research Committee headed by Dr. Vannevar Bush. Plans were framed here for the development of the atomic bomb and establishment of the Manhattan Project and the Los Alamos National Laboratory. After the war, the first meetings to attempt to bring the bomb under international control and direct it to peaceful purposes were held here. The mansion was also the site of the Dumbarton Oaks conferences in 1944, when Allied leaders developed plans that were the basis for the United Nations charter in 1945.

㉝ 3238 R Street NW

HALLECK HOUSE—Home of Civil War Union chief of staff Gen. Henry T. Halleck and a summer home after the war for Ulysses S. Grant. Toward the end of the 19th century, according to writer

High-level Reservoir. The Georgetown Branch Library occupies the site at Wisconsin Avenue and R Street once used by a reservoir connected with the Washington Aqueduct System, as shown in this 1864 *Harper's Weekly* illustration.

Map on page 193

Soda Fountain. Heon's Pharmacy, shown here in about 1935, operated at the southeast corner of Wisconsin Avenue and M Street NW.

Grace Ecker, Col. John J. Joyce lived here while debating Ella Wheeler Wilcox, author of the lines, "Laugh, and the world laughs with you/Weep, and you weep alone." (Bartlett's *Familiar Quotations* awards the honor to Wilcox.)

During the 1930s Thomas "Tommy the Cork" Corcoran, Benjamin Cohen, and other New Deal presidential aides and reformers shared the house.

In 1984 the house was bought by Robert Bass, chairman of the National Trust for Historic Preservation, for his residence, along with several adjacent houses.

34 3402 R Street NW

BOB'S PLACE—Residence of H.R. (Bob) Haldeman, key aide to President Richard M. Nixon, before and during the Watergate revelations that shook the nation in the early 1970s.

35 3304-3310 R Street NW

MOUNT HOPE—The original 19th-century home once on this site was called Mount Hope. It served as the Dumbarton Club in the early 1900s. In 1951 writer Grace Ecker remembered its "very good tennis courts" and nine-hole golf course, located "where the suburb of Burleith is now." The home was acquired in 1942 by Washington socialite Mrs. Evalyn Walsh McLean, who was in her final years. She and husband Ned McLean, according to James M. Goode's *Capital Losses,* had "managed to dissipate almost all of the vast McLean and Walsh fortunes, amounting to 100 million dollars, on entertaining and traveling." McLean transferred the name Friendship from her former summer estate farther up Wisconsin Avenue. (She sold that property to the government, and it was razed to build the McLean Gardens apartment complex during World War II.) After her death in 1947, the house was enlarged and the land subdivided.

36 **West side of 34th Street, between Reservoir Road and R Street NW**

BURLEITH—This land was originally part of the 1,000-acre estate of Henry Threlkeld, purchased after his arrival in America from England in 1716. Called Burleith, the tract stretched north from the Potomac and included what became Georgetown University and the neighborhood today called Burleith. Located on this spot in the 19th century was the home of Col. John Cox, an enterprising veteran of the War of 1812, who married a Threlkeld descendent and gained the estate. Georgetown extended its boundaries to include the property in 1823 so Cox could serve as mayor. He stayed on the job a record 22 years, pursuing business and real estate along the way. Georgetown chronicler Grace Ecker remembered the estate as a young ladies' finishing school "kept by the Misses Earle...a quaint and lovely old cream-colored mansion, a portico on its north front, two long piazzas as usual, along the south side of the house." The 20th century brought Western High School, now the Duke Ellington School for the Arts.

37 **2500 Q Street NW**

FRESHMAN DIGS—Apartment residence of future President Gerald Ford while he was a freshman member of the House (1949-51). From this location the Fords moved to northern Virginia.

38 **Behind apartment building at 2511 Q Street NW**

MOUNT ZION CEMETERY—In 1879 Mount Zion United Methodist Church leased a burial ground for blacks here from the Montgomery Street (now Dumbarton United Methodist) Church. It adjoined a cemetery for free blacks operated by the Female Union Band Society, and the two together were known as Mount Zion Cemetery. Burials ceased in 1950. In the 1970s the cemetery was

Washington's Water. The Pennsylvania Avenue Bridge over Rock Creek now has a modern facing, but it still contains the arched conduits of the Washington Aqueduct System, visible in this 1870s photograph. The conduits actually supported the 19th-century bridge, built about 1862. Water was pumped from this location to the high-level reservoir at Wisconsin Avenue and R Street NW.

Map on page 193

NEW NAMES. In 1880, Georgetown became part of Washington and was renamed West Washington. Many of its streets were also renamed to conform with Washington's pattern. For instance, according to *Keim's Illustrated Handbook* (1884), Bridge Street became M Street, Congress Street became 31st Street, and First Street became N Street. Some of the streets that have retained their original names are Dumbarton, Prospect, Olive, Grace, and Potomac.

saved from being replaced by a town house development and placed on the National Register of Historic Places. Today it is being restored and can be interpreted as evidence of the historical role of African Americans in Georgetown's development.

39 2715 Q Street NW

COLONIAL DAMES—Relocated from nearby grounds in 1915 to permit the extension of Q Street across Rock Creek, this house since 1928 has served as the headquarters of the National Colonial Dames of America and is now operated as a museum. The building was the home of Joseph Nourse, first registrar of the treasury, in 1805. Among other duties, Nourse was in charge of moving the government's early financial records from Philadelphia to Washington in 1800. He held office from 1789 to 1829, and played host to Thomas Jefferson and other prominent officials. After 1813 it was the home of Charles Carroll, who operated a paper mill on nearby Rock Creek.

40 2804 N Street NW

TOUCH OF HOLLYWOOD—This was the home of actress Myrna Loy in 1952 while her husband, Howland H. Sargeant, was assistant secretary of state for public affairs and she was serving in UNESCO (United Nations Educational, Scientific, and Cultural Organization).

41 1334 29th Street NW

MOUNT ZION UNITED METHODIST CHURCH—This church building was dedicated in 1884 but has its roots in an earlier church at 27th and P Streets NW, erected in 1816 when black worshippers split off from the nearby Montgomery Street (now Dumbarton

United Methodist) Church, which was segregated. The earlier church burned in 1880. The church was a station on the underground railroad for escaping slaves, with the "vault in the nearby Old Methodist Burying Ground" serving as the hiding place until safe passage to the North was assured. The church also played a key role in educating black children prior to the establishment of public education for Washington, D.C.'s blacks in 1862.

The Mount Zion Church is a vivid reminder that Georgetown had a thriving black community for nearly two centuries. A third of Georgetown's antebellum population was black and half of the blacks were free. Beginning in the 1930s, rapidly rising demand for the town's historic ambience caused an influx of affluent whites, and rising property values encouraged long-time black homeowners to sell. Kathryn Schneider Smith reports in *Washington at Home* that Georgetown's population was 22 percent black in 1940, 13 percent in 1950, and 3 percent in 1960.

42 2906 O Street NW

MOUNT ZION UNITED METHODIST COMMUNITY HOUSE— This simple brick building, erected in 1810-11, served the surrounding black neighborhood as a community center and the first black library in the District. According to the Mount Zion United Methodist Church fact sheet, it was built in the then-popular style of an English medieval cottage and is thought to be the only building of that type remaining in the District. It was the residence of a number of black families in the 19th century, beginning with a freed woman named Abigail Sides who purchased it in 1849. The fact sheet indicates that the church bought the building in 1920, has restored it, and uses it for meetings and the church's historical collections.

Corner Store. United Meat Market occupied the prominent corner building at 30th and M Streets NW when this photo was taken in 1951.

Map on page 193

Early Panorama. View labeled "Bird's-eye view of Georgetown, D.C.," an extremely early photograph of the area by W.M. Smith of Washington.

43 2805 P Street NW (alternate address 1516-1518 28th Street NW)

GUN-BARREL FENCES—The fence around this and adjacent property was supposedly fashioned from surplus gun barrels purchased by the owner after the Mexican War in the 1840s. Gunsmith/businessman Reuben Daw is said to have inserted spear-shaped tips into the open ends of the tapered gun barrels. A variant story is that, as a gunsmith, Daw had a number of left-over or defective barrels and used them for this practical purpose. For many years this was the home of Dean Acheson, Secretary of State under President Truman from 1949 to 1953.

44 1239 30th Street NW

FOR SPITE—Sometimes called the "Spite House," this 11-foot-wide building was supposedly erected in a side yard to shut off a neighbor's view after a squabble.

45 3014 N Street NW

MILLION-DOLLAR HOUSE—Robert Todd Lincoln, son of the President, lived in this house from 1918 until his death in 1926. He served as secretary of war and ambassador to Great Britain. Reynolds Tobacco Company heir Smith Bagley bought the 40-room home for a million dollars in 1976.

46 3038 N Street NW

JACKIE KENNEDY #1—Mrs. John F. Kennedy lived in this house after the President's assassination in 1963. It was owned at the time by Averell Harriman, ambassador to the Soviet Union, secretary of commerce, governor of New York, statesman, and Democratic Party wise man.

47 3017 N Street NW

JACKIE KENNEDY #2—Mrs. John F. Kennedy purchased this house after leaving the Harriman residence and lived here briefly prior to moving to New York.

48 3018 Dumbarton Street NW

MONGREL HOUSE—Although its new owner was reported in a 1978 *Washington Post* article to have described the house as a "mongrel house on a street of mongrels," it apparently sufficed for New Deal-era Supreme Court Justice Felix Frankfurter, Nixon administration Secretary of State Henry Kissinger, and Carter administration Secretary of State Cyrus Vance.

49 1517 30th Street NW

DODGE HOUSE—This was the home of Francis Dodge, Jr., erected about 1850 from designs by Andrew Jackson Downing and Calvert Vaux, introducing the Italianate villa into Georgetown architecture during the vanguard of the Victorian era. Francis' brother Robert erected a similar residence by the team at the same time on the southwest corner of 28th and Q Streets NW. An architectural writer in 1852 cited the houses as models for the community. They were the latest in fashionable design and upscale amenities: "gas lighting, speaking tubes, ventilators, hot and cold water...bathroom, hot-air furnace, and dumbwaiter between dining room and kitchen." Both homes have been altered. Henry D. Cooke occupied the former and built the row of Italianate and French Second Empire-styled double town houses along the north side of Q Street between 30th and 31st Streets (1868-69), supposedly to provide residences for his 12 children.

Reclamation. This 1885 view from the Washington Monument shows largely treeless Roosevelt (then Mason's) Island and semirural lands beyond Georgetown and in Virginia. The light industrial area of Foggy Bottom would eventually be erased by highway and apartment construction, and the areas being reclaimed from the Potomac and graded in the foreground would in time receive a variety of governmental buildings and park areas.

Map on page 193

50 1215 31st Street NW

GEORGETOWN POST OFFICE—Built by the United States government in 1857, this building initially served as the Washington, D.C., custom house, and is a reminder of Georgetown's history as a port entry point for foreign goods. It is a local example of the 19th-century public buildings constructed by the Office of the Architect of the Treasury across the nation, as federal services were extended to newly settled areas. According to the Treasury Department's 1901 history of buildings under its control, the Georgetown Custom House then contained a post office on its first floor and processed $209,000 worth of imports, on which duties of $97,900 were paid to the federal treasury. Now the building is operated as the Georgetown Post Office.

51 1226-1236 31st Street NW

HAMILTON ARMS—For over 40 years the buildings clustered on this site, dating from the early 1800s to the 20th century, comprised the Hamilton Arms Village apartments, named of course after Alexander Hamilton, from whom the owners were said to be descended. The most prominent structure was the former west exchange building of the C&P Telephone Company, built in 1900. Assembled by Col. Milo Hamilton Brinkley in the 1930s, the pink, yellow, and turquoise complex was cited by the *Washington Post* in 1978 as one of Georgetown's "most eccentric landmarks." Until 1958 it sported the Hamilton Arms Coffee House, site of the first salad bar in Washington, and decor created by Brinkley's daughter and self-styled artist-in-residence "Molly" Reid, featuring intricately integrated building parts and tiles illustrating the tale of *Ferdinand the Bull* and characters from *Cinderella* and *Snow White and the Seven Dwarfs*. In a 1969 *Washington Post* article, Reid unabashedly declared the complex an "artwork. The world needs more of this in everyday living. I wanted to get away from plain things." One resident described the result as exuding "a kind of inspirational decadence." Residents claimed it was the location of Georgetown's first pot party in the 1950s and the source of the idea for Clyde's restaurant in the 1960s. Good times came to an end after the Reids died in 1977; the property was upscaled in the 1980s and is now called Hamilton Court.

52 1528 31st Street NW

JFK BACHELOR—John F. Kennedy lived here as a bachelor.

53 1644 31st Street NW

TUDOR PLACE—Merchant Thomas Peter and his wife, Martha, granddaughter of Martha Washington, used her $8,000 bequest from George Washington to buy this city block in 1805. The home, a national historic landmark designed by Dr. William Thornton, descended through the family until 1984 and is now open to the public by appointment. It is noted for its excellently preserved building as well as its gardens. Lafayette and other notables were entertained here, and it is supposedly the last place Robert E. Lee visited in Washington. In the 1880s, according to writer and Tudor Place neighbor Grace Ecker, President Cleveland's wife would drive him to the White House by carriage from their summer home in what is now known as Cleveland Park. On her way home she would stop opposite Tudor Place to watch tennis matches on the courts.

54 32nd and O Streets NW

SCHOOL GROUNDS—The Curtis School building, completed by Adolf Cluss in 1875, incorporated the Linthicum Institute and the Peabody Library, benefactions respectively of Georgetown merchant Eli Ward Linthicum ($50,000 to educate poor white boys) and Massachusetts philanthropist and erstwhile Georgetown

Old Stone House. Today operated by the National Park Service, this venerable house at 3501 M Street NW was being used as a sign-painter's shop when photographed in 1909 by Willard R. Ross.

Map on page 193

Writer's Cottage. Prolific Victorian novelist E.D.E.N. (Emma Dorothy Eliza Nevitte) Southworth lived in this cottage overlooking the Potomac at 36th and Prospect Streets in Georgetown. Her 70, mostly blood-curdling, melodramas included such long-forgotten titles as *Capitola's Peril*, *The Deserted Wife*, and *Cruel at the Grave*. Photo by Willard R. Ross, ca 1909.

resident George Peabody. The building served as a public school until 1946, a Hebrew academy until 1951, and was then razed to make way for the Hyde Elementary School playground.

55 3240 O Street NW

KEY'S CHURCH—St. John's Church, Georgetown Parish dates from 1796 and the present building from 1806, after designs by William Thornton, architect of the U.S. Capitol. Church vestryman Francis Scott Key wrote the inscription on a tablet inside memorializing first rector John J. Sayre. President Thomas Jefferson gave $50 for the building fund.

56 3271 P Street NW

JFK NEWLYWED—Sen. and Mrs. John F. Kennedy moved here when first married in September 1953.

57 3307 N Street NW

PRESIDENT-ELECT—Sen. John F. Kennedy bought this house when Jacqueline Kennedy was in the hospital having their first child, Caroline. The family lived here when JFK was elected to the presidency in 1960. From this house he named his Cabinet members and made sundry announcements on the administration that would change Washington forever. This series of impromptu announcements created a press-corps-in-waiting and more than a few traffic jams.

58 3302 N Street NW

IMPROMPTU PRESS CENTER—During the pre-inaugural period when John F. Kennedy was announcing his appointments, a friendly neighbor named Helen Louise Montgomery lived in this house and took pity on the reporters working the Kennedy story. She invited the frost-bitten reporters in for coffee and offered them the use of her phone. Before it was all over, she had installed two extra phone lines, and the reporters gave her a plaque for the house that read:

> *In the cold winter of 1960-61 this house had an important role in history. From it was flashed to the world news of pre-inaugural announcements by President John F. Kennedy.*
> *Presented by*
> *The grateful newsmen who were given warm haven here by Miss Helen Montgomery and her father, Charles Montgomery.*

59 Southwest corner of Prospect Avenue and 34th Street NW

HALCYON HOUSE—Col. Benjamin Stoddert, an established merchant and landowner, built this house in 1789, dubbing it Halcyon House. In 1793, Stoddert was one of the men who incorporated the Bank of Columbia to finance land transactions for the new capital city. He himself invested heavily in the city's early development. Called to Philadelphia in 1798 to serve as the first secretary of the navy, he helped start the Marine Corps before returning to Washington when the government relocated in 1800. Early federal and local leaders frequented the Stoddert house.

A century later an eccentric owner, Albert Adsit Clemons, a nephew of Mark Twain and a compulsive renovator living in the basement with a carpenter, is said to have spent 40 years in non-stop alterations. According to a Historic American Buildings Survey report, the pair enclosed the entire original building, subdividing the interior rooms, adding new stairwells, a chapel, even a theater and a ballroom, neither of which was ever used. Clemons amassed such a collection of antiques and bric-a-brac that he

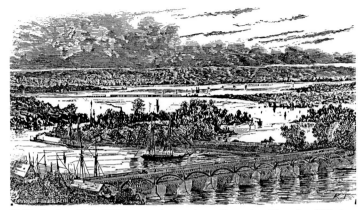

Idyllic Setting. This 1875 engraving captures the natural beauty of Washington's waterfront setting. Aqueduct Bridge, conveying the C&O Canal's extension to Alexandria, is in the foreground at Georgetown, and Mason's (now Roosevelt) Island, linked by causeway to Virginia, is in the center. Long Bridge, precursor to today's 14th Street Bridge, crosses the Potomac in the background.

purchased two nearby houses for storage. He offered apartments for rent, stipulating no children, dogs, or electricity. Reports were that his money came from "New England utilities." A *Washington Times-Herald* report posited that his ample means were "provided by his wife on condition that he stay away from her." Two subsequent occupants spent a decade apiece discovering new rooms-within-rooms and endless corridors before the building was turned into an apartment house in the 1960s. More recently the building has been restored to its 18th-century splendor over a 17-year period by sculptor John Dryfuss and his wife, photographer Mary Noble Ours. The house includes rental apartments and elegant spaces and gardens for events.

60 3508 Prospect Street NW

PROSPECT HOUSE—According to the Historic American Buildings Survey records, this house was built between 1788 and 1793 by James Maccubbin Lingan, a tobacco merchant who had been wounded and captured in the Revolutionary War. He returned to become a prominent civic leader, named by President Washington as customs collector for the Port of Georgetown. (Ironically, he met his demise two decades later when unruly mobs in Baltimore stoned him to death because of his opposition to America's entry into the War of 1812, expressed in a Federalist paper he and others printed.)

Another leading citizen, John Templeton, bought the house from Lingan in 1793. Templeton superintended construction of the Georgetown bridge over the Potomac, ran the Bank of Columbia for a while, and helped arrange the welcome for President John Adams when he arrived with the federal establishment from Philadelphia in 1800. His family owned the house for over 50 years. One occupant after the Civil War was George Upham Morris, whose Union ship, the *Cumberland,* was attacked, rammed, and sunk by the Confederate navy's steel-plated *Merrimac.* Morris survived.

The house was painstakingly restored in the 1930s, and 20th-century occupants included James Forrestal, Secretary of Defense under President Truman. When the Trumans renovated the White House and relocated temporarily to Blair House in 1949, Prospect House was used to entertain official foreign guests, including the Shah of Iran and Field Marshal Viscount Montgomery, raising eyebrows in the press. A *Washington Times-Herald* reporter accused the State Department of sponsoring private parties for VIPs at public expense, favoring "scores of Congressmen and their secretaries," closely akin to "stag entertainments...featuring liquor and feminine companionship as well as honeyed words from back-slapping diplomats."

61 Southwest corner of 36th and Prospect Streets NW

EXORCIZED—Native Washingtonian and author, Mrs. E.D.E.N. (Emma Dorothy Eliza Nevitte) Southworth, resided in a house on this site and died here in 1899. Immensely popular in her day, Southworth and her works long ago drifted out of favor. In her advancing years (after she published 65 books), journalist Frank Carpenter wrote candidly, "She is not, like some writers, subject to fits of genius. She can write at any time, and she turns out books as others manufacture machinery." The Victorian carpenter-Gothic house was demolished in 1941 and replaced in the early 1950s by two small brick houses. This site was used in the 1973 movie *The Exorcist* because of its proximity to a long set of steps (75, in three tiers) made famous by the film. In the movie the house abuts the steps because of a temporary addition built for cinematic effect.

62 Northeast corner of 35th Street and Volta Place NW

VOLTA LABORATORY—Alexander Graham Bell received the $10,000 Volta Award from the French government in 1880 for his invention of the telephone and used it to establish the Volta Laboratory in the carriage house of his parents' house across the street (1527 35th Street NW). Profits from his subsequent invention of a flat phonograph record yielded the present building, home for the Volta Bureau for the Increase and Diffusion of Knowledge relating to the Deaf. Helen Keller turned the first soil in 1893. *Rider's Washington* praised the bureau as the "World's Clearinghouse" on the subject.

Sinclair Lewis, who in 1930 became the first American to win the Nobel Prize for Literature, worked here for $15 a week in 1911, according to his biographer Mark Shorer. Lewis was employed as an "assistant chief clerk and office boy" to editor F. K. Noyes, his former classmate at Yale. Finding the job stifling, Lewis left after six months to write novels, returning to Washington ten years later to write his famous work *Main Street* while he was living at 814 16th Street NW.

63 West side of 35th Street, opposite Volta Place NW

GEORGETOWN VISITATION—Founded in 1799 by the Right Reverend Leonard Neale, the convent here is the oldest in the United States operated by the Order of the Visitation. Its buildings include an academy, convent, and chapel. The 1873 academy building was gutted by fire in 1993 and has been restored.

64 Entrance at 37th and O Streets NW

GEORGETOWN UNIVERSITY—Founded in 1789, Georgetown is the oldest and largest Jesuit institution of learning in this country. Its astronomical observatory, founded in 1848 and located at the rear of the university's field house, was one of two then operating in the District of Columbia, the other being the National Observatory then located at 23rd and E Streets NW.

Crowded Waterways. Stereoview taken by Mathew Brady on July 12, 1864, shows canal boats and government vessels on the C&O Canal hiding from Confederate raiders. The arched conduits of Washington's water supply system then under construction are at lower left. In the background, Aqueduct Bridge carries the canal across the Potomac toward Alexandria.

Map on page 193

Civil War Defenses. In the 1860s, Battery Kemble was one of the dozens of defenses set on the high ground surrounding Washington. Today it is known better as an idyllic park along Chain Bridge Road between Loughboro Road and MacArthur Boulevard NW. Some of Battery Kemble's earthworks are still visible.

Out West

❶ Three Sisters Islands, in the Potomac River above Georgetown

SPAN DENIED—Highway-building interests, which had paved most of Foggy Bottom and unsuccessfully threatened to build a four-lane highway through Glover Archbold Park, proposed a highway bridge across the Potomac with routes through the park, Georgetown University grounds, and into downtown Washington. As construction began on the bridge pilings in 1969, hundreds of local citizens marched and picketed, students occupied the rocky islands on all-night vigils, and lawyers and politicians joined in battle. The bridge and the highway through downtown were defeated.

❷ West side of Foxhall Road at P Street NW

V-GARDENS—*The Foxhall Community at Half Century,* by community resident Richard Conn (1979), recounts that the present playground was the site of World War II victory gardens in which "sixty plots of about 6x10 square feet each" were planted by local residents.

❸ Foxhall Road and P Street NW

SPRING HILL—Near this intersection was the summer house and 60-acre farm of Henry Foxall. It was described in the *Records of the Columbia Historical Society* in 1918, when the landscape was much more open than today, as overlooking "the city, the canal, the Virginia hills, the Aqueduct Bridge over the Potomac, at site of present Key Bridge, and the river for many miles distant." The

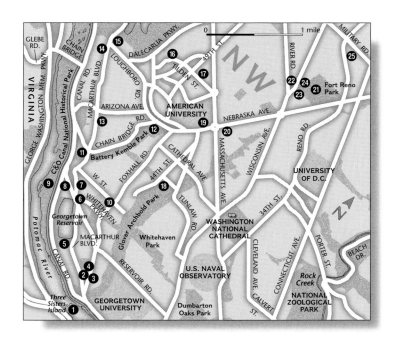

FOXHALL ROAD. Named for Henry Foxall, whose foundry just north of Georgetown supplied the nation's armaments for the War of 1812. An early mistake on a road sign changed the spelling from Foxall to Foxhall, an error that still prevails.

property was sold in 1908 and the house torn down in 1921, before construction of Foxhall Village by Harry K. Boss began in 1927.

④ Foxhall Road across from Volta Place NW

OCTO-GONE—A rare octagonal house was built here about 1800 by Georgetown merchant James M. Lingan. It lasted until about 1932 when it was torn down to make way for the District's Hardy School playground.

⑤ MacArthur Boulevard and Eliot Street NW

CASTLE BY THE LAKE—The castlelike structure built here in 1899 is actually the gatehouse for the reservoir and reflects the emblem of its builders, the Army Corps of Engineers. According to a 1957 *Washington Daily News* article, the gates control 150 million gallons of water a day moving at two feet per second on its way to the McMillan processing plant near Howard University.

⑥ Whitehaven Parkway and MacArthur Boulevard NW

DROVERS TAVERN—Where Our Lady of Victory Roman Catholic Church is located today was the site in the 19th century of Drovers Rest Tavern. Drovers taking cattle to the half-dozen neighborhood slaughterhouses rested here after delivering their charges to the fattening yards at MacArthur Boulevard and Reservoir Road, across from the reservoir.

⑦ U Street and MacArthur Boulevard NW

MACARTHUR THEATER NO MORE—From 1946 to 1997 the MacArthur Theater graced this site until the building was converted into a CVS Pharmacy despite a storm of community opposition. It was a prime feature of the small cluster of commercial enterprises—Safeway, pharmacy, frame shop, gas stations, liquor store, dry cleaner, and frame shop—that with the nearby public library branch helped sustain this neighborhood within a city. Longtime Palisades resident Harold Gray recalled for a *Washington Post* article written by Michael Dolan (March 23, 1997) that with the theater's arrival, it was no longer necessary to "go down to F Street" for a movie. "It was elegant and exciting...a newsreel, then...a cartoon or a short with actors, then the main feature." Over the years offerings and attendance changed. Theater owners threatened to replace it with an office building in 1981, and new owners partitioned it into three units in 1982. Gone was the original 900-seat space with the big screen. With declining business in the 1990s, economic interest prevailed over community sentiment and the theater's fate was sealed.

❽ 4928 Reservoir Road NW

MANOR HOUSE—Thought to have been erected in 1754, the house standing on this site—somewhat altered over the years—was the manor house for Whitehaven Plantation, derived from the 759-acre Whitehaven land grant of 1689 from Maryland's colonial governor, Lord Baltimore. An early resident was Thomas Maine, a horticulturist who frequently entertained Thomas Jefferson. Visiting American expatriate David Baillie Warden described Maine in 1816 as a Scottish immigrant who leased 60 acres and "employs five or six young blacks to cultivate his nursery, whom he nourishes, educates, and rewards with the annual sum of sixty-four dollars." Warden recalled that Maine taught his workers to read and write and that "Joseph Moor, a manumitted black, who lived with him several years, is now a respectable grocer in Georgetown."

C&O Canal. Begun in 1828 as a commercial artery, the 184.5-mile canal today has become a national park, popular with hikers, bicyclists, and anglers.

Map on page 223

STREET LORE

MACARTHUR BOULEVARD. This thoroughfare was named Conduit Road in 1863 because it covered the aqueduct carrying the District's water supply from above the Great Falls of the Potomac. In 1942 Congress and the White House agreed to rename the street for Gen. Douglas MacArthur, who was fighting in the Pacific. Today there is a law on the books that prohibits D.C. streets from being named for living people. In his April 1990 *Washingtonian* article, "The Great Outdoors," Howard Means tells us, "Drive along MacArthur Boulevard west from Georgetown to Great Falls, and you are driving along an old Potomac River bottom. The hills that loom to your right were all carved by water receding as the sea level fell."

❾ Along the Potomac River

WASHINGTON AND GREAT FALLS ELECTRIC RAILWAY— For more than a half-century after 1902, this line—extending from the car barn at Georgetown—offered the most spectacular rail excursion in the metropolitan area. *Rider's Washington* reported in 1924: "After leaving Georgetown the road steadily rises, skirting the verge of the Palisades of the Potomac, with constant picturesque glimpses of the Potomac River and the Chesapeake and Ohio Canal far below...." After a "good view" of Little Falls, Rider continued, "the road runs inland through farming lands until Glen Echo Park is reached." The line crossed high trestles, sometimes at harrowing speeds, according to some memories, and a favorite pastime, as recounted in a report in the *Evening Star* of November 27, 1950, was "standing on the running board and grabbing leaves from the trees as the car speeds through the woods...." Travel anywhere in the District in Rider's day cost eight cents, with a slight additional charge beyond the District line to reach Glen Echo. A 1959 timetable for the streetcar service then operated through the Palisades by D.C. Transit gave the time from Dalecarlia as 30 minutes to 15th Street and New York Avenue and 46 to Union Station. Cars passed at 8-to 20-minute intervals weekdays, more frequently on weekends. Streetcars were discontinued in 1962.

❿ Southwest corner of Foxhall Road and W Street NW

FROM FARM TO COLLEGE—Land now occupied by Mount Vernon College was once grazed by the cows of the Palisades Dairy Farm, operated by the Malone-Shugrue family. While the farm had its chief location on what is now MacArthur Boulevard (see Urban Dairy, p. 227), the family used the house at 2207 Foxhall Road as its summer house, and cows grazed in the surrounding fields. The college relocated here in 1946 from temporary quarters in Garfinkel's department store at 4820 Massachusetts Avenue NW.

⑪ 4954 MacArthur Boulevard NW

CONDUIT ROAD SCHOOL HOUSE—Erected about 1864 as a one-room schoolhouse, this building became the Palisades Branch Library in 1928. By 1932 the librarian reported circulation of over 25,000 volumes. After the library relocated in 1964, the building served as a children's museum, a language school, and in 1999 was the Discovery Creek Children's Museum of Washington.

⑫ Off Chain Bridge Road west of Foxhall Road

BATTERY KEMBLE PARK—Former resident James B. Jenks wrote the authors of remembering "of the times in the 30's when my friends and I walked up the stream from the Conduit Road library to what we called the Old Zoo...with barred cages and ponds made of concrete." A contemporary, Grace McGrath, shared the memory. This site was a serious project by Victor J. Evans, who ran a nationwide patent agency and other enterprises headquartered in the Victor Building at 724-726 Ninth Street NW. According to a letter from his nephew published in the *Potomac Current* (September 21, 1972), Evans bought what is now Battery Kemble Park to preserve it from development in the 1920s, called the spot "Acclimation Park," and started a zoo to provide for "field animals that needed open space, such as zebra, springbok, gnu, and others." Following Evans' death and the stock market crash in 1929, a portion of the property was conveyed to the National Park Service and the zoo animals to the National Zoo. Concrete foundations today mark the site of the zoo buildings, and the park has become a recreational and social center for urban dog owners and their pets.

⑬ 5201 MacArthur Boulevard NW

URBAN DAIRY—The Shugrue family ran the Palisades Dairy Farm on this site for five generations. According to a historical sketch prepared by the Palisades Citizens Association in 1966, the farm was one of several in the area that supplied dairy goods and produce to the city. Today the site is occupied by a branch of First Union Bank.

⑭ Newark Street and Sherier Place NW

BIKER PARK—Between here and the present grounds of the filtration plant was the 1890s location of the International Athletic Park. The park was built during the heyday of the bicycle, and Conduit Road (now MacArthur Boulevard) was a favorite excursion area because of its winding, scenic course and because it was paved and maintained by Army engineers to protect the city's water supply in the aqueduct below. In addition to competitions on Conduit Road, races were held day and night on dirt and board tracks before crowds in the grandstands.

⑮ Northeast corner of Loughborough Road and MacArthur Boulevard NW

INSTITUTIONAL SITE—A Victorian-era mansard-roofed building remains behind the present Sibley Memorial Hospital as a remnant of the former National Training School for Girls that existed here from 1893 (renamed from Reform School for Girls in 1912). *Washington, City and Capital* (1937) noted there were "four buildings on 20 acres of land and a staff of 24 teachers who have the care of about 50 girls on parole from the juvenile court." Sibley Hospital was built over part of the site in 1959 following transfer of 12 acres for the purpose authorized by act of Congress. Patients were transferred from the old hospital on North Capitol Street in May 1961.

STREET LORE

TUNLAW ROAD. Walnut spelled backward. Several stories have circulated about this odd street name. The most prevalent is that Gen. Ulysses S. Grant suggested the name to Thomas L. Hume, whose land had a memorable walnut tree on it. Another is that it was a Civil War code name for the Union Army route out of Washington, which ran through a walnut grove. One story we can put to rest is that the street was formerly known as Walnut Street for a grove of walnut trees on the property; the trees supposedly were claimed by the U.S. government in 1917 during World War I to be turned into rifle stocks. Since the name Tunlaw appears in city street directories beginning in the 1880s, this story clearly is bogus.

During the Civil War, Battery Vermont was located here as part of the defense for the city of Washington.

16 5101 Tilden Street NW

HOSTESS WITH THE MOSTEST—Perle Mesta, famed Washington hostess in the 1940s and 1950s, lived here. Nicknamed the "hostess with the mostest," she was played by Ethel Merman in the hit musical *Call Me Madam.*

17 4801 Tilden Street NW

NIXON #1—This was the first District residence of Richard and Pat Nixon. They moved from an Alexandria, Virginia, garden apartment in 1951, shortly after his election to the Senate, and stayed for six years.

18 4308 Forest Lane NW

NIXON #2—Richard and Pat Nixon moved into this 21-room stone Tudor house in 1957 while he served as vice president.

19 Intersection of Massachusetts and Nebraska Avenues NW

A.U.—The American University was established here as a postgraduate coed institution in 1893 by bishops of the Methodist Episcopal Church. Its current enrollment is about 11,000 and the campus covers 84 acres. Since the campus was not yet fully occupied when World War I began, it became a training center for Army chemical warfare units. According to the 1937 guide *Washington, City & Capital,* the poisonous lewisite gas was developed there and "pits for chemicals and explosives" were still evident in the 1930s. The grounds and facilities were again used by the military during World War II. When an artillery shell was unearthed in 1993, resident fears unleashed a 22-million-dollar three-year effort by Army engineers to locate ordnance left behind after the wars. On March 17, 1999, the *Washington Post* reported the third and what was hoped to be the last phase of "Operation Safe Removal," behind the South Korean Ambassador's residence on nearby Glenbrook Road.

20 3801 Nebraska Avenue NW

EARLY SEMINARY—Mount Vernon Seminary, a boarding school for women, relocated here from downtown Washington in 1917. In 1942 the property was taken over by the Navy, forcing the school to relocate temporarily to the upper stories of Garfinkel's department store at 4820 Massachusetts Avenue NW. Judith Beck Helm's *Tenleytown, D.C.* relates that over 5,000 Navy WAVES worked at the Navy facility and lived in nearby buildings flanking Massachusetts Avenue. One of the officers, stationed there for four years, wrote the authors that the mission was intelligence and that hers was the only shore unit to get a commendation, for its work reading Japanese codes. She recalled that favorite social spots were the "Hot Shoppe on Wisconsin Avenue south of Nebraska for dinner, and a bar on Warren St. I believe just east of Wisconsin, where we went for beer and sandwiches after work. We worked watches: a week from 4 to 12 p.m., a week from 12 to 8 a.m., and a week from 8 to 4, after which we got 48 hours off." The Navy has retained the site as the Naval Security Station.

21 Area bounded roughly by Reno Road, Nebraska Avenue, and Chesapeake and Fessenden Streets NW

FORT RENO—This tract was the site during the Civil War of Fort Pennsylvania. Its name was changed to Fort Reno after the death of Maj. Gen. Jesse Lee Reno at the Battle of South Mountain in Maryland. It was strategically located on the highest point in the District and positioned along the Frederick Pike (now Wisconsin Avenue), one of two routes downtown from the north (Seventh Street was the other). The fort's dozen heavy guns and 3,000 troops made it the most formidable of several protecting the District. While undermanned at the time, its apparent strength persuaded Confederate Gen. Jubal Early's forces to concentrate on Fort Stevens instead during Early's unsuccessful attack of July 10-12, 1864.

Historian Judith Beck Helm relates that many freed blacks acquired lots and built houses on and around the property of the fort after the war, attracted by "the availability of cleared land; a growing number of families, farms, and businesses that would employ them; a school; and eventually three churches." Interdependent black and white communities with segregated institutions evolved, as was the prevailing pattern.

At the turn of the century the high grounds of Fort Reno were given over to the District's water supply and distribution system with the construction of two covered reservoirs. A 60-foot-high water tower, completed in 1903, is a landmark visible for miles around. An additional tower and reservoir were added 20 years later. The elevation of the site also attracted many of the metropolitan area's television transmitters.

Alice Deal Junior High School and Woodrow Wilson High School were opened on the grounds in the 1930s as whites-only schools, two decades before integrated schools came to the District. Rising land values and restrictive real estate practices squeezed most black homeowners out of the area by the 1950s, an ironic change from the promising conditions facing the freed blacks who had come to Fort Reno a century earlier.

Today Fort Reno's grounds serve as the site of recreational activities ranging from weekend soccer matches to summer evening rock concerts.

Map on page 223

BRIDGE LORE

CHAIN BRIDGE. The present bridge is the eighth built since 1797 at the Potomac narrows above Washington. Donald Beekman Myer's book, *Bridges and the City of Washington* (1983), tells us that the third, built in 1810, was suspended by two chains of thick iron bars from two stone towers, thus giving the name to all its successors. Floods ravaged the site, requiring new suspension-type bridges in 1812, 1815, and 1840. Stone piers constructed in the 1850s have supported all subsequent bridges there including the current one, built in 1939, which clears the river by some 45 feet. Many's the time area residents have flocked to the bridge during a flood, to see the raging water come to within 15 to 20 feet from the base of the roadway and the wild river stretching from its normal 100-foot-wide channel to cover the more than 1,300-foot breadth of the gorge.

 Wisconsin Avenue and River Road NW

TENNALLY'S TAVERN—Just north of this intersection was the location of John Tennally's Tavern about 1790, in local historian Judith Beck Helm's opinion the "first business establishment above Georgetown where food and liquors could be bought" on the route north to Fredericktown (Frederick), Maryland. Helm writes that another tavern was built in 1805 by Henry Riszner in the southwest corner. Residents of the high ground here could observe the smoke when the British burned the federal buildings downtown in August 1814, and one story has Dolley Madison taking refuge in a tavern in "Tennallytown," possibly Riszner's, on her flight from the city. After 1829 a toll booth was located near this intersection, possibly adjacent to one of the taverns, where through traffic was taxed to pay for the improved road to Frederick and the intersection with the National Road (today's U.S. Route 40), the nation's chief east-west artery. Riszner's was replaced by Godfrey Conrad's Tavern in the 1850s, a three-story building later purchased by Washingtonian brewer Christian Heurich, and then was William Achterkirchen's saloon. During Prohibition it was an auto parts store and filling station for cars, instead of people. In 1939 it was razed to make way for a Sears, Roebuck and Company store. Sears occupied the site until the mid-1990s, when Hechinger's relocated there from across the street.

Helm recounts in *Washington at Home* that the village's name was spelled and pronounced various ways—Tennallytown, Tennellytown—until the post office stipulated in 1920 that the official name would be Tenleytown.

23 **4539 Wisconsin Avenue NW**

SEVENTH PRECINCT—Between 1905 and 1926, this was the site of the police sub-station of the 7th Precinct in Georgetown. After the police left, the building was used as a public library branch until 1959, later as the Waffle House diner and then as a Domino's Pizza facility.

㉔ 4555 Wisconsin Avenue NW

ROOFTOP PARKING—The locally established Giant supermarket company opened an innovative store here in 1939 with parking on the roof. It later was the site of Hechinger's, a Washington-based homeowners' supply company that relocated across Wisconsin Avenue in the mid-1990s. The adjacent property to the south, formerly the lumberyard, was once the site of the Tennally-Lightfoot House, possibly lived in by John Tennally, whose tavern across the street gave its name to the community. The house was razed in the 1950s.

㉕ 3916 Jenifer Street NW

POET IN RESIDENCE—Residence of poet Randall Jarrell during his tenure as poet to the Library of Congress (1956-58).

STREET LORE

LOUGHBORO ROAD. This street was named for Nathan Loughborough, who bought a home in Georgetown when the government moved to Washington in 1800. The *Washington Star* looked into the variation in spelling between the man and the road in 1956 and came up with this report: "Just when the name was shortened to Loughboro is not clear, but it is not the first corruption of the Loughborough name. When he served as Comptroller of the Treasury he found it necessary to change his name temporarily to 'Luffborough' because of the confusion in mail deliveries addressed to him that way."

Map on page 223

Klingle Bridge
Washington D.C.
West Side South End
W.P.Thurston Co. Inc. Contrs.
September 1 1931

Modern Bridge. Connecticut Avenue's Klingle Bridge under construction in 1931.

Cleveland Park, Woodley Park, and Vicinity

1 **National Zoological Park (popularly known as the National Zoo), entrance at 3000 Connecticut Avenue NW**

ZOO STORIES—Once the home of forest fire prevention mascot Smokey Bear. The first Smokey was brought here as a cub in 1950 after being rescued from a forest fire in New Mexico. Early in his stay it was reported that he received as much fan mail as President Eisenhower, some 600,000 letters per year. (The Forest Service's Smokey of poster fame was created in 1944.)

The zoo boasts many attractions, ranging from the giant panda Hsing-Hsing to a varied lot of animal-oriented architectural details and sculpture, including the "Giant Anteater," a product of the New Deal's Works Progress Administration and the work of Erwin French Springweiler. It was completed in 1938.

Now the National Zoological Park is transforming itself into a BioPark, according to its brochure, focusing "on the interdependence of all life forms," with the aim of increasing awareness "of the delicate balance of the earth's ecosystems and of our vital role in conserving and protecting them."

2 **Connecticut Avenue and Ordway Street NW**

EARLY STRIP MALL—Site of the Park and Shop, described by Kathleen Sinclair Wood in *Washington at Home* (1988) as an early prototype for "today's ubiquitous strip shopping centers." It was designed by Arthur B. Heaton in 1930 in a patriotic colonial revival style. According to architectural historian Richard W. Longstreth,

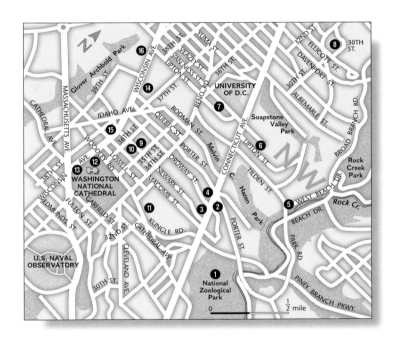

War and Peace. The Peace Cross, located behind St. Alban's Church at the northeast corner of Wisconsin and Massachusetts Avenues NW, commemorates the conclusion of the Spanish-American War in 1898.

the Park and Shop was the first influential establishment to combine an integrated group of separate businesses with off-street parking. In 1991 neighborhood preservationists saved it from destruction and it underwent an extensive renovation.

3 3426 Connecticut Avenue NW

UPTOWN THEATRE—One of the area's few remaining art deco movie houses, located on the site of an old granite quarry. The salt-and-pepper stone from the quarry was used in many of the buildings that now are neighbors of the National Zoo.

The Uptown opened in 1936 after construction from a design by noted theater architect John Jacob Zinc. It was established as a "move over" house to show second runs of films that had debuted at the Ontario Theatre on Columbia Road. The theater's first feature was *Cain and Mabel*, starring Marion Davies and Clark Gable.

A big hit at this theater can snarl the neighborhood in traffic. When *Star Wars* played here in 1977, the *Washington Post* called it "the movie that ate Cleveland Park." In 1988 the *Hollywood Reporter* conducted a survey to establish the best single-screen movie theaters in America. The Uptown, with its large screen and superior acoustics, came in second.

4 3524 Connecticut Avenue NW

YENCHING PALACE—This restaurant played an important role in the warming of relations between the U.S. and China in the 1970s. Visiting Chinese ping-pong players dined here during their American tour, and in April 1972, when the two Chinese giant pandas were brought to the National Zoo, a press conference was held here.

The 1940s-style blue mirrors have reflected more than their share of intrigue. Perhaps the most momentous came in the fall of 1962 during the Cuban missile crisis, when two men began meeting here secretly. One was John Scali, ABC newsman and later

U.S. ambassador to the United Nations, the other was Aleksander Fomin of the Soviet Embassy. Known only to a few people in the White House and the Kremlin, Scali represented President Kennedy and Fomin represented Premier Khrushchev. With their first and last meetings held here, the two men worked out the terms that ended the crisis that brought the two superpowers to the brink of war.

A reader from the neighborhood, Carl A. Saperstein, noted that the Yenching was started by a chef from the Peking, farther up Connecticut, "the first Northern Chinese restaurant in town." It was first called the Peking Palace. A lawsuit developed over the rights to name similar dishes, "focusing on '00/Zero Zero Soup'. Initially one title was used in both restaurants, but as part of the settlement one restaurant called it '00,' the other 'Zero Zero.'"

⑤ Rock Creek Park at Beach Drive and Tilden Street NW

PIERCE MILL—A preserved, restored, and workable mill now under the care of the National Park Service. It was a productive mill from 1820 to 1897, capable of stone-grinding 70 bushels of grain a day. The significance of the mill to the body of water that it was built on was neatly spelled out in the 1932 *Washington Sketch Book* by J. Frederick and Helen Essary: "Rock Creek was originally a racing stream, deep enough where it flowed into the Potomac to anchor seagoing ships while they received their cargoes of tobacco. But the Potomac changed its channel. Gradually the little harbor filled up. Once the force of the stream turned the wheels of many flour mills. Now only Pierce Mill is left...."

⑥ 2900 Van Ness Street NW

THE ACADEMY—In the 1920s this site was the home of the Academy of the Holy Cross, a Catholic institution for the education of young women under the care of the Sisters of the Holy Cross. It later became Dumbarton College. The main building is now occupied by Howard University Law School, and the former chemistry building at 2955 Upton Street NW has been used since 1973 by the Edmund Burke School, a college preparatory school established in 1965.

⑦ Between Upton and Van Ness Streets from Connecticut Avenue on the east to Reno Road on the west

STANDARDS—The federal government assembled various properties about 1900 to form the grounds for the National Bureau of Standards, which operated a campuslike complex of laboratories and offices here until relocating to the suburbs in the 1960s. The standards adopted here were used in commerce, science, manufacturing, and engineering. One of the properties, at the intersection of Van Ness and Reno, was the former summer estate of James Wormley, a free black who ran one of the most prominent hotels in 19th-century Washington. Wormley purchased a number of tracts and built three houses in this area.

The Bureau of Standards expanded between and during the world wars and eventually occupied some 28 buildings covering a 70-acre area as far north as Yuma Street. These buildings were razed in the 1980s. Now the area north of Van Ness Street is occupied by the campus of the University of the District of Columbia and other new structures. To the south along Connecticut Avenue is Intelsat, completed in 1985 and one of the first computer-oriented "smart" buildings in the city, designed to be energy-efficient. Embassies now line a street called International Drive; they include those of the governments of Israel, Jordan, Swaziland, Bahrain, and Ghana.

STREET LORE

RENO ROAD. Named for Fort Reno, which was in the vicinity, it illustrates the point that a street called a "road" is almost always named for some prominent local feature. In the late 1950s, a serious attempt was made to get this street renamed Washington Avenue for the state of Washington, but the move was thwarted.

8 4936 (formerly 4926) 30th Place NW

G-MAN HOME—J. Edgar Hoover, powerful and long-serving head of the Federal Bureau of Investigation, bought this house in 1939 and lived here until his death in 1972. In 1895 he was born in a house once standing at 413 Seward Square SE, and lived there with his mother until her death in 1938. A reader, Carl A. Saperstein, sent the authors an interesting anecdote about the address that speaks to everyday folks prevailing over the high and mighty. He grew up at nearby 4926 30th Street, where mail for Mr. Hoover was often misdelivered. His father, who was there first, insisted that Hoover change his address, and Hoover eventually did, to 4936 30th Place. Saperstein pointed out as well that Lyndon B. Johnson lived at 4921 30th Place when he was Senate majority leader in the 1950s and debated many a political issue with his cronies (then referred to as his "Board of Education") late on summer nights sitting in his screened-in back porch. "This was before air-conditioning was in general use and it was a necessity to keep the windows open for ventilation. As you might expect sleeping was most difficult."

9 3501 Newark Street NW

ROSEDALE—Older than President Cleveland's Red Top Farm next door, this 1793-1794 farmhouse is still standing. Called Rosedale, it was built by Gen. Uriah Forrest, a friend of George Washington. In 1973 the residence was designated a District of Columbia landmark and listed on the National Register of Historic Places. The site is now owned by Youth for Understanding, sponsor of an international youth exchange program.

10 3542 Newark Street NW

RED TOP—Former site of Grover Cleveland's 27-acre retreat from the downtown heat. Originally called Oak View, the house was christened Red Top after Cleveland remodeled it with Victorian porches, towers, and balconies, and painted the roof red. The first Democratic President in 24 years, he needed such a place to get away from office seekers. Cleveland bought the property for $21,000 in 1886 and—after putting about $10,000 into it—sold it to developers for $140,000 in 1890. The home is no longer there.

⑪ 3225 Woodley Road NW

TWIN OAKS—Once the summer home of Gardiner G. Hubbard, father-in-law of Alexander Graham Bell, who taught and later married Hubbard's deaf daughter Mabel. Hubbard helped Bell develop his telephone enterprises and was the first president of the National Geographic Society, serving from 1888 to 1897. The house is the only remaining example of the Cleveland Park summer residence.

⑫ Wisconsin Avenue NW, between Massachusetts Avenue and Woodley Road

WASHINGTON NATIONAL CATHEDRAL, THE CATHEDRAL OF SAINTS PETER AND PAUL—Although the land for a cathedral was set aside in the later 19th century, work did not begin on the building until the 20th. Theodore Roosevelt officiated at the groundbreaking in 1907, using the same silver trowel that George Washington used to lay the cornerstone of the Capitol. The construction of this 20th-century version of medieval Gothic architecture was completed on September 28, 1990. Before the cathedral, there was a frame house on this location that belonged to Joseph Nourse, an Englishman born in 1754 who served as the registrar of the Treasury from 1789 to 1829. He called his estate Mount Alban

Standards. The Bureau of Standards buildings were razed after the bureau relocated to suburban Maryland beginning in 1966. The campus depicted here featured such structures as the Hydraulics Building, the X-ray Plant, and the Sound Reverberation Chamber. Old-time Washingtonians were amused by the fact that the laboratories inside cost more to build than the buildings that housed them.

Map on page 233

after the Mount Saint Alban of his Hertfordshire birthplace.

Woodrow Wilson is interred here in a marble sarcophagus, the only president buried in the District of Columbia (Taft and Kennedy are buried in Arlington National Cemetery). The remains of Bishop Claggett, the first bishop of the Protestant Episcopal Church to be consecrated in the United States, and of Bishop Satterlee, the first bishop of Washington and founder of the cathedral, are also here. Adm. George Dewey is here, as well as Helen Keller and Anne Sullivan.

Although affiliated with the Episcopal Church, it is known as the National Cathedral and is used for services by many denominations and for ceremonies that are national in nature.

Rocks brought back from the moon are incorporated in the stained-glass window dedicated to space exploration.

13 On the grounds of the Washington National Cathedral on Wisconsin Avenue NW

BRADDOCK'S BOULDER—This memorial was erected in 1907 by the Society of Colonial Wars, to commemorate the march of the colonial forces under General Braddock past this spot. They were on their way to Fort Duquesne (now Pittsburgh) to protect the frontier against the French and Indians.

14 3825 Wisconsin Avenue NW

SIDWELL FRIENDS—The stone house used by Sidwell Friends School as an administration building was erected about 1820 by Charles and Rebecca Nourse. Charles, given the property by his father, Joseph, a long-time Treasury Department official, built the house with stone from local quarries, possibly on his own land, that extended east nearly to Rock Creek.

⑮ West side of Wisconsin Avenue at intersection with Macomb Street NW

McLEAN GARDENS—Former site of the 70-acre estate of *Washington Post* owner John R. McLean, acquired in 1898. He named it Friendship because part of it was included in the land grant of 1713 made by Charles Calvert, Lord Baltimore, to James A. Stoddert and Thomas Addison, close acquaintances who named their tract Friendship. Before 1898 the property was a Jesuit retreat for Georgetown College. The McLeans added a 30-foot-high water tower at the Porter Street entrance to the property that included the neighborhood's town clock.

McLean's son, Ned, who was married to socialite Evalyn Walsh, transformed the house into one of the city's premier expressions of lavish living and entertaining during the 1920s. Judith Beck Helm's book, *Tenleytown, D.C.,* relates that the McLean's exotic cars, animals, and parties ruled the day. Their menagerie included over three dozen dogs, peacocks, geese, sheep, a burro, a monkey, and Tom Thumb's miniature horses (with coach). The Ringling Brothers circus was brought in to entertain their son, Vinson. A nine-hole golf course and enormous swimming pool supported an endless round of gala parties, especially during the Harding Administration.

After Ned's death in 1941, Evalyn sold the estate to the federal government for one million dollars. Garden apartments were built to house approximately 3,500 civilian workers during World War II, and the tract became known as McLean Gardens. In 1953 part of the grounds were sold off and converted to a 3 1/2-acre shopping center at Macomb Street. Twenty-five years later residents, community figures, and developers combined to renovate the remaining McLean Gardens apartments and convert them to condominiums.

STREET LORE

KLINGLE ROAD. A move in 1961 to get this renamed Tennessee Avenue by a representative from that state failed. It was argued, unsuccessfully, that the existing Tennessee Avenue (running from 15th Street NE to Lincoln Park) did not do the state full justice.

---

⑯ 3900 Wisconsin Avenue NW

FANNIE MAE—When the Equitable Life Building was erected in 1958 it was modeled after the colonial capitol building in Williamsburg, Virginia. It is now the headquarters of the Federal National Mortgage Association—popularly known as Fannie Mae.

Tourist Haven. This 1950s postcard shows the continued attraction of Washington, D.C. Hall's "Homey" House For Tourists, seen here, was located at 2357 Rhode Island Avenue, N.E. Homes with rooms to rent for tourists have been a Washington staple since the middle of the 19th century.

HALL'S "HOMEY" HOUSE
For Tourists
2357 RHODE ISLAND AVENUE, N. E.
WASHINGTON, D. C.

Private home conveniently located on main route between New York and the South. 8 minutes from heart of city. Hot and cold running water. 12 bedrooms, 4 baths, free parking. Rates $1.00 per person, more than one in room. Parties up to 25 solicited.

East of Rock Creek Park to Georgia Avenue

1 **1212 T Street NW**

DUKE'S HOUSE—A man many call one of the world's great composers, Edward "Duke" Ellington, grew up in this house. (He was born at 2121 Ward Place NW.) At the turn of the 20th century, the area now referred to as Shaw, centered at 12th and R Streets NW, was a thriving cultural, commercial, and residential center for Washington's black population. Marcia M. Greenlee in *Washington at Home* notes that Ellington worked as a soda jerk and played the piano at such spots as Jack's Place and the Poodledog Cabaret. By 1920 he had formed a popular society band, and by 1930 he relocated permanently to Harlem's Cotton Club in New York City.

2 **1839 13th Street NW**

WHITELAW HOTEL—Brought back to life in the 1990s after closing in the 1970s, the Whitelaw Hotel is credited in James M. Goode's *Best Addresses* with having been the first "apartment hotel in the nation's capital and one of the first in the United States" to be "developed, financed, designed, and built by blacks," when it first opened in 1919. Goode notes that its developer and namesake, John Whitelaw Lewis, came to Washington as a laborer in 1894 and went on to develop the Industrial Savings Bank, another successful and early black-owned enterprise. Designed by Washington architect Isaiah T. Hatton, the building, according to Goode, served for many decades as the city's only luxury apartment house for blacks. It was about equally divided between hotel rooms

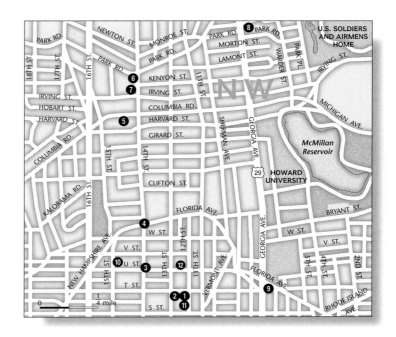

HARVARD STREET. This was part of the original Columbia Heights subdivision, in which many of the streets were given the names of colleges and universities. When the District began alphabetizing the streets around the turn of the century, Harvard fit in but others did not. Yale was changed to Fairmont, Princeton to Girard, and Dartmouth to Lamont. Princeton survived as Princeton Lane (originally Princeton Street) in the Park View area east of Columbia Heights. At the same time, Columbia Street became Columbia Road. Once this street was called Tayloe's Road, or Tayloe's Lane, after Gen. John Tayloe, the wealthy Virginia landowner who built Octagon House at New York Avenue and 18th Street NW.

and one-bedroom apartments, all with the most modern amenities, and its appointments included a ladies' parlor, a billiard room, convenience shops, and a grandly detailed 100-seat dining room that could be converted into a ballroom and used for debutante balls and other elegant events. A *Washington Post* article (November 12, 1992) noted that its hotel register listed a galaxy of notable African Americans including future Supreme Court jurist Thurgood Marshall, boxing champion Joe Lewis, and musicians Paul Robeson, Louis Armstrong, and Cab Calloway. Journalist Nancy L. Ross noted Calloway's comment that the Whitelaw was one of the few hotels where African Americans could stay in the then-segregated city. The building has been renovated and restored by the nonprofit developer Manna Inc. and divided into 35 apartments.

3 Intersection of 14th and U Streets NW

TURMOIL—Once the thriving center of local black commerce and social life, this was the site at which riots began on April 4, 1968, at about 9:30 p.m., when word reached Washington of the assassination of the Rev. Martin Luther King, Jr. In *Ten Blocks From the White House*, the *Washington Post*'s book on the riots, this is how the moment was described: "The feared response wasn't long in coming. It began in the area around the intersection of 14th and U streets NW—a bus transfer hub, one of Washington's most congested inner-city intersections, a place notorious for tensions and trouble." The official *Report on Civil Disturbances* noted that the first violent act was the breaking of a Safeway store window at 14th and Chapin Streets NW.

Before the riots ended, fire had destroyed shops along H Street NE and 7th and 14th Streets NW. Ten people were killed and 7,470 arrested.

This area has been revitalized in the 1990s with the extension of Metro keying both public and private investment in the area.

4 14th Street at Florida Avenue NW

TRACK—This was the site of Holmead's race track, established about 1802 by Gen. John Tayloe and designed by William Thornton, better known as the original architect of the Capitol. During the 1820s and 1830s, crowds as large as 10,000 watched mile-long horse races staged here by the National Jockey Club.

5 1458 Columbia Road NW

RESIDENCE OF INVENTION—After 1870 this was the home of Emil Berliner, inventor of the telephone transmitter, the microphone and the gramophone, an early version of the phonograph that led to the formation of the Victor Talking Machine Company.

6 14th Street at Park Road NW

WASHINGTON'S GARDEN—A 1927 directory advertised the Arcadia at this location as "Washington's Madison Square Garden," with dancing classes, boxing exhibitions, basketball, fashion shows, billiards, exhibitions, track meets, ceremonials, and dances. It was a complex located at 3134-3138 14th Street and operated in the 1920s and 1930s. Dr. Neil P. Campbell, who grew up in the neighborhood, remembered the building as the Arcade and noted that it "started its life as a carbarn at the Park Road end of the Capitol Traction streetcar line," and was converted to entertainment purposes when the line was extended.

Anticipating the projected opening of the Columbia Heights Metro station, several major developers were competing in 1999 to develop retail and commercial enterprises on this and nearby sites, including restoration and adaptive reuse of the historic Tivoli Theater, which in its heyday operated at 3301 14th Street. It was designed by renowned theater architect Thomas White Lamb and opened in 1924. It closed in the 1970s.

7 3128 14th Street NW

HOT SHOPPE—On this site in the 1920s, J. Willard Marriott opened a nine-seat root beer stand with his wife, Alice. The stand soon served hot food and became known as the Hot Shoppe, the beginning of a nationwide chain and a worldwide hotel empire.

8 3509 Georgia Avenue NW

SUPER IDEA—On this site on February 6, 1936, two Pennsylvania entrepreneurs, N.M. Cohen and Sam Lehrman, brought the supermarket to Washington. Business historian Thomas V. DiBacco recounted in the *Washington Post* on March 9, 1990, that eager shoppers gathered in a blizzard to try the new approach—"a cash-only, self-service, price-conscious food market with everything under one roof." Despite the skepticism of traditional grocers, the store was a great success.

9 624 T Street NW

HOWARD THEATER—Following its opening in 1910, this renowned 1,200-seat theater became Washington's center for black entertainers, featuring Ella Fitzgerald, Duke Ellington, Cab Calloway, Pearl Bailey, and other stars from Washington's black community as well as famous visiting artists, both black and white. Audiences were integrated as well. The theater's celebrity spread, and white Washingtonians ignored segregation codes to share in what many thought the best entertainment in town. Donald Lief, a reader who once patronized the Howard, reminded the authors that it "was second only to the Apollo in Harlem—in my opinion—for the quality of its stage shows. I used to go to midnight Saturday shows: a terrific experience, the shows and the audiences. You have to remember that segregation was often one-way and

Map on page 241

AFRICAN AMERICAN CIVIL WAR VETS. The Cardozo-U Street metro stop, located on the north side of the intersection of Vermont Avenue and 10th and U Streets, is the site of the African-American Civil War Memorial, recognizing the more than 200,000 blacks and their 7,000 white officers who voluntarily served the Union Army in the Civil War. The "Spirit of Freedom," by Louisville designer Ed Hamilton, was installed on July 18, 1998. Plaques engraved with the 209,145 names of those who served are being installed. The 3.5-million-dollar project has been championed by the African-American Civil War Memorial Freedom Foundation and funded by Metro, and various public and private sources. When completed, it will be maintained by the National Park Service.

foolish. I could attend the Howard, or go to a black club. Blacks could attend concerts at Constitution Hall but couldn't perform there."

⑩ Northeast Corner of 15th and U Streets NW

DUNBAR HOTEL—Originally an elegant apartment building opening in 1897 as the Portner Flats, this building, as recounted in James M. Goode's *Best Addresses,* was strategically located a block from the then recently extended 14th Street streetcar line. It sported tennis courts and a swimming pool, the first such amenities for an apartment building in the city. It was sold and converted to the Dunbar Hotel in 1945, eventually becoming briefly in the still-segregated 1950s the leading hotel for African Americans. As integration expanded the range of accommodations and competition, the Dunbar declined in prominence, eventually to be bought by the city, razed over the protests of preservationists, and replaced by the Campbell Heights apartments in the 1970s.

⑪ 1816 12th Street NW

ANTHONY BOWEN YMCA—The Twelfth Street Branch of the YMCA opened in 1912 as the home of Washington's "Colored" YMCA, which had previously been located in several other locations after being established by former slave Anthony Bowen in 1853. It provided the Shaw neighborhood with a library, swimming pool, and gymnasium where basketball greats Elgin Baylor, Dave Bing, and John Thompson played in their youth. It was named for Bowen in 1972. It deteriorated and closed in 1982, but is being renovated and is to reopen at the end of 1999 as the Thurgood Marshall Center for Service and Heritage.

⑫ 1215 U Street NW

LINCOLN THEATER—The Lincoln Theater opened in 1922 and was one of the premier theaters serving Washington's African-American community in segregated Washington during the first half of the 20th century. It closed in 1984 and was restored and reopened in February 1995 following an investment of nine million dollars by the city. The renovated theater features a stage for live performances, a tiered balcony, and one of the largest movie screens in the area.

Washington's Garden. The Arcadia at the southeast corner of 14th Street and Park Road NW was billed as "Washington's Madison Square Garden."

St. Paul's. The oldest church in the city, located in Rock Creek Cemetery, as it appeared at the turn of the century.

Brookland and Upper Georgia Avenue

❶ On the hills about 3 miles north of the Capitol, at Rock Creek Church Road and Upshur Street NW

U.S. SOLDIERS' AND AIRMENS' HOME—Founded in 1851 by Gen. Winfield Scott as the Soldiers' Home, it was created with war tribute that Scott collected in 1848 in Mexico City.

For more than a hundred years it was described by this simple sentence: "Here comfortable quarters are provided for men who have served for 20 years in the United States Army or who have been disabled by wounds or disease." In the home's cemetery is the tomb of John A. Logan, general in the Union Army and congressman and senator from Illinois.

It is an immense and attractive estate with more than 10 miles of roads on the grounds.

❷ Just inside the grounds of the Soldiers' Home at Rock Creek Church Road and Upshur Street NW

ANDERSON COTTAGE—Dating from 1843 when it was built by banker George Washington Riggs, who named it Corn Riggs, this residence became the first building of the Soldiers' Home in 1851. Beginning with James Buchanan, it was used as a summer White House by several Presidents. Before there was a Maryland mountain retreat (now known as Camp David), this was often alluded to as the Presidents' Cottage. Abraham Lincoln prepared the final draft of the Emancipation Proclamation here in 1862.

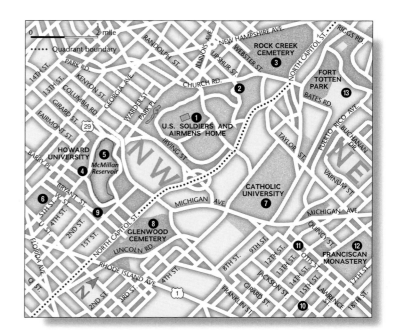

STREET LORE

UPSHUR STREET. This street was named for Abel Parker Upshur, the secretary of state who was killed on the Potomac River on February 28, 1844, when a gargantuan 27,000-pound cannon—the "Peace Maker"—exploded aboard the U.S.S. *Princeton.*

The ship was the first of its kind—a screw-driven steam warship—fast, well-engineered, and a dream to maneuver. She boasted 14 guns, including the Peace Maker, reputed to be the world's largest.

The new ship arrived in Washington on February 13, 1844, and quickly became the center of attention. As interest grew the captain of the ship decided to arrange a cruise for President Tyler, his fiancee, the Cabinet, and about 400 others to demonstrate its prowess. It was a festive day of feasting, dancing, and test firings of the mammoth gun. During one display of power, a 225-pound cannonball was fired more than a half-mile downriver, at which point it hit the water and skipped along until it disappeared from sight.

The demonstration ended, but Secretary of the Navy Thomas Walker Gilmer, who had become quite infatuated with the gun, asked for one more shot. On

continued on next page

❸ Northeast of the Soldiers' Home between the 5000 block of North Capitol Street and New Hampshire Avenue NW

ROCK CREEK CEMETERY—Celebrated local figures of the past, such as Mayor Peter Force and Alexander "Boss" Shepherd, are buried here, as are Supreme Court Justices John Marshall Harlan and Harlan Fiske Stone. This is also the site of St. Paul's, the oldest parish church in the District of Columbia. It was founded in 1719, rebuilt in 1775, remodeled in 1868, and rebuilt again in 1921.

The most striking feature of the site is the beautiful bronze statue of a young woman by Augustus Saint-Gaudens. It was commissioned in 1891 by Henry Adams as a memorial to his wife, Marian Hooper Adams, a suicide. The memorial has no inscription—not even the sculptor's identity—and no title (others have tagged it "Grief," "Despair," or "Mourning"). Critic Alexander Wolcott called the seated statue the "most beautiful thing ever fashioned by the hand of man on this continent." Soames Forsyte, the fictional hero of John Galsworthy's *Forsyte Saga,* thought her "the best thing he had ever come across in America." First Lady Eleanor Roosevelt once said that she came here and sat in front of the memorial during times when she was troubled. In his book *Footnote Washington,* Bryson Rash tells of Mark Twain writing to his good friend Henry Adams to ask him what the statue meant. Adams' terse reply: "Any 12-year-old knows what it means."

Rock Creek Cemetery lies a distance from Rock Creek Park, which is one of the reasons so many people find it hard to locate.

❹ 2400 6th Street NW (between W and Fairmont Streets)

HOWARD UNIVERSITY—Site of the institution regarded as the nation's most important and diverse center for the education of blacks. The university was created on March 2, 1867, by President

Andrew Johnson, and during its early years primarily served as a school for ministers. It was named for Gen. Oliver Otis Howard, commissioner of the Freedman's Bureau and strong supporter of the school. The land was bought from John A. Smith, whose farm has been traditionally described as a "slave plantation." The record is far from exact. In *Howard University: the First 100 Years—1867-1967,* author Rayford W. Logan notes, "It may have been at one time; since slavery, however, was abolished in the District of Columbia by act of Congress on April 16, 1862, this...was not a slave plantation in 1867."

During its early years, most of the university's presidents were white ministers, but that tradition was broken in 1926 with the appointment of black Baptist minister Dr. Mordecai W. Johnson.

The school has distinguished itself in many areas, but none more dramatic than providing the lawyers for the civil rights movement, including Thurgood Marshall, who was counsel to the NAACP, solicitor general of the United States, and an associate justice of the Supreme Court. As early as 1963, Haynes Johnson was able to write in his book *Dusk at the Mountain:* "From the Howard Law School have come the men who have carried the burden of legal argument in segregation cases throughout the nation...."

⑤ The McMillan Reservoir, on the heights just east of Howard University

SPRING—In full service since 1913, this body of water was created to service Capitol Hill and the eastern section of the city. It was built on the Smith Spring and completed the modern water system that still serves the city.

Map on page 247

STREET LORE

continued from previous page

this last firing the gun blew apart, and when the smoke cleared Upshur, Gilmer, and 11 others were dead or dying.

The incident was profoundly shocking. The city literally shut down for several days to mourn what a newspaper termed "Our Most Awful and Lamentable Catastrophe!" It stood as the city's worst river disaster until the *Wawaset* ship fire of 1873. Upshur Street is one of the few reminders of it today. If there was a lesson in the story of the U.S.S. *Princeton* disaster, it was that giant guns could not be made from iron and steel of uneven quality.

Howard University Begins. This 1870 photo depicts students on the campus of the newly established (1867) Howard University, one of the few higher education institutions of the time offering equal educational opportunity to black and white, men and women students alike.

6 **Area bounded by W Street, Georgia Avenue, U Street, and 5th Street NW, containing the Howard University Hospital**

THE OLD BALLFIELD—Originally a forest, this site was cleared in 1891 of 125 immense oak trees, the stump holes were filled, and National Park Stadium was created. Later named Clark Griffith Park and then Griffith Stadium after the owner of the Washington Senators baseball team, the site was used for baseball for the next 71 years. (There was no professional baseball here during 1911 and 1912.) In 1913 the American League Senators made it their home. Negro league teams, including the Homestead Grays and the Black Senators, also played here.

A number of memorable events took place on this spot:

A Ladies' Day was held in 1897 during which women were given free admission so that they would become more familiar with the game. The free admission attracted a particularly unruly female element. When an immensely popular Senators pitcher named Winnie Mercer was thrown out of the game for abusive behavior toward an umpire named Bill Carpenter, a riot ensued and a group of women charged the field and beat Carpenter. Seats were ripped out and windows were broken in nearby buildings. The players had to rescue Carpenter and escort him from the field in disguise.

The first presidential season opener took place here in 1910 with William Howard Taft throwing out the first ball.

Mickey Mantle's April 17, 1953, hit off hapless Senators pitcher Chuck Stobbs is generally recognized as the longest home run of all time. The distance of the homer has been officially measured at 565 feet. The back wall of the left bleachers here was cleared only three times: once by Mantle and twice by Josh Gibson, Negro league star.

The last game played here was on September 21, 1961, between the new Senators, an expansion team headed for D.C. Stadium, and the old Senators, which had become the Minnesota Twins. The stadium was demolished in 1965. Commemorative plaques honoring the great pitcher Walter Johnson, some say the greatest right-hander in the history of the game, were removed and installed at a special memorial erected to him at Walter Johnson High School in Bethesda.

Griffith Stadium also served as home of the Washington Redskins football team (until it moved to the new D.C. Stadium), as well as the location of celebrated championship boxing bouts.

7 Michigan Avenue and Harewood Road NE in Brookland

CATHOLIC UNIVERSITY OF AMERICA—Founded in 1887, it is, the national university of the Catholic Church and is the only university in the United States established by the U.S. Catholic bishops. Located on the university campus, the Shrine of the Immaculate Conception, with its towering polychromed dome, is a prominent local landmark and one of the largest church buildings in the world.

8 2219 Lincoln Road NE

GLENWOOD CEMETERY—Originally spread over 91 acres, 52 acres of the cemetery were sold to Trinity College for part of its campus. This is the final resting place of photographer Alexander Gardner and artist Emanuel Leutze, who painted "Washington Crossing the Delaware."

9 100 block of Bryant Street NW

OPEN HOUSING—Restrictive covenants that prevented sale of the houses on this street to black people became the target of *Hurd vs. Hodge,* prepared by Howard University law professor Charles

Urban Retreat. The entrance to the portico and grounds of the Franciscan monastery. The 44-acre tract is part of an original grant from George Calvert, first Lord Baltimore, to an early colonist.

Map on page 247

Houston. The suit eventually led the Supreme Court in 1947 to deny the legality of restrictive covenants. This action helped end the widespread use of such covenants to prevent equal access for all prospective purchasers to residences offered for sale.

10 1510 Jackson Street NE

BUNCHE RESIDENCE—This was the home of United Nations mediator Ralph Bunche, the first African American to win the Nobel Peace Prize. In their *Guide to Black Washington*, Sandra Fitzpatrick and Maria R. Goodwin point out that when the Bunche family built the house in 1941 the children had to be driven three miles to a black school, although there was a whites-only school around the corner.

11 1221 Newton Street NE

RAWLINGS HOME—Site of the childhood home of Marjorie Kinnan Rawlings, author of *The Yearling* (1938).

12 1400 Quincy Street NE

SACRED GROUND—A 44-acre tract containing the Franciscan Monastery Memorial Church of the Holy Land and full-scale reproductions of Christian shrines such as the Bethlehem Manger, the Grotto of Lourdes, and the Catacombs of Rome. It is one of a group of Catholic institutions in this part of town, which gave rise to the area's nickname, "Little Rome." The 1983 edition of *The WPA Guide to Washington, D.C.* (first printed in 1937) notes the property was originally granted by "George Calvert, first Lord Baltimore, to an early colonist, and was probably a part of the Turkey Thicket or Cuckold's Delight area." In 1897 Father Godfrey Schilling of the Order of St. Francis visited and urged its development as a site where the order could promote public interest in the preservation of early Christian shrines in Jerusalem. Long a favorite tourist attraction, the grounds are extensively landscaped and the rose garden has many world-renowned varieties.

⓭ Along the Baltimore and Ohio Railroad line, approximately halfway between today's Metro stops at Brookland and Takoma Park

GHASTLY WRECK—Late on the foggy afternoon of December 31, 1916, a small but packed holiday excursion train that had stopped to unload a few passengers at the Terra Cotta station (a minor flag-stop station on the B&O's metropolitan branch) was hit from behind by a larger train running at 61 miles an hour and pulling empty passenger cars. "The impact was like an explosive shell," said an early report in the *Washington Star*. "Of the rear end of the local there was simply nothing left. Telescoping does not describe it. The car was simply burst into splinters, and the monster engine, its speed scarcely slackened by the blow, split the next car lengthwise like a cardboard box."

The rest of the local was either telescoped or sent hurtling down the track toward Brookland. The little train's smoking car skidded a half-mile down the track on its back. Its locomotive ran off screaming with its whistle stuck at full blast. Residents of the area said it sounded like some terror-stricken beast running away in the fog. Rescuers equipped with lanterns found a full quarter-mile of roadway littered with debris and people dead, dying, and wounded. The total effect was so ghastly that when historian Francis deSales Ryan wrote about it 51 years after the fact he said, "The first early streaks of dawn on the morning of Monday, December 31, 1916...revealed a scene probably more terrible than anything

Soldiers' Home. The Soldiers' Home as it appeared in 1911. Created in 1851 by an act of Congress, it is the oldest army veterans' home in the United States. The Lincoln (Anderson) Cottage appears on the left.

Map on page 247

Ruthian Finale. Babe Ruth at Griffith Stadium in a ceremony marking his final trip to Washington as a Yankee in 1934.

ever seen in Washington." What most shocked those who came to see the wreckage was the blood that seemed to cover everything.

In all, 46 died and 79 were injured. The next day, as New Year's Eve approached, railroad workers set fire to the wreckage (as was the custom in the days before detailed investigations of disasters). As clouds of smoke drifted over the city, the *Evening Star* appeared with an editorial that read in part, "The year closes with the Capital in the depths of an agony of suffering such as it has never known before."

The cause of the wreck was determined to be inadequate signal lights.

Unnamed. One of the city's most revered sculptures, located in Rock Creek Cemetery. It is Henry Adams's memorial to his wife. In a 1908 letter written by Adams to the son of sculptor Augustus Saint-Gaudens, Adams underscores the fact that the figure does not have a name: "I have only one favor to ask of you....Do not allow the world to tag my figure with a name! Every magazine writer wants to label it as some American patent medicine for popular consumption—*Grief, Despair, Pear's Soap,* or *Macy's Mens' Suits Made to Measure.*"

Map on page 247

Hospital Complex. Buildings on the grounds of Walter Reed Army Medical Center, seen about 1925.

Upper Northwest

1 **West side of Beach Drive, 1/4 mile north of the Military Road overpass in Rock Creek Park**

WASHINGTON'S ONLY LOG CABIN—This cabin was formerly located on Meridian Hill (16th Street NW between Belmont and Crescent Streets) and was occupied by Joaquin Miller, the "Poet of the Sierras." Miller told journalist Frank C. Carpenter in the 1880s, "The President's house is at one end of Sixteenth Street and mine is at the other, but while I own a cabin, the President has only his cabin-et." Carpenter wrote of the cabin, "It is built on the wild Western plan without a nail in it. The oak logs are hewn on the inside, but left rough on the outside. They are notched and joined, one on the other, until they have risen a story and a half. A ridge roof covers them, and from the two windows in front there is a beautiful view of the whole city."

2 **Fort Stevens Park, with entrances from either Piney Branch Road and Quackenbos Street NW or Georgia Avenue**

SITE OF WAR—The only battlefield in the District of Columbia during the Civil War. The advance of Gen. Jubal Early's Confederate forces was stopped and Lincoln stood under fire here during the attack on July 12, 1864. Union Gen. Lew Wallace, the future author of the novel *Ben Hur,* played a crucial role by delaying the Confederate forces by engaging them at Monocacy, thus allowing time for the reinforcement of Washington's defenses. A marker shows where Lincoln stood and notes this is the only case

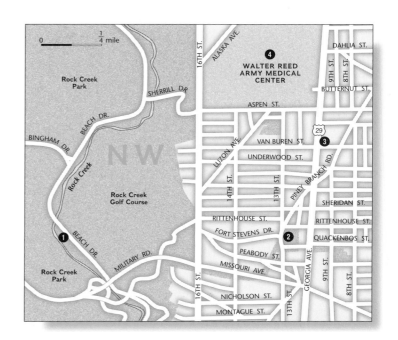

STREET LORE

BOTANICAL STREETS. Irish horticulturist John Saul came to Washington in the 1850s to assist Andrew Jackson Downing with the landscaping of the Mall. Eventually he developed about 140 acres of nurseries on his own, in the area of today's Walter Reed Army Medical Center and Shepherd Park. Many of the streets in those Upper Northwest neighborhoods are named after trees, also in alphabetical order (Aspen, Butternut, Cedar, etc.), reflecting the former presence of the nurseries.

Saul's son inherited the land as Washington began to expand into the suburbs, and a real estate empire was born in 1892. B.F. Saul Co. now employs 3,000 and operates in 14 states and is still family owned and operated.

MILITARY ROAD. A most aptly named road that was built in September 1862 to connect the various forts in the area during the Civil War. At the time Professor George C. Schaeffer observed, "When the defenses are swept away, the road may remain as a lasting benefit."

in which a President of the United States has been under the fire of enemy guns while in office.

③ 6625 Georgia Avenue NW

BATTLEGROUND NATIONAL CEMETERY—Here are buried the remains of some 41 of the soldiers killed in the defense of Washington, when Gen. Jubal Early made his attack on the capital in 1864. It is the smallest national cemetery in the country. A letter from John I. White published in the *Washington Post* (May 27, 1990), recounted the Memorial Day celebrations held at the cemetery during the first decade of the 20th century. Brightwood School students "placed flowers and small American flags on the circle of white gravestones around a tall flagpole in the center of the cemetery. There were patriotic speeches" and the singing of "a lachrymose Civil War song titled 'Just Before the Battle, Mother...,'" Band music and artillery salutes finished the event after which elderly veterans of the battle gathered at White's grandfather's house to swap stories and "fight the battle all over again," while children strained "to hear history related by these greying heroes who once had made it."

④ Georgia Avenue and Butternut Street NW

WALTER REED ARMY MEDICAL CENTER—Named in honor of Dr. Walter Reed, United States Army, who risked his life to demonstrate that yellow fever germs were communicated to man by mosquitoes. Beginning with a small hospital established on this site in 1909, the complex expanded dramatically on its 113 acres during and after World War I. Numerous specialized buildings developed in the post-World War II period, including a shop for manufacturing artificial limbs and, in the 1950s, the "first deliberately planned atomic-resistant structure in Washington," according to a history of Washington area projects of the Army Engineer Corps by Sacket Duryee. Built to house records and activities of the Armed Forces Institute of Pathology, the 11-story (3 below ground), supposedly atomic-bombproof building is "windowless, of heavily reinforced concrete," and includes "two expendable' office wings...separated from the main core by steel blast doors." This special oasis from nuclear war was constructed at a cost of 6.5 million dollars and dedicated on May 23, 1955, by President Dwight D. Eisenhower, who, coincidentally, died at the hospital on March 28, 1969.

On the grounds is a plaque marking the site of the "Sharpshooter's Tree," used by Confederates as a perch for sharpshooters and as a signal station during General Early's attack on Washington in 1864.

Near the medical center is the former site of Bleak House, the country estate of Alexander R. "Boss" Shepherd. The house was located near 14th and Geranium Streets NW and was torn down in 1916. Shepherd used his power on the Board of Public Works during the District's period of territorial government in the 1870s to modernize the city's streets and public works systems. Within three years his efforts paved miles of streets, built a city-wide sewer system, filled in the City Canal and Tiber Creek to create Constitution Avenue, and planted 25,000 trees. The city was transformed but 20 million dollars in debt, and local citizens and Congress erupted in indignation. Shepherd left for Mexico in 1874, made a fortune in silver mining, and was eventually honored by the city.

The Boss. The District Building when it featured a bronze statue of Alexander R. "Boss" Shepherd (1835-1902).

Map on page 257

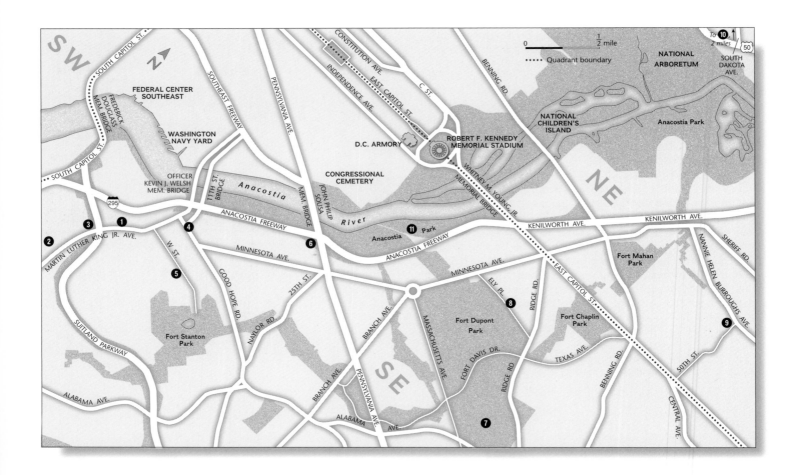

SW

FEDERAL CENTER
SOUTHEAST

WASHINGTON
NAVY YARD

FREDERICK
DOUGLAS
MEM. BRIDGE

SOUTH CAPITOL ST.

SOUTHEAST FREEWAY

PENNSYLVANIA AVE.

CONSTITUTION AVE.

INDEPENDENCE AVE.

EAST CAPITOL ST.

C ST.

BENNING RD.

Quadrant boundary

0   ½   1 mile

To ⑩
2 miles   50

NATIONAL
ARBORETUM

SOUTH
DAKOTA
AVE.

NATIONAL
CHILDREN'S
ISLAND

Anacostia Park

SOUTH CAPITOL ST.

OFFICER
KEVIN J. WELSH
MEM. BRIDGE

11TH ST. BRIDGE

MEM. BRIDGE

JOHN PHILIP SOUSA

Anacostia

River

D.C. ARMORY

CONGRESSIONAL
CEMETERY

ROBERT F. KENNEDY
MEMORIAL STADIUM

WHITNEY M. YOUNG JR. MEMORIAL BRIDGE

NE

295

③

①

④

⑥

⑪ Park
Anacostia

KENILWORTH AVE.

KENILWORTH AVE.

②

MARTIN LUTHER KING JR. AVE.

W ST.

⑤

MINNESOTA AVE.

ANACOSTIA FREEWAY

ANACOSTIA FREEWAY

MINNESOTA AVE.

Fort Mahan
Park

SHERIFF RD.

NANNIE HELEN BURROUGHS AVE.

SUITLAND PARKWAY

GOOD HOPE RD.

NAYLOR RD.

25TH ST.

BRANCH AVE.

ELY PL.

RIDGE RD.

EAST CAPITOL ST.

⑧

Fort Chaplin
Park

⑨

Fort Stanton
Park

Fort Dupont
Park

MASSACHUSETTS AVE.

FORT DAVIS DR.

RIDGE RD.

TEXAS AVE.

BENNING RD.

50TH ST.

SE

ALABAMA AVE.

BRANCH AVE.

PENNSYLVANIA AVE.

ALABAMA AVE.

⑦

CENTRAL AVE.

Across the Anacostia River

❶ 2405 Martin Luther King Jr. Avenue SE

PIONEERING MUSEUM—In the Carver Theater formerly on this site, John Kinard established the Smithsonian's Anacostia Neighborhood Museum in 1967. A "storefront museum," it was considered innovative in its time as an institution whose programs reflected its community and engaged community members in training, exhibits development, and public programs. In Kenneth Hudson's 1987 book *Museums of Influence,* it was cited as one of 37 such institutions in the world established over the past 200 years. The museum's provocative exhibition "The Rat: Man's Invited Affliction" would have been shunned by traditional institutions of the time and reflected the then-severe rat infestation in the inner cities. Kinard considered it vital that the museum involve young people in developing projects concerning their own history and in so doing to train them in museum work and build pride in their cultural experience. In 1987 the museum relocated to 1901 Fort Place SE and changed its name to the Anacostia Museum.

❷ 2700 Martin Luther King Jr. Avenue SE

ST. E'S—Formerly the Government Hospital for the Insane, now known as St. Elizabeths Hospital. Established under pressure from Dorothea Dix and other reformers campaigning for humane treatment of persons with mental illness, the hospital opened in 1855. District citizens had also petitioned Congress in 1851 to help care for the "many persons from various parts of the Union, whose

St. E's. This 1918 postcard shows part of the complex of buildings comprising St. Elizabeths Hospital at 2700 Martin Luther King, Jr., Avenue SE.

STREET LORE

GOOD HOPE ROAD. Notoriety came to this thoroughfare in 1865 when John Wilkes Booth used it as an escape route after shooting President Lincoln.

MARTIN LUTHER KING JR. AVENUE. Originally known as Asylum Avenue—alluding to St. Elizabeths, which it bisected—it became Nichols Avenue, after hospital Superintendent Charles Henry Nichols, and then was renamed for the slain civil rights leader.

63RD STREET NE. The highest-numbered street in the District.

minds are more or less erratic [who] find their way to the metropolis of the country and ramble about... poorly clad and suffering for want of food and shelter."

Designed by Architect of the Capitol Thomas U. Walter and based on advice from its first superintendent, Dr. C.H. Nichol, the building was erected on 419 elevated acres. According to the hospital's history, because of the urgent needs of the Civil War, the hospital received military wounded. Many of these men did not wish to write home that they were being cared for in a hospital for the insane, and simply called it St. Elizabeth's Hospital after the tract on which it is located. The name stuck, and in 1916 Congress formally changed the name, leaving out the apostrophe.

During the Civil War the Grand National Race Course opened on these grounds. After World War II, Ezra Pound was confined to St. E's, as it's known locally, when he was found "unfit" to plead to the charges that he broadcast pro-Fascist propaganda over Italian radio while Italy was at war with the United States. He was released in 1958, returned to Italy—where he declared "all America is an insane asylum"—and died there in 1972. In recent times, the inmate of note has been John Hinckley, the man who shot President Ronald Reagan on March 30, 1981. The hospital was transferred to the jurisdiction of the District of Columbia in the 1980s.

❸ On either side of Suitland Parkway SE at and just beyond the intersection with Martin Luther King Jr. Avenue

FREED BLACKS SETTLEMENT—Barry's Farm was established in 1865 by the Freedman's Bureau to provide land for the freed blacks who migrated heavily into the city after emancipation in 1863. It was a self-help, build-your-own-house approach, with residents provided lumber and one-acre lots at a nominal fee and expected to erect their own houses, streets, stores and community buildings. After Suitland Parkway bisected the 375-acre development in the 1940s, public housing complexes replaced the simple residences that had characterized Barry Farms.

4 Site in front of 1807 13th Street SE

AIR CRASH—On November 9, 1938, two Army fliers were killed here when their plane crashed into a row of parked cars, avoiding houses and the nearby business district.

5 1411 W Street SE

CEDAR HILL—Home of black abolitionist, orator, escaped slave, and journalist Frederick Douglass for 18 years before his death in 1895. He bought the property in 1877 while serving as U.S. marshal for the District of Columbia. The precedent-setting purchase broke the covenant in Uniontown that restricted property sales to whites, although segregated housing patterns persisted. Douglass named the house for cedar trees on the property that are now gone.

An interesting insight appears in *Historic Buildings of Washington, D.C.* (1973) by Diane Maddex: "Situated on the heights of Anacostia and commanding a superb view of official Washington below, Douglass' house may have been built as a temporary construction office for a 237-acre parcel then being subdivided for development. Together with clauses forbidding such nuisances as 'soap boiling, piggeries, and slaughter houses,' the real estate partnership's deed restriction, ironically, also reserved the lots for the use of 'white persons only.'"

It was first dedicated as a memorial to Douglass in August 1922 in accordance with the wishes of his wife, Helen Pitts Douglass, who wanted the house and its adjoining nine acres to serve as a "Mount Vernon to the black community." Financial problems led

Art Center. The Anacostia Neighborhood Museum operated an arts center shown in this ca 1970 photo, as well as a pioneering exhibition program involving and reflecting the Anacostia community.

Map on page 260

NEIGHBORHOOD LORE

ANACOSTIA. Uniontown (as it was first called) was established in 1854 as a whites-only working-class residential neighborhood across the Anacostia River (then called Eastern Branch) from the Navy Yard. Howard Gillette in *Washington At Home* calls Uniontown Washington's first consciously designed suburb, accessible by bridge to jobs in the Navy Yard and close to St. Elizabeths Hospital as well. After the Civil War, when many other cities were named Uniontown, the community was renamed Anacostia in 1886.

to deterioration of the site and a campaign to preserve the 21-room Victorian mansion began in 1960. The National Park Service agreed to take responsibility in 1962, but restoration did not begin again until 1969. It opened to the public in 1972.

6 23rd Street and Pennsylvania Avenue SE

PIE LANDMARK—For 38 years the site of the James G. Stephanson Co. pie-baking plant, a Washington landmark. The plant was razed in 1961 for the Anacostia Freeway. A picture printed in the *Washington Post* shows Mr. and Mrs. Stephanson standing on the rubble of their demolished building.

7 Fort Dupont Park on Alabama Avenue between Ridge Road and Massachusetts Avenue SE

FORT DUPONT PARK—One of the Civil War forts purchased by the government in the 1930s to preserve as a park. A mile to the south at Fort Stanton Park, the masonry, magazine, and tunnel of another fort are still visible.

8 37th Street and Ely Place SE

HISTORIC LAWSUIT—John Philip Sousa Junior High School was a brand-new modern facility restricted to white students when black student Spottswood T. Bolling, Jr., was denied admission on September 11, 1950, despite many empty classrooms. The ensuing legal challenge, developed by Howard University law professor James M. Nabrit, maintained that segregated schools in the District were unconstitutional and that the District's black students were denied due process of law as allowed by the Fifth Amendment, because Congress had never passed a law providing for segregated schools. After an adverse lower court ruling, Nabrit's case was attached to *Brown vs. Board of Education of Topeka,* to be considered by the United States Supreme Court. In a unanimous decision announced May 17, 1954, the high court held for the plaintiffs in both *Brown* and *Bolling vs. Sharpe,* declaring unconstitutional racial segregation in the nation's public schools.

9 **50th and Grant Streets NE**

NATIONAL TRAINING SCHOOL—This was the site of Nannie Helen Burroughs' National Training School for Women and Girls, a private boarding school for blacks established in 1909. The school provided a liberal arts education combined with training in home economics, accounting, dress and hat making, printing, secretarial, and other job skills. An enterprising laundry business started by the school provided training, performed laundering for the school, and helped raise money to sustain the school during the Depression. On this site today is a private religious academy named for Nannie Helen Burroughs.

10 **Bladensburg, Maryland, northeast of Washington, along Md. Route 450, beyond Fort Lincoln Cemetery at 38th Street**

BLOODY GROUND—In 1814 the Battle of Bladensburg was fought here, preceding the burning of Washington in the War of 1812. A detachment of 4,500 British troops fresh from victory over Napoleon's forces in Europe disembarked from ships on the Patuxent River, 35 miles southeast of Washington. They won an easy victory at Bladensburg, which opened the capital to a night of burning and looting that destroyed most of the public buildings in the city. A fierce storm and fear of an American counterattack caused the British to return to their ships the next day.

According to the *Records of the Columbia Historical Society,* the

Tire Shop. Photograph taken on 11th Street SE in 1939 by Farm Security Administration photographer John Vachon, which epitomizes the humble but essential businesses that were so much a part of the area.

Map on page 260

NO SWIMMING. A City of Washington act of June 8, 1826, mandated that "from and after the first day of August next, it shall not be lawful for any person…to bathe or swim in the Anacostia river, between Sixth street east, and First street west, or in the canal, or any part of the Tyber, east of Fifteenth street west, at any time of the day between the rising and setting of the sun." Today, swimming is still not encouraged, but boating and fishing are thriving. River clean-up expeditions are gaining support, and boat and canoe clubs are springing up along the Anacostia, including the Anacostia River Rowing Center and the relocated Capital Rowing Club.

dueling ground where Stephen Decatur fell was in Bladensburg at the sixth boundary stone near a stream that crosses Bladensburg Road and flows through a park just east of Fort Lincoln Cemetery about a mile from the District line. A historical marker along Md. 450 (Bladensburg Road) indicates the dueling ground site in Anacostia River Park.

⑪ Along the Anacostia River from Frederick Douglass Memorial Bridge to beyond the District line

ANACOSTIA PARK—This extensive riverfront embraces Langston Golf Course, National Children's Island, and the Kenilworth Aquatic Gardens, and adjoins the United States National Arboretum, significant treasures of the city and region. The Kenilworth Aquatic Gardens derive from the 19th-century farm of W.B. Shaw, whose 37 acres of ponds now contain some 75 varieties of water lilies, according to *Buildings of the District of Columbia* by Pamela Scott and Antoinette J. Lee (1993). The arboretum was purchased by the federal government in 1927 to be an experimental forest preserve. In addition to its arboreal offerings, it preserves a forest of 22 of the original columns used to build the U.S. Capitol building, arranged and installed here in 1990 to delight the eye.

Future Pentagon Site. Aerial photograph taken on the Virginia side of the Potomac by the late *Times-Herald* photographer Joe Roberts in June 1931. In the upper left is the new low-arched Arlington Memorial Bridge gleaming white with its veneer of North Carolina granite. The bridge sits low as a consideration to aircraft safety and to give a clear view of the Lincoln Memorial at one end and Arlington National Cemetery at the other.

Map on page 260

BIBLIOGRAPHY

The authors have relied on a variety of general histories, visitor accounts, business directories, specialized studies of neighborhoods and Washington, D.C.'s development, reports of government bureaus, institutional histories, tourist guides, newspaper and magazine articles, maps, city directories, and biographies.

The *Oxford Companion of American History* served as a general guide for biographical and historical facts. Invaluable references on Washington, D.C. and its changing history were standard works by Wilhelmus Bogart Bryan, Constance McLaughlin Green, Frederick Gutheim, and James M. Goode cited below. Particularly useful guidebooks were those by DeB. Randolph Keim (1884), Fremont Rider (1924), and Rand McNally & Co.(1902). Much material was found or checked in the pages of the *Records of the Columbia Historical Society*. References to specific articles and volumes are cited in the text. Information on Smithsonian buildings and the mall was found in Smithsonian annual reports. We have also relied upon many newspaper and magazine reports and publications of various organizations and National Park Service sites referred to in the text but too numerous to cite here.

Finally we have drawn on our individual collections of somewhat idiosyncratic reference materials including for Evelyn information on markets, the mall, Smithsonian, public buildings, and parks and, for Dickson, baseball, recreation, saloons, ice cream, disasters, and cemeteries. The authors have each lived in the area for over three decades and assiduously collect visual materials and ephemera related to Washington, D.C. history.

Adler, Bill. *Washington: A Reader*. Meredith Press, New York, 1967.

Allen, William C. *The United States Capitol: A Brief Architectural History*. U.S. Government Printing Office, Washington, D.C., 1990.

Ames, Mary Clemmer. *Ten Years in Washington, Life and Scenes in the National Capital*. A.D. Worthington & Co., Hartford, Conn., 1875.

Applewhite, E.J. *Washington Itself*. Alfred A. Knopf, New York, 1983.

Ashworth, Marjorie. *Glory Road: Pennsylvania Avenue Past and Present*. Link Press, McLean, Virginia, 1986.

Atwood, Albert T., ed. *Growing with Washington*. Washington Gas Light Company, Washington, D.C., 1948.

Barton, E.E. *Historical and Commercial Sketches of Washington and Environs—Our Capital City*. E.E. Barton, Washington, D.C., 1884.

Betts, James. *Historic Sketches at Washington*. James Betts & Co., Hartford, Conn., 1879.

Bigler, Philip. *Washington in Focus*. Vandamere Press, Arlington, Virginia, 1988.

Bowling, Kenneth R. *Creating the Federal City, 1774-1800: Potomac Fever*. The American Institute of Architects Press, Washington, D.C., 1988.

Brinkley, David. *Washington Goes to War*. Random House, New York, 1988.

Brooks, Noah. *Washington, D. C. in Lincoln's Time*. Collier Books, New York, 1962.

Brown, George Rothwell. *Washington: A Not Too Serious History.* Norman Publishing, Baltimore, 1930.

Bryan, John M., ed. *Robert Mills, Architect.* The American Institute of Architects Press, Washington, D.C., 1989.

Bryan, Wilhelmus Bogart. *A History of the National Capital.* 2 vols. The Macmillan Company, New York, 1914.

Bryce, James. *The Nation's Capital.* Byron S. Adams, Washington, D.C., 1913.

Bushong, William B. *Uncle Sam's Architects: Builders of the Capitol.* U.S. Capitol Historical Society, Washington, D.C., 1994.

Bustard, Bruce I. *Washington, Behind the Monuments.* National Archives and Records Administration, Washington, D.C., 1990.

Cable, Mary. *The Avenue of the Presidents.* Houghton Mifflin, New York, 1969.

Caemmerer, H. Paul. *A Manual on the Origin and Development of Washington.* U.S. Government Printing Office, Washington, D.C., 1939.

Cameron, Robert. *Above Washington.* Cameron and Co., San Francisco, 1980.

Carpenter, Frank G. *Carp's Washington* (edited by Frances Carpenter with an introduction by Cleveland Amory). McGraw-Hill, New York, 1960.

Christman, Margaret C.S. *Fifty American Faces.* Smithsonian Institution Press, Washington, D.C., 1978.

Clark, Elizabeth Gertrude. *Reports of the Chronicler from Records of the Columbia Historical Society,* Washington, D.C. 1951-1961. Columbia Historical Society, Washington, D.C., 1976.

Coffin, John P. Washington. *Historical Sketches of the Capital City of Our Country.* John P. Coffin, Washington, D.C., 1887.

Cole, Donald B. and McDonough, John J., eds. *Benjamin Brown French, Witness to the Young Republic, A Yankee's Journal, 1828-1870.* University Press of New England, Hanover and London, 1989.

Conn, Richard. *Foxhall Community at Half Century, A Fond Look Backwards.* Foxhall Community Citizens Association, Washington, D.C., 1979.

Cowdrey, Albert E. *A City for the Nation, The Army Engineers and the Building of Washington, D.C., 1790-1967.* Historical Division, Office of the Chief of Engineers, U.S. Army, c.1978.

Croggon, James. "Old Washington." Serialized articles appearing in *Washington Evening Star* in 1918, bound volume at the Washingtoniana Division, D.C. Public Library, Washington, D.C.

Cutler, David, *Literary Washington: A Complete Guide to the Literary Life in the Nation's Capital.* Madison Books, Lanham, Maryland, 1989.

D.C. Daughters of the American Revolution. *Historical Directory of the District of Columbia.* Daughters of the American Revolution, Washington, D.C., April, 1922.

D.C. History Curriculum Project. *City of Magnificent Intentions.* Published for the Associates for Renewal in Education by Intac., Inc., Washington, D.C., 1983.

DiBacco, Thomas V. "*Washington Business,*" in "*A Time to Reflect, A Time to Grow.*" Advertising Supplement to the Washington Post, March 9, 1990.

Duryee, Sacket L. *A Historical Summary of the Work of the Corps of Engineers in Washington, D.C. and Vicinity, 1852-1952.*

Eastman, John. *Who Lived Where.* Bonanza Books, New York, 1983.

Ecker, Grace Dunlop. *A Portrait of Old George Town.* The Dietz Press, Inc., Richmond, 1951.

Ellis, John B. *The Sights and Secrets of the National Capital.* United States Publishing Company, New York, 1869.

Essary, J. Frederick and Helen. *Washington Sketch Book.* Ransdell Incorporated, Washington, D.C., 1932.

Evans, James Matthew. *The Landscape Architecture of Washington*, D.C. Landscape Architecture Association, Washington, 1981.

Ewing, Charles. *Yesterday's Washington D.C.*, Seemann Publishing, Miami. 1976.

Executive Office of the President, Office of Administration. *The Old Executive Office Building, A Victorian Masterpiece*. U.S. Government Printing Office, Washington, D.C., 1984.

Federal Writers' Project, Works Progress Administration. *Washington, City and Capital*. U.S. Government Printing Office, Washington, D.C., 1937. Also 1983 edition published by Pantheon Books, entitled *The W.P.A. Guide to Washington, D.C.*

Fitzpatrick, Sandra and Goodwin, Maria R. *The Guide to Black Washington*, Hippocrene Books, New York, 1990.

Froncek, Thomas, ed., *The City of Washington*. Alfred A. Knopf, New York, 1977.

Gilbert, Ben W. and the staff of the Washington Post. *Ten Blocks From the White House*. Frederick A. Praeger, New York, 1968.

Goode, James M. *Capital Losses: A Cultural History of Washington's Destroyed Buildings*. Smithsonian Institution Press, Washington, D.C., 1979.

—————. *The Outdoor Sculpture of Washington, D.C.* Smithsonian Institution Press, Washington, D.C., 1974.

Greathouse, Charles H. *Historical Sketch of the U.S. Department of Agriculture; Its Objects and Present Organization*. Government Printing Office, Washington, D.C., 1907.

Green, Constance McLaughlin. *Washington: A History of the Capital, 1800-1950*. 2 vols. Princeton University Press, Princeton, N.J., 1962.

Gutheim, Frederick. *The Federal City: Plans and Realities*. Smithsonian Press, Washington, D.C., 1976.

—————. *The Potomac*. Rinehart and Co., New York, 1949.

Hahn, Thomas F. *Towpath Guide to the Chesapeake & Ohio Canal*. American Canal and Transportation Center, Shepherdstown, W. Va., 1987.

Haley, William D. *Philp's Washington Described*. Philp & Solomons, Washington, D.C., c.1861.

Helm, Judith Beck. *Tenleytown, D.C.* Tennally Press, Washington, D.C., 1981.

Hepburn, Andrew. *Complete Guide to Washington, D.C.* Nicholas Vane Publishers, London, 1964.

Herman, Jan K. *A Hilltop in Foggy Bottom*. Department of the Navy, Washington, D.C., 1984.

Herman, Jan K. and Miller, Elizabeth J. *Lighthouse of the Sky: The U.S. Naval Observatory 1844-1893* (exhibition pamphlet). National Academy of Sciences, Washington, D.C., 1984.

Hilker, Helen-Anne. *Ten First Street, Southeast: Congress Builds a Library, 1886-1897*. Library of Congress, Washington, D.C., 1980.

Hodges, Allan A. and Hodges, Carol A. *Washington on Foot*. Smithsonian Institution Press, Washington, D.C., 1977.

Humphrey, Robert L. and Chambers, Mary Elizabeth. *Ancient Washington: American Indian Cultures of the Potomac Valley*. The George Washington University, Washington, D.C., 1977.

Hurd, Charles. *Washington Cavalcade*. E. P. Dutton & Co., New York, 1948.

Johnson, Thomas H. *The Oxford Companion to American History*. Oxford University Press, 1966.

Kane, Joseph Nathan and Alexander, Gerard L.. *Nicknames of Cities and States of the U.S.* The Scarecrow Press, New York, 1965.

Kelly, Charles Suddarth. Washington, D.C., *Then and Now*. Dover, New York, 1984.

Keim, DeB. Randolph. *Keim's Illustrated Hand-book of Washington and its Environs*. DeB. Randolph Keim, Washington, D.C., 1884.

Kimmel, Stanley. *Mr. Lincoln's Washington*. Coward-McCann,

New York, 1957.

Kiplinger, Austin H. *Washington Now*. Harper & Row, New York, 1975.

Knapp, George L. *Uncle Sam's Government at Washington*. Dodd, Mead and Company, New York, 1933.

Lee, Richard M. *Mr. Lincoln's City*. EPM Publications, McLean, Virginia, 1981.

Leech, Margaret. *Reveille in Washington 1860-1865*. Harper & Brothers, New York and London, 1941.

Lewis, David L. *The District of Columbia: A Bicentennial History*. W.W. Norton, New York, 1976.

MacMahon, Edward B. M.D. and Curry, Leonard. *Medical Cover-ups in the White House*. Farragut Publishing, Washington, 1987.

Madden, Louise Mann and Ruffine, Sheila Dressner. *Cleveland Park: Washington, D.C. Neighborhood*. The American University, Washington, D.C., 1977.

Maddex, Diane. *Historic Buildings of Washington D.C.* Ober Park Associates, Pittsburgh, 1973.

McLean, Evalyn Walsh. *Father Struck it Rich*. Little Brown, Boston, 1936.

Means, Howard, "*The Great Outdoors*," The Washingtonian, April, 1990.

————. "*L'Enfant Terrible*," The Washingtonian, January, 1990.

Moore, Joseph West. *Picturesque Washington: Pen and Pencil Sketches*. J.A. & R.A. Reid, Providence, 1888.

Nicolay, Helen. *Our Capital on the Potomac*. The Century Co., New York & London, 1924.

Myer, Donald B. *Bridges and the City of Washington*. U.S. Commission of Fine Arts, Washington, D.C., 1974.

Pepper, Charles M. *Everyday Life in Washington*. The Christian Herald, New York, 1900.

Post, Robert C., ed. *1876, A Centennial Exhibition*. Smithsonian Institution Press, Washington, D.C., 1976.

Rand, McNally & Co. *Pictorial Guide to the City of Washington*. Rand, McNally & Co., Chicago and New York, 1902.

Rash, Bryson B. *Footnote Washington*. EPM Publishing, McLean, Virginia, 1983.

Reed, Robert. *Old Washington, D.C. in Early Photographs 1846-1942*. Dover, New York, 1980.

Reynolds, Charles B. Washington. *A Handbook for Visitors*. B.S. Reynolds Company, Washington, D.C., 1946.

Rider, Fremont, ed. *Rider's Washington, A Guidebook for Travelers*. The Macmillan Company, New York, 1924.

Roose, W.S. *Roose's Companion and Guide to Washington and Vicinity*. Gibson Brothers, Printers, Washington, D.C., 1887.

Russell, Francis. *The Shadow of Blooming Grove*. McGraw Hill, New York, 1968.

Scott, Pamela and Lee, Antoinette J. *Buildings of the District of Columbia*. Oxford University Press, New York and Oxford, 1993.

Smith, Kathryn Schneider. *Port Town to Urban Neighborhood: The Georgetown Waterfront of Washington, D.C., 1880-1920*. George Washington University, Washington, D.C., 1989.

————, ed. *Washington At Home*. Windsor Publications, Inc., Washington, D.C., 1988.

Smith, Margaret Bayard, and Hunt, Gaillard, ed. *The First Forty Years of Washington Society*. Charles Scribner's Sons, New York, 1906.

Smith, Peter H. *Commercial Archeology in Downtown D.C.* Society for Commercial Archeology, Washington, D.C., November, 1979.

Smith, A. Robert and Sevareid, Eric. *Washington: The Magnificent Capital*. Doubleday, Garden City, New York, 1965.

Solit, Karen D. *History of the United States Botanic Garden, 1818-1991*. Congress of the United States, Washington, 1993.

Staten, Vince. *Unauthorized America.* Harper and Row, New York, 1990.

Stevens, William O. *Washington: The Cinderella City.* Dodd Mead & Co., New York, 1943.

Stewart, George R. *Names on the Land.* Random House, New York, 1945.

Thomas, Bill and Thomas, Phyllis. *Natural Washington.* Holt, Rinehart and Winston, New York, 1980.

Tilp, Frederick. *This Was Potomac River.* Published by the author, Alexandria, Virginia, 1978.

Townsend, George Alfred. *Washington, Outside and Inside.* James Betts and Co., Hartford, 1873.

United States Department of the Interior, Geological Survey. *Building Stones of Our Nation's Capital.* U.S. Government Printing Office, Washington, D.C., 1975.

U.S. Government Printing Office. *100 GPO Years, 1861-1961; A History of United States Public Printing.* U.S. Government Printing Office, Washington, D.C., 1961.

U.S. Treasury Department. *A History of Public Buildings Under The Control of the Treasury Department.* U.S. Government Printing Office, Washington, D.C., 1901.

————. *History of the Bureau of Engraving and Printing, 1862-1962.* Treasury Department, Washington, D.C., c. 1962.

Van Dyne, Larry. "*The Making of Washington.*" The Washingtonian, November, 1987.

Viola, Herman J. *Diplomats in Buckskins, A History of Indian Delegations in Washington City.* Smithsonian Institution Press, Washington, D.C. 1981.

Walker, John and Katherine. *The Walker Washington Guide.* Guide Press, Bethesda, Maryland, 1975.

Warden, David B. *A Chorographical and Statistical Description of the District of Columbia, the Seat of the General Government to the United States.* Paris, 1816.

Washington Board of Trade. *The Book of Washington.* Underwood and Underwood, Washington, 1927.

The Washington Star. The Washington Star's First l00 Years in the Nation's Capital. Centennial supplement published Tuesday, December 16, 1952.

Whyte, James H. *The Uncivil War: Washington During Reconstruction.* Twane Publishers, New York, 1958.

Wilroy, Mary Edith and Prinz, Lucie. *Inside Blair House. Doubleday,* Garden City, 1982.

Worth, Fred L. *Strange and Fascinating Facts About Washington, D.C.* Bell Books, New York, 1988.

ACKNOWLEDGMENTS

This book was inspired by and modeled on early historical guidebooks to Washington, the last of which was published in 1933. In our view, the best of them is Fremont Rider's 1922 guide, *Rider's Washington*. Other favorites, relied on heavily in this book, are *Keim's Illustrated Hand-book of Washington and Its Environs* (1884) and *Points of Historic Interst in Washington and Vicinity*, issued in 1933 for Franklin Roosevelt's first inauguration. Much of the charm of these early books stems from the fact that they are so specific in telling the reader exactly where a building once stood or an event took place. We have followed the same format and supplemented it with old photographs to assist our readers in reconstructing the past.

A number of people were of great help in developing the original edition of this book and in preparing this updated version. Thanks to all of the following:

- John T. and Mary Gibson of Washington, D.C.
- Morrison Hansborough of Washington, D.C.
- Michael Plant, formerly of This 'n' That Antiques of Olney, Maryland, friend and purveyor of historical Washingtoniana.
- The late Walter Reynolds, who taught us a lot about the history of the local guidebook business.
- The staff of the National Geographic Society Library.
- James M. Goode, author of the incomparable testament to lost Washington, *Capital Losses*.
- Robert A. Truax, whose fascination for and knowledge of the city extends over a lifetime.

- The staff of the Washingtoniana Division of the Martin Luther King Memorial Library.
- David F. Haberstich, Keith Melder, William Worthington Jr., and Robert M. Vogel of the National Museum of American History.
- The staff of the Smithsonian Institution Archives.
- Sam Daniel of the Prints and Photographs Division, the Library of Congress.
- The late Robert Lyle of the Georgetown Branch of the D.C. Public Library.
- Philip Ogilvie, former Public Records Administrator of the District of Columbia.
- Agent Robert Shepard for making sure that this work would live on.
- Elizabeth Webber and Merideth Menken, formerly of Farragut Publishing Company, for many hours of dedicated help at every stage of this project and on both editions of the book.
- And our families, for their patience and good humor throughout.
- Finally, we would like to thank scores of letterwriters who contacted us after the first edition of the book to add, embellish, and correct us. Many of these are listed in the text. Among them are: Joe Brooks, Francis W. Brown, Neil P. Campbell, Essie Grohs, Pat Hollyfield, David H. Hugel, Paul W. Keve, Jimmy Lake, Don Lief, Robert M. Morris, Florence M. Prender, Jim Stasny, and Francis A. Young

ABOUT THE AUTHORS

The authors have been friends since first meeting at Wesleyan University in Middletown, Connecticut, more than 35 years ago.

Douglas E. Evelyn has been a Smithsonian Institution manager since 1969 and a student of Washington history since his arrival in the city in 1963. He and his wife, Martha, live in the Palisades section of the city, where they raised their daughters Sarah and Elizabeth.

Paul Dickson is a full-time freelance writer living in Garrett Park, Maryland, with his wife, Nancy, where they raised their sons Andrew and Alex. He has written or co-authored more than 30 books.

The authors would like readers to send suggestions, additions, corrections or the like to them, not only for this book, but also for furthur expansion of the On This Spot series to other cities. You can contact us directly at:

On This Spot, P.O. Box 80, Garrett Park, MD 20896

DEDICATION

To my parents, Everett and Marie Evelyn,
who gave me a sense of place.
D.E.E.

To my mother, Isabelle C. Dickson (1912-1988),
and her infectious fascination with local history.
P.A.D.

PICTURE CREDITS

Author's Collection—3, 15, 18, 46, 52, 58, 62, 66, 67, 69, 80, 87, 97, 110, 115, 119, 121, 128, 133, 143, 148, 149, 154, 159, 164, 166, 167, 169, 173, 189, 199, 211, 214, 221, 222, 225, 234, 237, 240. 246, 250, 251, 253, 255, 256, 259, 261

Author's Collection, Joe Roberts Photograph—254, 267

Author's Collection with permission of Chase Studios—158

E.E. Barton, *Historical and Commercial Sketches of Washington* (1841)—131, 191

***Keim's Illustrated Hand-Book*, 1884**—219

Kiplinger Washington Collection—49. 55, 65, 75, 90, 98, 185

Kiplinger Washington Collection, Joe Roberts Photograph—92, 156, 175

Library of Congress—13, 15, 17, 18, 21, 22, 25, 27, 29, 34-35, 43, 51, 56, 61, 64, 68, 71, 73, 77, 83, 96, 102, 107, 113, 114, 117, 123, 124, 126, 141, 146, 147, 160, 161, 162, 177, 182, 194, 201, 265

Peabody Room, Georgetown Branch Library—192, 195, 198, 204, 207, 208, 209, 210, 213, 217, 218,

Tinker Collection, Peabody Room, Georgetown Branch Library—202

Robert A. Truax—30, 37, 40, 45, 60, 63, 111, 120, 138, 144, 197

Smithsonian Institution—39, 57, 78, 84, 93, 103, 104-105, 112, 116, 205, 215, 232, 263

D.C. Public Library, Washingtoniana Division—53, 54

J. F. Jarvis Publishing Company—152-153

***The Book of Washington* (1927)**—245

INDEX